GRAVE
SECRETS

GRAVE SECRETS

A Leading Forensic Expert
Reveals the Startling Truth About
O.J. Simpson,
David Koresh,
Vincent Foster,
and Other Sensational Cases

CYRIL WECHT, M.D., J.D.

with Mark Curriden and Benjamin Wecht

Foreword by Michael M. Baden, M.D., and Henry C. Lee, Ph.D.

This book is dedicated with love and pride to Leah Darby Curriden and Dylan Nathan Wecht. Their recent entrances into the world may have caused some delay in the publication of *Grave Secrets,* but they also added immeasurably to the pleasure of writing it. We hope they will enjoy reading this book in future years.

Published by Graymalkin Media, LLC

www.graymalkin.com

Copyright © Cyril Wecht, 1996

This edition published in 2019 by Graymalkin Media.

ISBN: 978-1-63168-245-2

Printed in the United States of America

1 3 5 7 9 10 8 6 4 2

CONTENTS

ACKNOWLEDGMENTS

There are so many people we'd like to thank for helping us with the research and preparation of this book that we hardly know where to begin. In each case, there were attorneys, medical and forensic scientific experts, and families who took time to assist us in our endeavors. We sincerely appreciate their gracious cooperation and courtesy.

A few people need to be specially acknowledged and thanked for their contributions. In the world of forensic science, the abilities and achievements of Henry Lee, Ph.D., Michael Baden, M.D., and Herbert MacDonell, Ph.D., are unequaled. They are also our dear friends.

Two eminent trial attorneys helped us immensely as well: F. Lee Bailey in the Simpson case and Stanley Chesley in the Beverly Hills Supper Club fire case. In addition, we'd like to express a special debt of gratitude to two courageous lawyers in Cleveland who helped us with the Glenville shoot-out chapter— Charles Fleming, who later became a trial judge, and Stanley Tolliver. Sadly, Judge Fleming died in the summer of 1994. His contributions to the justice system were many.

A thank-you also goes out to Richard Whitt, a former reporter with the *Louisville* (Kentucky) *Courier-Journal* who is now with the *Atlanta Constitution*. Rich's coverage of the

Beverly Hills Supper Club fire was so outstanding that it won him a Pulitzer Prize. His insight into the details of that event was extremely helpful.

A special acknowledgment also goes out to Maribeth Blettner, who worked countless hours searching for decades-old case files and preparing the manuscript for submission. Finally, we are extremely grateful to Michaela Hamilton, our editor at Dutton, whose expert advice and wise counsel assisted us immeasurably in the writing of this book.

FOREWORD

by

MICHAEL BADEN, M.D.
Director, New York State Police Forensic Sciences Unit

and

HENRY LEE, PH.D.
Director, Connecticut State Police Forensic Science Laboratory

In this engaging chronicle, Cyril Wecht—physician, lawyer, lecturer, teacher, and author of countless professional treatises—has selected a number of investigations from his thirty-five-year career to explain the ways of the forensic scientist to the general public. From his vast professional experience, he has been able to cull a fascinating batch of cases in which his knowledge as a forensic pathologist was crucial in exposing official mistakes or otherwise illuminating weaknesses in the criminal justice system.

As the reader will quickly become aware, no shrinking violet is Cyril. By utilizing skills carefully honed since his days as a national debating champion in college, he succeeds in presenting persuasive analyses of everything from the shooting death of Black Panther Fred Hampton in Chicago in the turbulent 1960s to the brutal stabbings of Nicole Brown Simpson and Ronald Goldman in 1994 Los Angeles. The subtle characteristics of gunshot wounds, stab wounds, and poisonings that speak to and inform the forensic pathologist are translated, in this volume, into eminently readable prose.

We are on the cusp of great technological advances in the forensic sciences and in the crime laboratory. However, as Cyril Wecht explains, the accuracy and fairness of the masses of information that the crime lab can now provide in the areas of DNA identification, hair and fiber analysis, footwear-impression examination, and studies of blood and semen are entirely dependent on the proper identification, protection, collection, and transfer of trace evidence from the crime scene to the lab. He repeatedly returns to the importance of the crime scene in determining cause of death and reconstructing what happened and how it happened. His findings make plain the need for better training of police, crime scene investigators, and medical examiners in order to keep pace with the scientific potential that has developed in the past ten years.

Not limited to investigating homegrown mysteries such as the Vince Foster case, Cyril takes us into the international orbits of forensic science as he describes his involvement in investigating the deaths of both the famous and mighty and the obscure and powerless—from leading politicians in Taiwan and a Pakistani general, to a Filipino maid in Singapore whose autopsy in the Philippines almost resulted in the breakdown of diplomatic relations between the two countries.

In addition to illustrating how the forensic sciences contribute to the public good in the traditional sense of providing information to hold accountable those who murder, to exonerate those who are innocent, and to determine why accidental deaths occurred, Cyril shows us how this noble profession can help us prevent untimely deaths in the future. He takes us into the investigations of the causes of death in the San Francisco earthquake of 1989, in a 1977 Kentucky nightclub fire in which more than a hundred persons died, and the Waco conflagration of 1993.

Of particular interest is his description of the 1976 swine flu immunization fiasco, in which many of this country's leading scientific and health professionals promoted the immunization of millions of people to stave off an epidemic—one that in fact had never had any potential of occurring. He shows us how the prestigious Centers for Disease Control in Atlanta and health departments throughout the United States, together with well-intentioned physicians and politicians, inadvertently created a major public health crisis in which many dozens of people died and hundreds became seriously ill. Indeed, it was left to Coroner Wecht to use his national reputation as an impartial ombudsman to call attention to the tragic errors of great medical minds.

While we may not always agree with Cyril's opinions and conclusions, all of them are well-informed, eloquently expressed, and relevant to an era in which new scientific advances are being applied to criminal justice investigations to a greater degree than ever before.

For the dedicated student of death, *Grave Secrets* is an invaluable text.

INTRODUCTION

WHERE MYSTERY MEETS SCIENCE

When Vivian Hoffman's life came to a sudden end on October 13, 1973, there didn't seem to be much to the incident.

It was the opening day of squirrel-hunting season in Reading, Pennsylvania. The forty-five-year-old bank securities agent had just taken a break to use a nearby outhouse when, according to her husband, her shotgun discharged.

"I called out to her, wondering if she had killed a squirrel," thirty-nine-year-old Fred Hoffman told the police. Receiving no response, he ran to the outhouse. There, he found her lying on the ground, blood gushing from a gunshot wound in her neck. By the time an emergency medical crew arrived, her heart had stopped beating. A few minutes later, doctors at a nearby hospital pronounced Mrs. Hoffman dead.

Initially, the police thought that Vivian Hoffman had taken her own life. Her husband, however, rejected the idea, arguing that she had shown no signs of being depressed or suicidal. Friends and other family members agreed. When the Berks County coroner declared the official cause of death to be "accidental," most people thought the investigation was over.

But the homicide detectives probing the death were less

than convinced. They remembered that Fred Hoffman, then an assistant to a hospital pathologist, had been a police officer himself until he was arrested for leading a burglary ring he was supposed to have been investigating. Now, they couldn't help but wonder whether he might be up to his old tricks. However, they had a problem: there was no physical evidence connecting him to his wife's death. In the end, Fred Hoffman was allowed to bury Vivian, who was his third wife, and collect $50,000 from her life insurance policy.

In September of 1974, still troubled by the case, the detectives contacted me for advice. I told them I'd be glad to review the file.

Within days of reading the investigative reports, I called the detectives back to tell them that there were some serious questions that needed to be answered. Most importantly, a key report from the Pennsylvania Crime Lab raised considerable doubt that the shooting was either accidental or a suicide. According to the report, the shotgun, which was found two feet from Mrs. Hoffman's body, was a pump-action gun. Firearm experts told me that when a gun like this is discharged, the pump mechanism moves backward. But when police found the weapon on the morning of the shooting, the mechanism was in a forward position. Someone had to have manually locked the lever in a forward position after the shooting in order for it to have been found the way it was.

There was another interesting piece of evidence as well: no fingerprints had been found on the shotgun—only a few smudge marks.

Although it was far too soon to say for sure, I told the detectives, this shooting did not appear to be either an accident or a suicide. Another look at the victim's body, I suggested, might yield some useful information.

After months of legal wrangling with Fred Hoffman, who had since remarried for the fourth time, police finally obtained court permission to exhume Vivian Hoffman's body. On June 6, 1975, the coffin was lifted from the ground and brought to a hospital in Reading, where a roomful of doctors, lawyers, and police officers sat waiting.

For the next three hours, I examined the mortal remains of Vivian Hoffman. The gunshot entrance wound was located on the right side of her neck, just beneath the chin. The pellets had exited high on the left side of her head. She had been shot only once. The X rays told me that there were fourteen pellets still lodged in her skull. Judging from the damage the gunshot had inflicted, I told the investigators that Mrs. Hoffman could have lived for up to five or six minutes after being shot, but that it was more likely she had lived only a minute or less. I also told them there was no way she could have moved herself after being shot.

Because the detectives had recovered additional pellets in the wood of the outhouse, I was able to determine that Mrs. Hoffman was sitting upright when the gun was discharged. After examining the size and characteristics of the entrance wound, I also could tell that the barrel of the shotgun was 6 to 12 inches from her neck when it was fired. With this in mind, I measured the distance from Mrs. Hoffman's armpit to her knuckles: 32 inches. I then measured the shotgun from muzzle to trigger: 35 inches. Adding the additional 6 to 12 inches, I determined that her arms would have to have been at least 42 inches long for her to have fired this weapon by herself. Since there was no evidence that a stick or any other object was used to trigger the weapon, I had my answer.

"This was no accident," I told the detectives. "Nor was it a suicide. There's no doubt about it: this was a homicide."

With my official findings in hand, the police tracked down Fred Hoffman and charged him with first-degree murder. Shortly thereafter, a jury found him guilty of killing his wife and sent him off to prison.

Welcome to the world of forensic pathology, where mystery meets science, law and medicine join forces, and amazing discoveries lurk around every corner. Most importantly, as the Hoffman case illustrates, it is a world where the application of fundamental scientific principles and sound investigative techniques can help to uncover the truth and ensure that justice is served.

Mention the term *forensic pathologist* and most people think of Quincy, the gruff but effective television sleuth. Unlike a typical plot from the TV series, however, not every murder or medical intrigue is solved in sixty minutes by looking through a microscope or examining the soles of a dead man's feet, as Jack Klugman's character was apt to do.

This book was written to take you inside some of the nation's most bizarre and intriguing medical-legal investigations and show you how forensic scientists help to solve crimes—and likewise how they sometimes fail to solve them.

The keys to cracking cases are always different. In the Hoffman case, the keys were the trajectory of the shotgun pellets and the logistics of the crime scene. Other cases have risen and fallen on such factors as the angle of stab wounds, the distance between a gun and its shooter's victim, the time or place a person died, the presence of drugs or poisons in a victim's body.

Technically defined, forensic pathology is that field of medicine that is concerned with the investigation of sudden, violent, suspicious, unexpected, unexplained, or medically unattended deaths. Three out of every four deaths referred to coroners and medical examiners are natural, meaning that the deaths directly resulted from old age or a known sickness or disease. Sometimes hospital pathologists will perform autopsies on these bodies, but never as part of an official medical-legal investigation unless specifically authorized to do so by the local coroner or medical examiner. Of the remaining 25 percent of all deaths, about 75 percent are accidental—a car or airplane crash, for example, or a fall down a set of stairs. Suicides and homicides each account for about 1.0 to 1.5 percent of all deaths, and a small number are classified as being due to "undetermined" causes.

There are many reasons beyond the needs of a homicide or accidental-death investigation to perform an autopsy, of course. Autopsies help us to identify genetic disorders. They uncover contagious diseases and environmental concerns. And through autopsies, pathologists furnish essential data to the scientific world about health and medicine in general.

While there have been many tremendous advances in the techniques of medical-legal investigation in recent years, the fundamental concept is not new. From history books we know that ancient medical men would pour water into stab wounds to determine their depth and severity, and records from Hippocrates' time show a general knowledge of poisons and an interest in such issues as the viability of premature births and the relative fatality of different wounds. Until the Roman era, however, autopsies were generally not performed, since most ancient cultures considered human remains to be sacred.

The first medical-legal autopsy on record was performed on Julius Caesar in 44 B.C. As the great Roman emperor was making preparations for another military invasion, he was attacked in the Roman Senate House by a group of noblemen led by Marcus Brutus. Antistius, a Roman physician, externally examined the general's body and identified twenty-three separate stab wounds. He was even able to tell which of these wounds was the fatal one. As a result, at least according to Shakespeare, Brutus and his co-conspirators were expelled from Rome.

Over time, the concept of forensic science evolved. The Justinian Code, which made its appearance in Rome around A.D. 550, stated that physicians are not witnesses for either party in a dispute before a tribunal or the government; they render judgments rather than testimony. This was the first recognition of the expert witness in history.

By the 1600s, legal medicine had advanced beyond the status of a theoretical pursuit and was actually being introduced into legal texts and courtrooms throughout Europe. Between 1621 and 1635, for instance, a physician to the Pope contributed a collection that discussed such issues as death during birth, feigned diseases, rape, virginity, and determination of parentage. And in Germany in 1667, a physician was able to show that the lungs of a newborn baby would float in water if the child had breathed after birth; if the infant had been stillborn, on the other hand, the lungs would not float, because no oxygen had been inhaled. Twenty years later, another physician used this test to prove that a girl who had been accused of murdering her illegitimate child had been falsely accused.

All the while, medical-legal clinics were being established in Germany, France, and Austria. Many developed educational programs as part of their medical schools. This does not mean that the discipline had entered an altogether enlightened era. As late as 1720, for example, there was serious debate in medical-legal circles about whether a woman could be impregnated by the Devil or a dream. In fact, a judge in France around this time legitimized an infant in a case where the mother and her husband had been physically separated for four years, the decision being made on the grounds that the child had been conceived in a dream. Early practitioners of forensic medicine were also known to have recommended that mentally retarded and insane people be persecuted, drowned, and burned because they were believed to be "firebrands of hell" who were "moved and seduced by instigation of the devil." Needless to say, we've come a long way since those days.

One of the key moments in the history of legal medicine occurred in 1858 in Hooghly, India, when an Englishman named William Hershall made the discovery that the markings on every individual's fingertips were unique. No two sets were alike, not even those of twins. Just as important was his discovery that these markings never changed over the course of a lifetime. Hershall devised a system by which people would dip their fingertips into common seal ink and then press their fingers against a piece of paper, leaving impressions. He first used this technique to prevent swindling in the pension system established for Indian soldiers. Little did he know the impact this discovery would have on the future of criminal investigation.

In 1891, a young Argentinean policeman named Juan Vucetich took fingerprinting to its logical next step by developing a registry of fingerprints for known criminals. A year later, he solved a sensational murder by finding and identifying a fingerprint at the scene of a crime. The print was matched with that of a suspect and used against him in court.

The first criminal case in the United States that involved fingerprinting occurred around the turn of the century, when a notorious burglar named Caesar Cella was on trial in New York City. The evidence gathered by police and prosecutors was rather scant. However, they did have an expert witness who was willing to testify that he had matched the defendant's fingerprints with fingerprints found at the scene of the crime.

The judge in the case was highly skeptical. As the jury watched, he had the state's fingerprint expert leave the courtroom and asked fifteen spectators to press their right index finger against one of the courtroom windows. The judge then asked one of the fifteen spectators to press his finger against the judge's glass desktop. When the expert returned to the courtroom, the judge asked him to match the fingerprints. To everyone's astonishment, the expert solved the mystery in a matter of minutes.

In the United States, we have developed two different kinds of medical-legal systems—the coroner and the medical examiner systems—both of which originated in Europe. In England, the coroner system was introduced by eleventh-century kings, who appointed loyal knights of the realm to go to the scene of a death to determine whether it was natural, accidental, or a homicide. As individuals appointed by the monarchy, they were called "crowners." Over the centuries, this title evolved into "coroner." Because it was a political patronage position, the coroner usually had little or no experience in, or knowledge of, legal medicine.

By comparison, the system established in various parts of the Continent was much more professional and remains the preferred method even today. This model calls for a "medical examiner" trained in forensic pathology and medical-legal practices to be appointed to a position that is designed to be independent from any political influence.

In the United States, English colonists early on established the coroner system, which remains in effect in most communities today. Under this system, a coroner is elected from the general public. However, there is no requirement that this person be a forensic pathologist, a clinical or anatomic pathologist, or even a medical doctor. In fact, as many as half of all elected coroners today have no scientific background at all. A survey of one state showed that only eleven of the eighty-two county coroners were physicians. Most were funeral home directors. A few were farmers, taxi drivers, and high school teachers.

In Hindman, Kentucky, a community of a thousand people located in the southeastern part of the state, residents usually face a choice in the race for county coroner. Every election two individuals, each from one of the town's two funeral homes, campaign hard for the position. Neither is a medical doctor. But the winner gets the gold prize: extra business for his funeral home. This system is fine for the coroner's pocketbook, but lousy when it comes to the administration of justice.

A good example of the kind of trouble this system can cause occurred in 1970 in the nearby town of Hyden, Kentucky, when thirty-eight coal miners died in an explosion. A medical doctor who assisted in the recovery of the bodies determined that five of the thirty-eight miners survived the initial explosion, but then succumbed to carbon monoxide poisoning. When the U.S. Bureau of Mines held hearings on the explosion, however, the physician was never called to testify. Instead, the local coroner, a funeral home director, was asked to speak. Despite his lack of medical training, this man told the federal agents that all of the miners died in the initial explosion.

What the coroner was concealing was the fact that the mine's operators had not equipped the miners with "self-rescuers," small gas masks that provide an extra hour or so of breathing time. Had this testimony come out at the federal hearings, the mine operators very likely would have been charged with criminal violations. It also would have provided evidence for the families of the miners with which they could have sued the owners of the coal mine.

It is important to understand, however, that these anecdotes are not necessarily offered as indictments of the coroner system. Indeed, it is not the name of the medical-legal investigative system that is important, but rather the manner in which the office functions, and the sense of professional responsibility that the person in charge adopts in his or her approach to the determination of cause and manner of death.

As I pointed out in my previous book, *Cause of Death*, many of the most controversial cases on record have involved medical examiner systems, in which, presumably, there were trained forensic pathologists at work. Some of these controversies have stemmed from sloppiness or negligence, while others have strongly suggested influence by district attorneys, homicide detectives, or others.

By the same token, there are many coroners' offices that perform their duties in an admirable fashion, often despite the fact that the coroner is a layperson. They do so by utilizing trained forensic pathologists for autopsies and experienced toxicologists to perform lab tests. More importantly, the officeholder has a keen sense of responsibility and a willingness to order autopsies even in situations in which the family might object. I have had the pleasure of working with several such coroners' offices, and it is my experience that these kinds of offices can function just as well as any medical examiner's office.

Whatever the merits and deficiencies of the coroner system, there is no doubt that the country is slowly shifting away from it. During the three and a half decades in which I have been a practicing forensic pathologist, we have seen hundreds of cities and counties replace their coroners with medical examiners. During the 1960s, there were still only a handful of trained forensic pathologists on the job in the United States, and only a few held degrees in both medicine and law. Today, by contrast, there are as many as 750 educated forensic pathologists in the country. However, only 300 to 400 are in full-time forensic practice, most in medium- and large-sized metropolitan communities that have medical examiner systems. This is a very small number when you consider that there are about 700,000 practicing physicians in the country.

Still, to take a look at the growing role of the forensic expert in our society is to recognize the need for even greater professionalism. In the United States today, nearly 80 percent of all civil cases and perhaps an even greater number of criminal cases involve some aspect of forensic medicine. When one thinks of how litigious and violent our society is, one gets an idea of the magnitude of this interface. Indeed, the term *forensic* has come to identify a growing number of medical and other scientific subspecialists who are called upon to provide and analyze evidence in courts of law. There are forensic psychiatrists, forensic toxicologists, forensic odontologists, forensic immunologists, and forensic anthropologists, to name but a few of these fields of endeavor.

Despite this proliferation of medical-legal specialties, the most widely used courtroom expert remains the forensic pathologist. Why? Quite simply, because there is no other medical specialist as critically integrated into the legal process. In theory, it has always been this way. But it was not until fairly recently that the usefulness of the forensic pathologist was fully appreciated. For better or for worse, there are an increasing number of cases in which individuals seek redress for injuries, for malpractice, and for harm done to them by all kinds of home and work products. Issues like survival time and determination of conscious pain and suffering have been thrust upon my specialty.

The criminal justice system, too, is constantly being made more sophisticated by the involvement of forensic scientists. Until thirty years ago, for example, child abuse was a little-recognized social ill. Even when it gained substantial recognition, legal action was still slow to evolve. Today, however, the number of such cases is truly amazing. Indeed, it is a whole area with which the forensic pathologist, a generation ago, had very little contact. This is also true of rape and sexual assault. Such crimes have always occurred, of course, but it was not until the feminist movement's success in expanding their legal definitions that these kinds of cases assumed such a prominent role.

As I look back over my nearly thirty-five-year career as a forensic pathologist, I am repeatedly reminded of the old French adage "The more things change, the more they remain the same." For all of the advances I have witnessed in my field over the past three decades, the discipline's fundamental concepts have not changed all that much. Even today, a shooting is still a shooting, a stabbing is still a stabbing, and a beating is still a beating. Every year, people die in plane crashes, in fires, in bombings, in falls. And it remains my job to determine just how these deaths occurred. It may sound like a horror story, but that's what forensic pathology is all about, and that's what it always will be about.

ONE

THE O.J. SIMPSON CASE
BEHIND THE SCENES OF THE "DREAM TEAM" DEFENSE

Two dark socks.
An old, shriveled-up glove.
Blood—big spatters of it here, small droplets of it there.
A missing hour in the middle of the night.

Gaffes—an amazing, almost incomprehensible number of stupid blunders.

And, quite possibly, a few intentional misdeeds. Or even outright corruption.

Mix it all up and you have the recipe for the murder trial of the century. But then, of course, *California v. Orenthal James Simpson* was much more than a court case. It was theater. It was soap opera. It was prime-time entertainment. And yet it was entertainment of a whole new variety.

To an extent perhaps never before encountered in the history of the American legal system, this trial focused on the significance of physical and scientific evidence. Some pointed strongly toward Simpson's guilt in the murders of his ex-wife, Nicole Brown Simpson, and her friend, Ronald Goldman. Surprisingly, however, there were enough lapses in the evidence to suggest his innocence—no eyewitnesses, no jailhouse confessions, not even a murder weapon.

Much like the assassination of President Kennedy, the murders of Simpson and Goldman have imprinted themselves on the nation's collective memory. It was the evening of June 12, 1994. Nicole had been to dinner with her family at Mezzaluna, a trendy southern California restaurant where she often ate. After a pleasant evening, she returned to her condo at 875 South Bundy Drive. No sooner had she walked in the door at about 9:35 P.M. than her telephone rang. It was her mother, Judith Brown, saying she had left her glasses at the restaurant. Assuring her mother that she would retrieve them, Nicole called Mezzaluna. Ron Goldman, a waiter with whom she had become friendly, offered to bring the glasses by her home when his shift ended at 9:50 P.M.

That's the last time anyone would see or hear from Simpson or Goldman again. At exactly midnight, neighbors came across Nicole's Akita, which had blood on its paws and was barking persistently in what they described as a "wail." They followed the dog to the walkway and garden area outside of Nicole's home. There, they discovered the bodies.

When Los Angeles police arrived on the scene about 12:15 A.M., they found thirty-five-year-old Nicole lying near the front gate of the condo at the foot of the stairs that led to her front door, her bloodied body curled up in a fetal position. She had been stabbed several times, including a gaping slash across the front of her throat. A few feet away, detectives spotted the body of twenty-nine-year-old Ronald Goldman backed up against a tree stump and an iron fence and slumped to one side. His face, arms, and hands had repeatedly been cut. Next to Goldman's right foot was an envelope containing a pair of eyeglasses. The Akita's bloody paw prints were also present on the sidewalk.

Within minutes, authorities identified the victims and learned that Nicole's ex-husband was O.J. Simpson. Almost immediately, the former football star became a suspect. And so it all began.

Everywhere I went in 1994 and 1995, the only topic people wanted to talk about was the O.J. case. Some were completely fascinated by it, openly admitting to being addicted to the nationally televised coverage by CNN or Court TV. Others talked about how bored or disgusted they were with the whole thing and how society was being oversaturated with information about the case. Clearly, the addicts outnumbered the bored or disgusted, for no other American news story has ever dominated the news ratings over such a long period of time.

Another interesting aspect of the Simpson case is the fact that almost everyone who knew anything about it took sides. There were those who believed that the evidence against the former football star was so overwhelming and so incriminating that he had to be guilty. And then there were those who took the position that there was so much evidence— especially circumstantial evidence—linking O.J. to the crime in such a simple, obvious manner that he must have been framed and that some of the evidence must have been fabricated.

Well, here's a novel thought: perhaps both positions were correct.

To be sure, there are several indisputable facts or arguments favoring each side of the coin. For example, prosecutors presented the following evidence:

- Bloodstains found at the crime scene genetically matched blood samples taken from Mr. Simpson.
- The socks found at the foot of Simpson's bed contained bloodstains that matched samples taken from the victims.
- A glove found behind Simpson's home matched a glove found at the crime scene and contained bloodstains that matched samples taken from the victims.
- Blood droplets found in Simpson's white Ford Bronco genetically matched the victims' samples.
- Hair found on the bloodied shirt worn by Ronald Goldman had the same characteristics as the samples taken from Simpson.
- A mysterious shoe print discovered at the crime scene matched a Bruno Magli shoe. There was evidence

that Simpson had purchased a pair of Magli shoes weeks earlier.

- Simpson does not have an alibi for about an hour of the time frame during which the murders are believed to have occurred.
- There is significant evidence showing that Simpson physically abused his ex-wife and threatened to kill her if he ever caught her with another man.

While this laundry list seems pretty damning, keep in mind that some or all of it may be dirty laundry. An inventory of the evidence and arguments supporting the defense's case is also quite staggering:

- A vial containing blood taken from Simpson subsequently revealed that 1.5 cubic centimeters had disappeared while in police custody.
- Two defense experts who examined the socks two weeks after the murders did not see any evidence of bloodstains. Furthermore, the prosecution says it didn't discover and report the stains until August, more than six weeks after the slayings.
- The bloodstains found on the socks also contained EDTA, a chemical preservative used to prevent blood samples from clotting. This would suggest that the blood was not directly transferred from the victims onto Simpson's socks.
- The gloves did not fit Simpson.
- Police allowed the bodies to lie outdoors at the crime scene for ten hours before permitting anyone from the coroner's office to examine them.
- The forensic pathologist who performed the autopsies admitted to making up to forty errors during his examinations.
- A lead detective in the case, who found the glove at Simpson's estate, was caught perjuring himself on the witness stand by claiming that he had not used a particular racial slur in more than ten years, when in fact he had used

racial and ethnic slurs frequently and most disparagingly in several hours of tape-recorded interviews with a screenwriter. The interviews took place over a period of years within the last decade.

What does all of this mean? It's hard to say, but it raises a possibility that neither the prosecution nor the defense was willing to admit: that Simpson was involved in the murders but either did not act alone or did not actually participate in them.

From day one and throughout the trial, the logical flaw in this case was the assumption that it was an all-or-nothing proposition—either Simpson went to Nicole's apartment by himself, killed her and Goldman, then quickly washed himself and discarded his clothes and the murder weapon; or he didn't do it at all and was conspiratorially framed by law enforcement officials. Rather than claim that either one of these scenarios is completely and absolutely incorrect, I suggest that there is another possibility that is reasonably supported by the evidence.

My involvement in the Simpson case was essentially twofold. First, as a friend and colleague of many of the key characters in this tale, I was privy to a great deal of information about the case. Trial attorney F. Lee Bailey and I have known each other for many years, and I've testified and given him expert opinions in dozens of homicide and wrongful-death cases. Similarly, I've worked closely with both DNA specialist Barry Scheck and appellate attorney Alan Dershowitz.

In addition, I am very close professionally and personally with four of the defense team's main expert witnesses: Dr. Michael Baden, director of the New York State Police Forensic Sciences Unit; Dr. Henry Lee, director of the Connecticut State Police Forensic Science Laboratory and a professor at the University of New Haven; Professor Herbert MacDonell, director of the Laboratory of Forensic Science, a first-rate private lab in Corning, New York; and Dr. Fredric Rieders, director of National Medical Services, a highly regarded toxicology laboratory in Willow Grove, Pennsylvania. All four of these men are considered to be among the top forensic scientists in the world.

Seldom would a week slip by when I did not have occasion to discuss some aspect of the case with a member of the defense crew. Of course, these discussions were always on a confidential basis. But because of them, I have gained a unique perspective on the evidence in question, the players involved, and the events as they unfolded backstage. On a few occasions, Lee Bailey or Michael Baden contacted me about officially joining the so-called O.J. "Dream Team." While I agreed to advise them privately and share ideas, I decided early on that it would be best if I did not become formally connected to the trial. One of my primary concerns was preserving my second connection to this case.

Beginning with the preliminary hearing in June 1994, I had become a regular commentator for several national news outlets. As a result, I had frequently expressed opinions about scientific evidence and other aspects of the case (though never on Simpson's guilt or innocence), and therefore did not think it would be proper for me thereafter to take sides by becoming an official forensic pathology consultant.

Besides, my newfound "career" as a media consultant was as time-consuming as it was exciting. Nearly every day, a producer at NBC, ABC, or CNN would call to ask me to go on the air that evening to help interpret a new piece of evidence or testimony. Somehow, my name must have gotten into the Rolodex files of reporters at the *Los Angeles Times* and *USA Today* as well, because they frequently called me at home or at my office for a quote or an analysis.

My favorite interviews were on those programs that were a bit longer and included other experts, such as prosecutors, defense attorneys, and judges. I was on NBC's *Today* show several times and found Bryant Gumbel and Katie Couric to be absolutely delightful. Peter Jennings and Tom Brokaw each had me on a few times and both were extremely gracious and professional. Similarly, I found Larry King, Geraldo Rivera, and PBS's Charlie Rose to be well-informed and talented interviewers.

The case affected many other people besides myself, of course. As a result of all the media attention and shared fascination, it took on a life of its own in the public mind. People began referring to the trial and all the legal wrangling simply as "O.J." Friends would ask one another not whether they had seen excerpts of the trial that day, but whether they had watched "O.J." It replaced the weather as the topic of conversation to fall back on.

At times, the lawyers seemed to be more like actors than advocates. Witnesses came across as if they were auditioning for parts rather than offering testimony. And the judge—well, let's just say that he seemed more interested in the high-profile guests who paraded through his courtroom daily (Ted Koppel, Larry King, and Diane Sawyer, to name but a few) than he did in running the trial in a tight, professional manner and keeping the lawyers under control.

One of the biggest problems with this trial was that, from an entertainment perspective, it had everything: suspense, celebrity, violence, sex, corruption. As the news media came to call it, it was, quite simply, "the trial of the century." But then again, it seems to me that we have a trial of the century every few years.

Throughout our country's brief history, Americans have shown a strange fascination with the courts, especially criminal trials. This intrigue dates back at least to the Salem witch trials of the late 1600s, when several female members of the Massachusetts colony were hanged or burned at the stake as Satan's accomplices. And then, of course, there was the all-consuming interest in the fate of Lizzie Borden, who, legend has it, "took an ax / And gave her mother forty whacks," then gave her father forty-one. Often forgotten in the telling of that tale is the fact that Borden was found not guilty.

Almost every recent decade, in fact, has featured at least one trial that could lay claim to this title. In the late 1940s, Charlie Chaplin's paternity suit in Los Angeles received nearly as much attention as the trials of twenty-one Nazi war leaders in Nuremberg, Germany. In 1951, the nation couldn't get enough news about Julius and Ethel Rosenberg, owners of a

New York machine shop who were turned in by Mrs. Rosenberg's brother on charges of selling nuclear secrets to the Soviets.

The cases of Jack Ruby and Sirhan Sirhan dominated legal headlines in the 1960s, as did the trials of the Black Panthers in Chicago and New Haven. In the 1970s, court enthusiasts were treated to the bizarre and gruesome murders committed by Charles Manson and to the ultimate in political crimes when several high-ranking officials of the Nixon administration were charged and convicted in the Watergate break-in. The 1980s, too, had a few celebrated cases. First, there was the Jean Harris affair. Then, of course, came the trial of John Hinckley Jr., the man who tried to kill President Reagan, and his successful plea of not guilty by reason of insanity. Later in the decade, courts focused on such characters as Marion Barry and Oliver North.

But for unforgettable trials, few decades will top the 1990s. First, there were the Menendez brothers in Los Angeles, whose novel defense in the murders of their parents painted them as victims rather than perpetrators. The largely unsuccessful prosecutions of the Los Angeles police officers who were caught on videotape beating Rodney King came next, and the Reginald Denny case that followed will long be remembered. And then, of course, there were the trials of Panamanian dictator Manuel Noriega, the former Philippines First Lady Imelda Marcos, and boxing champ turned rapist Mike Tyson.

The major difference between the pre– and post–World War II cases, of course, is television. More recently, Court TV and CNN have allowed people to follow legal proceedings closely while sitting in their La-Z-Boy recliners instead of on hard, wooden benches. They have also served to educate the public about many of the intricacies of our legal system.

And then came O.J. Simpson.

To understand the attention this case received, one needs to understand the place the defendant occupies in the American psyche. My wife, Sigrid, and I sat down one evening and tried to think of a more famous and respected American who had been accused of murder. All of the names previously mentioned and more were tossed around. But while many of those people became famous for their alleged crimes, very few of them had previously been as well-known, and loved, as Simpson.

Orenthal James Simpson was born to Eunice and Jimmy Lee Simpson in San Francisco in 1947. From the start, the person we affectionately called "The Juice" had a roller-coaster upbringing. In the months shortly after his birth, Simpson's parents noticed that something was wrong with his legs. Doctors said their son was ravaged by rickets—a vitamin D deficiency that weakens and disturbs the growth of bones. The physicians had an answer: break his legs and reset them with braces. But because the Simpsons were poor, they rejected the surgery, opting instead for a homemade brace using special shoes that O.J. often wore on the wrong feet. As a result, when his bones grew, he ended up bowlegged and with legs so thin that friends called him "Pencil Pins."

A below-average student, Simpson focused on athletics instead and soon found himself running as fast as the other boys. But socializing was at least as important, and by the time he reached high school, his extremely outgoing and friendly personality had gained him positions of leadership. He headed a group called The Superiors, which organized school dances and community projects for young people. But he also created the Persian Warriors, a street gang that was a bit less community-minded than The Superiors, specializing in stealing and drinking.

At the age of fifteen, these antics landed O.J. in juvenile court. Going home and facing his parents that afternoon would be a defining moment in Simpson's life. Instead of his father waiting at the front door, there stood Willie Mays, the all-star outfielder for the San Francisco Giants. Mays, a friend of Simpson's football coach, had heard of O.J.'s athletic promise and agreed to try setting him on the right track. The legendary slugger talked with the teenager for a while, then took him to Mays's home, which was located in one of the wealthiest sections of town.

"This is the way to live," young O.J. is said to have remarked that day.

It was as if he had seen his road to success. Family members say he cleaned up his act and immediately decided to make athletics, especially professional football, his life and his ticket to fame and stardom.

This new attitude soon displayed itself on the football field. O.J.'s high school, Galileo High, had never been known for its athletic teams. That changed in Simpson's senior year. One of the first games of the season was against football powerhouse St. Ignatius, winners of their previous 23 games. The first half was dominated by St. Ignatius, which took the lead 25-10. But then O.J. went to work, scoring touchdowns on 60-, 80-, and 90-yard runs.

So impressed was the coach at St. Ignatius that he immediately called someone he knew on the coaching staff at the University of Southern California to tell him about the potential recruit. USC was more than a little interested, but because of poor grades, Simpson was forced to attend a junior college for two years before USC would offer him a full scholarship. When he finally got there, O.J. wasted no time breaking almost every USC rushing record. Then, in 1968, he won the Heisman Trophy, college football's most prestigious award, and became the first selection in the NFL draft, taken by the Buffalo Bills.

For the next decade, O.J. dazzled fans of professional football. Like no other running back in history, he could find a hole in a defensive line and explode through it. I remember watching him play against the Detroit Lions one Thanksgiving in the early 1970s. It was the day he set the single-game rushing record. At times it seemed as if he could change direction in midair.

In 1973, he set the single-season rushing record with 2,003 yards—an incredible achievement, especially considering that he was a member of a rather mediocre team. In fact, there are many football buffs who believe that if Simpson had played with a great team of that era, such as the Baltimore Colts or the Miami Dolphins, he might have become known as the greatest football player of all time.

Nevertheless, football was rough on O.J., and by the late 1970s his knees had started to give out. I remember reading an article that quoted Simpson as saying that he was so sore, bruised, and beaten up after Sunday football games that he couldn't even practice again until Thursday. Finally, in 1978, he hung up his cleats and turned his gaze in other directions.

Throughout his football career, The Juice had become known to the public and to friends alike as one of the nicest guys on earth. He always made time to spend with children. He was generous to a fault with charities. And never did he turn away or charge money for an autograph. Once retired, this "good-guy" image, coupled with O.J.'s limitless ambition, guaranteed him a smooth transition into the commercial world.

First, Hertz made him its national spokesman, and O.J. became famous all over again, this time for running and leaping through airports to catch a plane. Then ABC, and later NBC, signed him on as a commentator on NFL games. Later still, he endeared himself to moviegoers everywhere by acting in such hits as *The Towering Inferno* and the *Naked Gun* series. By the time Simpson divorced Nicole, his second wife, in 1992, his annual income from football commentary, movies, and Hertz ads was estimated at about $700,000 a year and his net worth at $10 million.

Long before that milestone, though, O.J. was wealthy and popular beyond his wildest dreams, married to his high school sweetheart and a proud father to two daughters and a son. But apparently, all was not as rosy as it seemed to be. Many friends, including Cleveland Browns superstar Jim Brown, say Simpson had a drug habit. Others, including his first wife, contend he was a womanizer who surrounded himself with young ladies readily willing to fulfill his sexual needs. And then there were stories about his temper, something that his millions of adoring fans never heard or read about before the murder trial.

Then, in 1980, tragedy struck. The Simpsons' daughter, Aaren, was only twenty-three months old when she was found drowned in the family's pool. Although neither one of the Simpsons was to blame, this was the last straw for their marriage. Shortly thereafter, the couple divorced.

Three years earlier, while still married, Simpson had met Nicole Brown, a waitress at a swank Beverly Hills nightclub called the Daisy. Eighteen years old, blond and beautiful, Nicole had been born in West Germany to a *Stars and Stripes* correspondent and his wife and raised in an unexceptional, middle-class atmosphere. In California, Brown had developed a reputation as a beach bunny, a free spirit who liked to dance and party. She and O.J. dated and then lived together for several years before marrying in 1985.

Even in Hollywood, they were a striking couple. He was good-looking and physically fit, showing no signs of age, and she was absolutely gorgeous. Together, they lived the good life. They frequented the hottest nightspots in southern California, drove white Ferraris, traveled in the most exclusive circles, and lived in million-dollar homes in Brentwood, Laguna Beach, and Manhattan Beach. Most importantly, say friends, he loved being with her and she simply adored him. And despite their busy lives, they even found time to have two children, a daughter and a son. To the public eye, they were the ideal couple, living in the perfect world.

Then came that notorious evening on New Year's Day, 1989—when police were called to an estate on Rockingham Drive. When they arrived, they found Nicole standing outside crying. Her eye was black and blood dripped from her lip. She ran toward the police officers, begging for help.

"He's going to kill me," she screamed.

At that moment, the front door opened and Simpson, wearing only a robe, walked out.

"I don't want that woman sleeping in my bed anymore," he yelled. "I got two women and I don't want that woman in my bed anymore."

Informed that his wife wanted to press charges and have

him arrested, Simpson retorted, "This is a family matter. Why do you want to make a big deal of it? We can handle it."

Eight times during their marriage, police were called to their house to intercede in the couple's domestic discord. Two of those incidents reportedly involved violence. We've all heard the 911 calls. We've all heard the threats from the defendant's own mouth. Most of us were shocked: this was not the O. J. Simpson we thought we knew. But after Nicole's death, several witnesses would come forward to say that Simpson had also stalked Nicole after their divorce. He was the ultimate in jealous ex-husbands, they claimed. These repeated incidents, of course, would become the basis for the motive to which police and prosecutors later attributed the murders.

I first came to learn about the slayings of Nicole Brown Simpson and Ronald Goldman the afternoon after they occurred. Like everyone else, my first thought was: Where was O.J.?

Simpson's supporters contend that the police unfairly targeted him from the start and didn't even consider other potential suspects or look for evidence that might lead them elsewhere. As it turns out, I think there is some evidence indicating that there were two assailants or an assailant with an accomplice. Still, I do not think it was improper for the detectives to take their first look at the ex-husband of one of the victims.

From experience, I can tell you that when something like this happens, the initial reaction of every police detective, every forensic pathologist, every lawyer, and every seasoned journalist is, Where's the spouse? It's a logical connection to make. In fact, one would be stupid *not* to think this way. Statistics show that in our country, more people are killed by relatives or close friends than by complete strangers. When you have a homicide and are searching for suspects, you always start with family members—a spouse or ex-spouse if the victim was married or divorced, parents if the victim was a child, even brothers and sisters.

In this case, of course, there was another factor driving investigators toward Simpson. Many of them were well aware of the couple's marital problems, and that made Simpson a prime suspect even without a stitch of evidence. Detective Mark Fuhrman, for one, certainly knew about their troubles; he had been one of the officers who responded to their residence on the evening of New Year's Day, 1989. In fact, it is fair to say that it was because of Fuhrman's and the Los Angeles Police Department's institutional knowledge of the Simpsons' squabbles that O.J., rightly or wrongly, became an instant suspect.

Having said that, I must add that bad reputations alone do not give police officers probable cause to go and arrest a person. We can thank our legal system that strong suspicions and gut instincts by police officers are not evidence in court. Fortunately, the Sixth Amendment to the U.S. Constitution requires a little thing called *evidence* before the government can make an accusation against one of its citizens.

From the beginning, there was nothing ordinary about this case. The ex-wife of a major celebrity and her male acquaintance were horrendously slashed to death, and all eyes, as in a made-for-television movie, were on the celebrity ex-husband. Simpson appeared grief-stricken. He hugged and kissed and cried with his children and their families. He even consented to additional police searches of his home and gave the authorities a lengthy statement. Throughout, he denied any involvement in the murders, stating that he had no idea why someone would want to kill his ex-wife or Goldman.

Even Simpson's eventual arrest was something only Southern California could dream up. On the evening of Friday, June 17, 1994, my family and I were at a restaurant in Pittsburgh. On my way to the rest room, I noticed dozens of people standing around a television set at the bar, their eyes glued to the screen as if the President were on the air announcing we were at war with China.

"What's going on?" I inquired.

"It's O.J.," one man responded, pointing his finger at a white Ford Bronco driving thirty miles an hour down an empty Los Angeles interstate. Behind the Bronco, and traveling at the same rate of speed, were dozens of police cars with their blue lights flashing. Lining the side of the highway were people cheering and holding signs reading, "Go O.J." and "We love you O.J."

"Why don't they just force him to pull over?" I asked.

"They say O.J. is in the back seat with a gun pointed to his head, threatening to kill himself if they get any closer," the man answered. "His friend A. C. Cowlings is driving."

Every major network had dropped its normal prime-time programming to broadcast this surreal scene. More than 95 million people watched Simpson run that night—more than had ever seen him carry a football! Friends and family took to the airwaves to beg the former football star not to harm himself and to turn himself in. Then, as if the entire episode were staged, Robert Kardashian, Simpson's close friend and lawyer, came forward to read a letter Simpson had written. Most interpreted it as a suicide note:

To Whom It May Concern:

First, everyone understand. I have nothing to do with Nicole's murder. I loved her, always have and always will. If we had a problem, it's because I loved her so much.

Recently, we came to the understanding that for now we were not right for each other, at least for now. Despite our love, we were different and that's why we mutually agreed to go our separate ways.

It was tough splitting for a second time but we both knew it was for the best. Inside I had no doubt that in the future we would be close friends or more. Unlike what has been written in the press, Nicole and I had a great relationship for most of our lives together. Like all long-term relationships, we had a few downs and ups.

I took the heat New Year's 1989 because that's what I was supposed to do. I did not plead no contest for any other reason but to protect our privacy and was advised it would end the press hype.

I don't want to belabor knocking the press, but I can't believe what is being said. Most of it is totally made up. I know you have a job to do, but as a last wish, please, please, please, leave my children in peace. Their lives will be tough enough.

At times I have felt like a battered husband or boyfriend but I loved her, make that clear to everyone. And I would take whatever it took to make it work.

Don't feel sorry for me. I've had a great life, great friends. Please think of the real O.J. and not this lost person.

Thanks for making my life special. I hope I helped yours.

Peace and love, O.J.

As we all know, Simpson finally turned himself in at his Brentwood estate later that evening. At that point, it certainly did not look good for the Hall of Famer. Under the law, intentionally running from police can be used in court as evidence of guilt. But five days later, on June 22, Simpson stood before Los Angeles Superior Court judge Cecil Mills and pleaded "Absolutely, 100 percent not guilty."

This marked the official beginning of one of the most bizarre murder cases I have ever encountered.

A week later, preliminary hearings to determine whether there was enough evidence to put Simpson on trial began. Officially called a "probable cause hearing," this is also an opportunity for defense attorneys to see just how strong a case the prosecution has. Likewise they get a chance to see if there are any major holes or errors.

As the hearings began, I was called by a producer with *NBC News* who wanted to know whether I'd be interested in flying to New York to help Tom Brokaw analyze the evidence. Despite the fact that I could have charged a paying client much more for the same amount of time, I readily agreed.

The next day, I was in my own room at Rockefeller Center, just down the hall from the main news studios. During breaks in the testimony or at key moments, Brokaw would cut in to ask me questions. Intellectually, it was very challenging. One of the requirements of speaking on live television is that you have to say everything in crisp, succinct sentences. There is very little time to elaborate on anything.

The first day of testimony in the preliminary hearing focused on a knife that Simpson had allegedly bought at a Los Angeles store. Police said they were still looking for the knife and believed it to be the murder weapon. While they didn't have the knife itself, they said, they did know exactly what it looked like and how long and wide it was. However, I had learned that not everything the L.A. stations were reporting was accurate. For example, one TV station reported—and many others later repeated the story—that police had found a ski mask used in the crime. Eventually it was revealed that there was no ski mask.

During a break in the hearings, I called my office to learn that a producer from CNN's *Crossfire* had called to invite me to appear on the show that evening. Of all the programs on which the Simpson case was being discussed, *Crossfire* was my favorite. Not only do I find Patrick Buchanan and Michael Kinsley to be highly entertaining individuals, but I also think of them as very astute and well-read. That being said, I must add that Buchanan should have stuck to his God-given talents as a television commentator and kept out of politics. I, along with millions of other Americans, would have a hard time ever accepting his political philosophies and agenda as president of the United States. At any rate, the chance to appear on *Crossfire* was not one I wanted to pass up. I told my administrative assistant, Maribeth, to call back immediately and accept the invitation.

A second message was from my good friend and colleague Dr. Michael Baden. The former chief medical examiner of New York City, Michael had served with me on the special medical panel that investigated the murder of President John F. Kennedy for the House Select Committee on Assassinations in 1978 and 1979. While we ultimately disagreed on the validity of the single-bullet theory and the question of whether President Kennedy could have been killed by a lone gunman, we had grown close over the years as fellow professionals and friends. I would venture to say that Michael is always correct in his findings—except, of course, when I am testifying for the other side!

A few days earlier, Michael and I had been testifying on opposite sides in a murder trial in Wilkes Barre, Pennsylvania, when Michael pulled me aside to tell me that Robert Shapiro, Simpson's lead attorney, had just asked him to travel to L.A. to review the O.J. case. Curious as to what Michael had discovered, I returned his call immediately.

"Hello, Michael," I said. "How are you?"

"They'll let just about anyone on television these days," he responded.

As we talked, Michael described his review of the autopsy findings and other medical evidence. His first conclusion was that they were a complete mess. But Michael had more interesting things to tell me about his trip to California. Upon his arrival, Bob Shapiro had taken him and Dr. Henry Lee to the home of O.J.'s personal attorney, Robert Kardashian, where O.J. had been staying since his return from Chicago. They arrived at Kardashian's home in the late morning hours of Friday, June 17, just as O.J. was preparing to surrender to police.

Together, Michael and Henry had examined and photographed the cuts on Simpson's hands. They also had taken blood and hair samples from Simpson for comparison with evidence police had collected at the crime scene.

"So what do you think?" I inquired.

"There are definite cuts," Michael said. "But the cuts are jagged. To me, they're more consistent with O.J.'s story that he cut his hands on a glass at his hotel when he learned of Nicole's murder. The cuts are not consistent with knife wounds."

Michael also informed me that Simpson had appeared to be very depressed, answering all of Michael's and Henry's questions with either a simple yes or no. While he had cooperated fully with them, Michael said, he did very little talking and came across as lethargic and apathetic.

"In fact," Michael said, "I was so concerned about his depressed state that as soon as I got a chance, I called the jail physician to ask him to put O.J. on a twenty-four-hour suicide watch."

In the meantime, unbeknownst to everyone but O.J., history was in the making. According to Michael, O.J. had just walked into a bedroom to make one last call to his mother when the police officers arrived. Meeting the officers at the front door, Shapiro called out for Simpson to come down. There was no answer. After a few more shouts, Kardashian and Shapiro started walking through the house looking for him. "Only after about five minutes of searching did it hit us," Michael said. "O.J. was gone. He had snuck out."

Immediately suspicious of everyone in the room, the officers had placed all of them under house arrest. "They thought that Henry and I had somehow helped O.J. escape," Michael said. As it turned out, however, one or two of the officers had attended lectures that Henry had conducted. "When they recognized Henry," Michael said, "they let us go."

"You certainly know how to pick the right cases, don't you?" I said.

On *Crossfire* that night, the knife and DNA were the hot topics of conversation. Neither Buchanan nor Kinsley had figured out whether the slayings were a right-wing or a left-wing event, and so they stuck to the facts.

KINSLEY: Cyril Wecht, explain to us about this knife. Now, police went to the store and asked for this specific knife. Can you reason backward from a knife wound to a particular kind of knife the way you can a bullet wound to a particular kind of bullet?

WECHT: No, Michael, not with that kind of specificity. You can get some general characteristics from examining the knife wounds, the size, the width, the depth, whether there are any hilt marks. These are the kinds of things that you determine with stab wounds. Are there any serrations? Are there any patterns that would suggest a particular kind of knife? But you do not have the specific characteristics that you would have with certain bullets that are recovered from the body or from the crime scene. I think that they did not get onto the trail of this particular knife from the autopsy findings. There had to have been something of a non-medical nature that led them in that direction.

KINSLEY: So, you think that they found out that the knife store had sold this guy the knife and they really have not tied it into the murder at all yet?

WECHT: Well, I expect next week, when the pathologist who did the autopsies comes forward, he or she is going to testify what the minimum length of the knife had to be, what the width had to be, the absence of serrations, whether the wounds are all consistent with a single-edged blade, all of those things. And then, during the hearing, the prosecutors will present the pathologist with that knife and ask, "Dr. X, is this knife consistent with the kind of instrumentality that could have inflicted the wounds you saw on Mrs. Simpson and Mr. Goldman?"

BUCHANAN: Dr. Wecht, Pat Buchanan here. We've been hearing all along that this was a serrated knife that did it. All of a sudden, we find out, it's a very sharp knife on one side and very blunt on the other, from all of these leaks that have been coming out. What does that tell you?

WECHT: Well, I guess, Mr. Buchanan, maybe the serrated knife went the way of the ski mask. You know, it tells me that this trial has been going on in the news media in a way that I cannot recall any other trial [going on]. . . . Any kid right out of law school practicing in East Podunk, Montana, or West Overshoe, Mississippi, would have known not to do this. I can't believe that the district attorney's office of Los Angeles, coming off the McMartin School child abuse case, or the Menendez brothers case, or the Rodney King case, would have wound up with another debacle like this. It's absolutely incredible.

BUCHANAN: All right, Dr. Wecht. Let's assume for the sake of argument that all of the evidence found at O.J. Simpson's house and his driveway and his Ford Bronco is thrown out because police didn't have a warrant to search any of it. That leaves the case resting almost totally on blood and hair samples at the crime scene. Now, how good is DNA and the blood testing in linking, again hypothetically, O.J. Simpson to the crime? Is the DNA, is that a lock or a definite match, or is it just probable?

WECHT: The DNA is essentially a lock. The basic scientific concept of DNA has not been challenged anywhere in the world. There have been challenges in the courts regarding the degree of mathematic conclusions that can be drawn. In other words, is it a one in 800,000 or a one in four or five million?

BUCHANAN: Let me follow up. There's blood all over the crime scene. There's Mrs. Simpson's blood, there's Mr. Goldman's blood, and presumably there's someone else's blood. If it's O.J. Simpson's blood, and it's his hair at that scene, and they can match it, they really don't need to bring in the blood in the house, do they?

WECHT: Well, sure. Let us say that these things do match up, Mr. Buchanan.

BUCHANAN: Right.

WECHT: Then it's going to be up to O.J. Simpson to say, "Well, I bled there two or three days before. I dropped my hair there the week before." How do you think that's going to fly? How are they going to explain all of those things being there? Now, you can only hope, if you're the prosecution, that these specimens were properly collected, that there is no contamination. You can only hope that you have the necessary expertise within the crime lab. Based on what I saw today, I would be a little concerned if I were the prosecutor.

The next day, I was back at the NBC studios with Brokaw. The big action of the day focused on a piece of mystery evidence. Lawyers were in mid-argument when another Los Angeles Superior Court judge entered at the back of the courtroom. In his hands he carried an envelope. As he approached the front of the courtroom, the jurist announced that defense attorneys had come to him privately with a potential piece of evidence and asked that it be sealed. This was done to guarantee that there had been no tampering. Immediately, people began speculating what was in the sealed envelope.

Just as the judge was handing the envelope over to the Simpson court, the telephone in my studio booth rang. It was F. Lee Bailey.

"Do you know what's in the package?" he asked.

"No clue."

"It's the knife—the knife they've been looking for."

In return for this piece of information, I shared one of my own discoveries, something that would rightfully become a big embarrassment to the Los Angeles authorities. Even though the time of death was estimated to have been between 10 P.M. and midnight, the official report said that a representative of the medical examiner's office did not examine the bodies until approximately 10:30 A.M.—more than ten hours after the slayings. Furthermore, the autopsies on the two bodies were not performed until the next day, more than thirty hours after being discovered.

In fairness, it should be noted that the police investigators had not called the office until 6:30 A.M. to notify it of a homicide. And even then, the medical examiner's office was told simply to stand by; in fact, it was not until 8:15 A.M. that police called back and requested that someone come to the crime scene. Even after an investigator arrived at the scene, she was not permitted to examine the bodies right away. And as it turned out, this individual was not a forensic pathologist or even an experienced medical-legal investigator.

"This is outrageous conduct," I told Bailey. "As you know, proper police investigative protocol is to call the medical examiner to the scene of a homicide immediately. I cannot explain to you in strong enough terms how important this is."

As it turned out, I did not have to explain anything to Lee. He was well-acquainted with the reasons that a medical-legal investigator must get to the crime scene as quickly as possible, including the need to ensure that the physical evidence is properly collected and preserved, and that the chain of evidence is properly followed. Most importantly, however, it is up to the medical examiner or coroner to determine the time of death in homicides to the closest degree possible.

There are three primary ways of gauging the time of death. None is precise on its own, but when calculated together, they can give a pretty solid estimate. The first is by determining the extent of algor mortis, which is the cooling of the body after death. The second is by looking at the degree of rigor mortis, or the stiffening of the corpse's muscles. Finally, there is checking the extent of livor mortis, the settling of blood in the body as a result of gravitational flow.

The sooner a medical expert can examine the body and assess these processes, the more reliable the estimate will be. Because police did not permit the medical examiner's office to be at the crime scene for more than ten hours, the best estimate for time of death that could be made by the deputy medical examiner who conducted the autopsy was between 9 P.M. and 12:45 A.M. This was a completely useless finding. It told us nothing.

As we concluded our conversation, Lee encouraged me to disclose my findings as soon as possible.

The next day, I was back on *Crossfire*. This time, however, Michael Kinsley's spot was being filled by Bob Beckel, a liberal commentator who lacked Kinsley's keen sense of humor. Pat Buchanan was there and was his usual cantankerous self.

> BECKEL: Dr. Cyril Wecht, let me ask you, this is the most extraordinary case. There's never been anything like this. Public opinion is playing a huge role in this thing. But it seems like the defense is getting their lunch eaten every day. They're looking small, evasive.
>
> WECHT: I've had the pleasure and opportunity to work with many great attorneys. As coroner of Allegheny County [a job to which I returned in January 1996], we handled all of the equivalents of preliminary hearings for homicides. As far as I'm concerned, this preliminary hearing is a media circus. It has been generated for many different reasons by the activities of both the prosecution and the defense, but I think more so the prosecution. Preliminary hearings in my

jurisdiction and in most other places take an hour, maybe two, or perhaps a whole day or two in a very complicated case. There's no question in my mind that this judge is no more going to dismiss the charges against O.J. than I'm going to jump off the Empire State Building in New York City tonight. He's going to be held over, and they're going to go to trial.

BUCHANAN: Dr. Wecht, let's talk about the dog that barked.

WECHT: Yes.

BUCHANAN: This fellow says he watches television, he's a very conscientious fellow, and it was about twenty minutes into the news he heard the dog wailing and crying up until 11 o'clock. . . . That sets the death of Nicole Simpson at 10:15 at the latest. Is that crippling to the defense of O.J. Simpson, which is that, you know, at 11 o'clock he was waiting for this car?

WECHT: Well, it certainly doesn't make him the villain, but it is not helpful. With regard to the establishment of the time of death, I think you're going to hear some shocking stuff next week with regard to that determination. You're going to hear that the medical examiner's office never had a forensic pathologist there to examine those bodies, and that it wasn't until almost 11 A.M., or about eleven hours after the deaths, that a forensic pathologist first examined the bodies to make determinations as to rigor mortis, livor mortis, and algor mortis. If those determinations had been made at one in the morning, right after the bodies were found, then they would have been able to pinpoint with much better accuracy whether the deaths occurred most likely at 10 P.M. versus 11 P.M. But eleven or twelve hours later, when they first saw those bodies, that kind of precise, temporal determination could not be made.

Some of the questions were so silly as to invite a facetious response.

BUCHANAN: Dr. Wecht, what's your take on the wailing dog?

WECHT: Yes, let me make a comment on the wailing dog. While all of you were on television, I called up six of the most eminent veterinary psychologists in the country, and this case is going to be resolved on Tuesday. That dog is going to be brought into the courtroom. If he snaps at O.J. or if he sulks away and is scared to death, O.J. is guilty. If, on the other hand, he goes up and kisses O.J. or just walks around the room and ignores him, O.J. is innocent, and that ends everything.

BECKEL: You know, I'll tell you, this profession you're in I thought was a gruesome one. Maybe that's why you've got such a good sense of humor about these things.

Perhaps Beckel's own taste in humor wasn't so bad after all.

I spent the July Fourth holiday weekend at my summer home near New Haven, Connecticut. In between visiting with family and friends and soaking up a little sunshine on the beach, I perused forty pages of autopsy materials and police investigative reports that Lee Bailey had sent to me. They painted a picture of two horrible murders. Here's how they read:

Case Report: Department of Coroner
Date: June 14, 1994
Mode of Death: Homicide
Victim: Simpson, Nicole Elaine Brown
Address: 875 S. Bundy Drive, Los Angeles, CA 90049
DOB: 5/19/59
Age: 35
Height: 65 inches
Weight: 129 lb.
Eyes: Brown
Hair: Blond
Scars: Breast

Place of Death: Outside of residence

Clothing: Decedent was wearing a short black dress, bloodstained. Also, black panties.

Evidence of Injury: Four stab wounds to the neck, three stab wounds to the scalp, two cut wounds on the right hand and one cut wound on the left hand.

Opinion: Death is attributed to multiple sharp force injuries, including a deep incised wound of the neck and multiple stab wounds of the neck. The sharp force injuries led to the transection of the left and right arteries, and incisions of the left and right internal jugular veins causing fatal exsanguinating hemorrhage. Injuries present on the hands, including an incised wound of the right hand, are compatible with so-called defense wounds.

The autopsy report also stated that the fatal neck injury was "gaping and exposes the larynx." In fact, the wound was more than five inches long and two inches deep. "The edges of the wound are smooth," the report continued, indicating that it was not inflicted with a serrated knife. The toxicology report showed no evidence of illegal drugs and a blood-alcohol level of only 0.02 percent, which could be accounted for by two glasses of wine or a couple of beers a couple of hours earlier.

Goldman's autopsy report was almost as gory. It read as follows:

Case Report: Department of Coroner
Date: June 14, 1994
Mode of Death: Homicide
Victim's name: Ronald Lyle Goldman
DOB: 7/2/65
Age: 29
Height: 69 inches
Weight: 171 lb.
Eyes: Hazel
Hair: Brown

Remarks: Tattoo on right shoulder

Clothes: The decedent was wearing a long-sleeved sweater (it was extensively bloodstained). Also, a pair of bloodstained Levi jeans, sweat socks and canvas type boots.

Evidence of Injury: More than two dozen stab wounds to the neck, face, scalp, chest, abdomen, thigh and hands.

The report also contended that a stab wound to the left side of the neck that severed the jugular vein was the fatal injury. This wound was three inches long with smooth edges. Like Nicole's toxicology report, Goldman's showed no signs of any illegal or prescribed drugs. Unlike Nicole's, however, it did not show any alcohol. Finally, both reports stated that the bodies showed evidence of numerous ant bites, apparently a consequence of their having been allowed to remain at the murder scene for several hours.

That Saturday, Sigrid and I drove up the coast to Branford to have dinner with Henry Lee and his wife at their beautiful home overlooking Long Island Sound. Frequently consulted by attorneys and government agencies investigating murders and other mysterious deaths, Henry is arguably the world's most respected forensic scientist. Born in China, he served as a captain in the Taipei police force before moving to the United States to receive specialized training in criminalistics. Since becoming director of the Connecticut State Police's forensics lab, he has worked diligently to make it one of the best in the country.

It has heretofore been a well-kept secret that, in addition to his being a wizard of a sleuth, Henry is a gourmet Chinese chef. That night, he and his wife prepared what may be the most delicious Oriental dinner I have ever eaten. He also gave me a signed copy of his new book on DNA testing, a book I will probably never read (it is written in Chinese).

Like Michael Baden, Henry had recently joined the defense team. That evening, we talked at length about some of the amazing discoveries he had made and what they meant. From the police department's sloppy work at the crime scene to possible evidence of an accomplice that was never investigated, some of what Henry had learned was startling. We agreed that his findings would make explosive testimony come time for the trial. In the end, it would be Henry's testimony that best supported my theory of there having been more than one participant in the murders.

While the first week of the Simpson hearing saw the prosecution producing seemingly endless physical evidence connecting the defendant to the crime scene and to the murders through blood-sample matches, the second week produced even more fireworks. But this time, it was bad news for the prosecution. Lawyers from the district attorney's office thought that calling Los Angeles Deputy Medical Examiner Irwin Golden to the witness stand would simply lead to routine questions and answers. It was not to be.

To be sure, everything went fine under direct examination. Dr. Golden quickly answered the key questions, giving the number of stab wounds on each victim, their length, and other pertinent information. He did, however, admit that it was a significant error not to have a medical-legal investigator or forensic pathologist at the crime scene on the night of the slayings.

But it was under cross-examination by defense attorneys that Dr. Golden and the credibility of the entire Los Angeles medical examiner's office took its biggest hit. The defense team had obtained a copy of the minutes of an internal meeting at the coroner's office which detailed between thirty and forty errors or incidents of mishandled evidence in this case. Several were very significant:

- Nicole Brown Simpson's bloodstained dress was improperly dried, hanging into a communal drip pan below the drying rack, where it could have soaked up impurities from the drying clothing of other dead bodies.
- A bottle of liver bile was improperly marked as containing urine.
- The bodies were stored in unlocked homicide crypts, allowing anyone access to tamper with the evidence.

- Personal effects were not immediately removed and placed in envelopes, as policy requires. Expensive jewelry was not removed from Simpson's body until it arrived at the coroner's office thirteen hours after the death.
- Simpson's stomach contents were mistakenly discarded. (Examining the victim's stomach contents offers yet another way for a forensic pathologist to estimate time of death, based on when the victim last ate and how much had been digested.)
- Simpson's body was never examined for evidence of sexual assault.
- The wounds to Simpson and Goldman were not adequately examined to see whether they could have been inflicted by the fifteen-inch knife prosecutors contended could have been the murder weapon.

On cross-examination by Mr. Shapiro, Dr. Golden seemed confused and embarrassed by the office's mistakes. He was especially humiliated when the questioning turned to the fact that tests which might determine whether the alleged murder weapon matched the stab wounds had not been conducted.

SHAPIRO: You understand a man is sitting in jail, faced with charges of double homicide, do you not? When would you suggest doing these tests?
GOLDEN: Now?

All afternoon, my office was bombarded with calls from the news media seeking a comment. I told them I was flabbergasted. If this is how the Los Angeles coroner's office handled the evidence in the Simpson case, I said, just imagine what they do in everyday cases. It is nothing short of incompetence.

"The very office that should be playing a major role in helping resolve this horrible crime has actually become an impediment to law enforcement and truth," *USA Today* quoted me as saying.

Eventually, all of these bungles led to the defense's position that Simpson had been framed for the murder by racist police officers. For example, the defense claimed that the blood at the scene that matched Simpson was taken from the sample he had voluntarily supplied the day after the slayings. While I am aware of what dirty cops are capable of doing, I must admit I was extremely suspicious of these claims. They seemed to be wildly conjectural and lacking any concrete physical evidence. To say that law enforcement had completely screwed up the case was one thing. But to claim that Simpson was actually being framed for the homicides was, I thought, a bit much.

From day one, I had said that the Simpson case rose and fell on the blood. Could the prosecution, using highly advanced DNA testing, match blood samples found at the crime scene with those of the defendant? Without DNA, this was a truly circumstantial case.

Little by little, law enforcement officials leaked reports of DNA matches to the news media. First, it was a match with blood found on the glove and on the socks. Then it was Simpson's blood at the crime scene and in the Bronco. A single drop of dried blood on a sidewalk or handrail or sweater might not appear to be much, but in reality it is a storehouse of information for modern-day scientists.

One of the first methods of linking Simpson to the crime scene was what is called an ABO blood-typing test, a method first used in the early 1900s for categorizing blood. There are four possible blood types: A, B, AB, and O. If a person has a special substance called "A antigen" on the surface of his or her red blood cells, he or she is said to have type A blood. If a person's red blood cells have "B antigen," then the person has type B blood. If both A and B antigens are present, then the blood type is AB. If there are no antigens, then that person is said to have type O blood. The blood found at the Simpson crime scene was type A, the same as Nicole's and O.J.'s. Goldman had type O blood.

Despite the supposedly strong evidence in the hands of the state, I was shocked to learn that prosecutors refused to allow experts hired by the defense to conduct their own tests.

As all of the DNA and blood evidence was becoming

public, I was once again asked by the producers of *Crossfire* to be on their evening program. Pat Buchanan was on again that night, but Michael Kinsley was still away, replaced this time by Juan Williams. Buchanan wasted no time getting into the case.

BUCHANAN: Good evening and welcome to *Crossfire*. Those drops of blood found at the murder scene of Nicole Simpson match perfectly the blood of O.J. Simpson. That's what the DNA tests reveal, the prosecution said today in court. It is the hardest piece of evidence yet, and it puts O.J. right at the scene of the double murder of his ex-wife and her friend. But O.J.'s defense team, apparently aware of what was coming, leaked a letter to the press suggesting the prosecution had handled the blood evidence so sloppily, it may have to be thrown out of court.

Dr. Cyril Wecht, if the prosecution, as they claim, has a perfect match in the so-called DNA fingerprinting, what are the odds that they are wrong, what chance is there they have the wrong person?

WECHT: If the specimen was not contaminated and there's no serious challenge to evidentiary custody, Pat, then it is, indeed, a very damning piece of evidence. The RFLP [restriction fragment length polymorphism], especially if they have done four to eight probes, is exclusionary. One in a million conservatively. The National Research Council in 1992 reported essentially up-to-everybody-in-the-world maximum exclusionary probabilities except your identical twin.

BUCHANAN: All right. Dr. Wecht, if the blood puts O.J. right at the murder scene, it's a perfect match. What if Robert Shapiro calls up Cyril Wecht and says, "I've seen you on *Crossfire*. I want you to be part of our team. What exactly should we do? Should we challenge this directly, or should we concede it and try a new defense?" What would you tell him is the best defense strategy?

WECHT: Obviously, they would already have undertaken every single conceivable legal argument, and they've got all the experts on board for that. I would stress the fact that the defense experts were never given the opportunity to test the specimens themselves. And by the way, Pat, I think that the prosecution is making a serious error here. If they feel so confident about their test results, they would be best served by making specimens available to Dr. Henry Lee to have the tests validated.

BUCHANAN: Quickly, if you were the defense—

WECHT: I would argue contamination.

BUCHANAN: If they gave you the samples, would you test the samples with the possibility that you could come up with the perfect match, too, and then you'd look foolish?

WECHT: Well, that may be true, but you can't be sure until you test the samples yourself. I would argue contamination in collection, contamination in preserving and maintaining the specimens there in California and transmission to Maryland.

WILLIAMS: Dr. Wecht, in fact, that seems to be what Robert Shapiro is already arguing. In the letter that he sent to the judge today, he talks about the blood evidence being compromised by potential mislabeling, switching, all this kind of thing. Have you ever heard of a case where that kind of procedure has led to evidence being excluded from consideration?

WECHT: Yes, indeed. Keep in mind that the incidence of laboratory error is significant. A study back in 1978 showed that 71 percent of the two hundred crime labs in America had errors in their blood sampling and errors in the 20 to 50 percent range with other kinds of specimens, including hair. So, a test done by a lab is not necessarily the gospel. It's not the word from on high.

WILLIAMS: What is going to allow Judge Ito to either include or exclude this evidence?

WECHT: I think that he will demand that testimony be given directly in his courtroom by everybody involved. He will have to determine whether or not all of these things have been properly handled. It will be his decision and I think that it is unlikely to be overruled by an appellate court.

The next four months were occupied by legal wrangling and strategy setting by both sides. Prosecutors took the position that Simpson and Simpson alone was the killer. Defense attorneys contended that a racist police detective planted evidence in an attempt to frame their client.

The trial, which began on January 23, 1995, lasted an amazing thirty-three weeks and involved 126 witnesses and more than one thousand exhibits. The case also broke the previous record held by the trial of Charles Manson for sequestering a jury, which was 225 days.

From the start, I believe this case was completely out of control. Judge Lance Ito of the Los Angeles Superior Court, generally given very high marks by those who had appeared before him over the years, had allowed pretrial publicity to get out of hand. But this had nothing to do with his having allowed television cameras into the courtroom. The problem rested with lawyers speaking outside of the courtroom. The anonymous leaks, especially by law enforcement, were absolutely inappropriate, and Judge Ito should have put a stop to them early on. Unfortunately, he did not.

The excesses began with the opening statements by Marcia Clark and Johnnie Cochran. I am a firm believer that if a lawyer cannot explain his or her case in less than two hours (and I prefer less than an hour), then that attorney does not have a good grasp of the facts in the case or the direction in which he or she wants to go. In the Simpson case, both Clark and Cochran took more than a day to describe to the jury the evidence they would present. My experience as a lawyer and expert witness is that after a couple of hours, the jurors start tuning the lawyers out. And there are some studies that show that jurors even resent lawyers who are too wordy.

I do believe the state did a good job in three portions of its case. First, it established with reasonable certainty that Simpson had a clear motive to kill his ex-wife. Witness after witness talked about how abusive Simpson was during the marriage and how, after their separation, he became violently jealous.

For me, two particular pieces of evidence drove this point home most effectively. One was a videotape of Simpson exercising, in which he instructed viewers as he ran in place and jabbed into the air to imagine that they were "working out with your wife, if you know what I mean." While this proved little, it certainly looked bad. The second, far more devastating piece of evidence came in the form of Nicole's diary. In it, she wrote that Simpson had beaten her while they were having sex and once demanded that she have an abortion. The diary also provided ammunition that Simpson was stalking his ex-wife. "O.J. is following me again, Mommy. I'm scared," she wrote. "I go to the gas station, he's there. I go the Payless shoe store, and he's there. I'm driving and he's behind me." This, I felt, was pretty damning stuff.

In addition to creating a motive for the murder, prosecutors did an excellent job of establishing means. Through a series of witnesses, they were able to show that Simpson had no alibi during a one-hour time frame in which the state contends the murders occurred. This was crucial, and not an easy thing to prove. However, the prosecutors were burdened by the fact that the police had not called the medical examiner to the crime scene immediately. As a result, an exact time of death could not be given.

Witnesses for the prosecution said that Nicole called Mezzaluna at 9:45 P.M. and that Goldman left with the glasses at 9:50 P.M. Five minutes away, O.J. Simpson and houseguest Brian "Kato" Kaelin were said to have driven to McDonald's in Simpson's Bentley to grab some dinner. They arrived back home at about 9:40 P.M. Kaelin testified that Simpson said he was going to his room to shower and prepare for a late flight to Chicago. Telephone records show that Simpson tried calling his new girlfriend, a model for Victoria's Secret, at 9:40 P.M. But no witnesses came forward to say they saw or talked with Simpson for the next hour or more.

At 10:15 P.M., neighbors told police they heard the dog's wail. Seven minutes later, limousine driver Allan Park arrived at the Simpson mansion early. He did not remember seeing the white Ford Bronco parked on the street outside of the estate. Park waited until 10:40 P.M., then buzzed the house's intercom system. There was no response.

About 10:45 P.M., Kaelin stated that he heard three thumps on the wall outside the house. At 10:55 P.M., Park claimed he saw a large, shadowy figure enter the front door of the house. Minutes later, Simpson responded on the intercom saying he had fallen asleep and would be down shortly. It also was at 10:55 P.M. that Nicole's neighbor, Steven Schwab, found her upset Akita a few blocks from Nicole's home.

"The dog seemed agitated," Schwab told the jury. "It was very unusual for a dog to be barking that way. I noticed that there was blood on the paws."

At 11:01 P.M., Simpson exited his home and got in the limo. Park said Simpson complained of being hot, even though it was a cool evening. Simpson's flight aboard American Airlines for Chicago left at 11:45 P.M.

At about midnight, neighbors of Nicole walked her Akita down the street. When they approached 875 South Bundy, the Akita led Sukru Boztepe and his wife, Bettina, to the bodies. At 12:10 A.M., they called the police and emergency crews.

It was important for the prosecutors to establish that the murders happened about 10:15 P.M. That would have given Simpson enough time to leave Kaelin, drive to 875 South Bundy Drive, commit both murders, clean up, dispose of evidence, and race back to his home a few miles away. Any later than 10:30 P.M., and there was no way for Simpson to have accomplished the feat.

To raise doubt about the time of death, defense attorneys tried to use a series of witnesses to suggest that the slaying could have occurred much later, around 10:45 or 11 P.M. They called four very credible witnesses who testified that they were walking along South Bundy Drive that evening between 10:20 P.M. and 10:30 P.M. and heard no wailing dog. In fact, one witness, Robert Heidstra, said that he heard two men arguing near the crime scene about 10:40 P.M. However, Heidstra also testified that he saw a car resembling Simpson's Bronco speeding away from the crime scene at about 10:45 P.M.

The third portion of the case in which the prosecution did an excellent job was in establishing Simpson's presence at the crime scene. They did this very keenly through the analysis of bloodstains and spatters found at the scene of the murder, in Simpson's Bronco, on a glove behind Simpson's house, and on two socks at the foot of his bed.

Gary Sims, a criminalist with the California Department of Justice laboratory in Berkeley, testified that blood on the right-handed glove found behind Simpson's guest house matched Goldman's. On the glove's middle finger, Sims said he found bloodstains that were a mixture of blood from Nicole and Goldman. Furthermore, Sims told the jury that blood spatters on the socks undoubtedly came from Nicole Brown Simpson.

Dr. Robin Cotton, director of Cellmark Diagnostics, the company that performed the DNA testing on the bloodstains and samples, spent two weeks on the witness stand explaining the ABCs of DNA. *DNA,* she explained, stands for *deoxyribonucleic acid,* a substance that contains an individual's genetic blueprint. Using samples of blood, hair, semen, skin, or other human tissue, scientists can map genetic patterns. Just like fingerprints, each person's DNA is different and can provide a unique identity marker (except in the case of identical twins). DNA is made up of four basic components, or chemical bases: adenine, guanine, thymine, and cytosine. Scientists abbreviate them using their first letters—A, G, T and C. Many people compare DNA to the alphabet. Just as the twenty-six letters from A to Z are used to form words, DNA bases are linked to form strands.

There are two kinds of DNA tests: RFLP [restriction fragment length polymorphism] and PCR [polymerase chain reaction]. PCR is the quickie test, taking about a week to get a result. However, it is not nearly as accurate or definitive as the RFLP test. The chances of a match in a PCR test range from one in 100 to one in 2,000. PCR is also the newer of the two tests. Here's how it works:

1. Crime-scene tissue or fluid—a pinhead amount of blood or one hair is sufficient—whose origin needs to be identified has DNA extracted from it and purified. DNA samples are likewise obtained from the crime-scene tissue's or fluid's possible source (e.g., the suspect).
2. The crime-scene DNA is combined with short fragments of another, known DNA, called primers, and with other chemicals, which cause the DNA to replicate. With thirty cycles of replication, the amount of DNA increases one million times. The DNA from the possible source is treated similarly.
3. Small quantities of the replicated DNA are then applied to eight to ten spots on reagent strips. Each spot contains a different segment of the other, known DNA. If the replicated DNA contains a segment matching the known segment, a blue color appears on the spot.
4. The pattern of spots from the sample taken at a crime scene is compared to that taken from a suspect.

PCR is so new that few state courts have allowed it to be admitted as evidence in criminal trials. On the other hand, the RFLP examination has been accepted by nearly every court in the country. Taking at least six weeks to perform, the accuracy of the RFLP test ranges from one in 1 million to one in 1 billion, or even higher. Here's how the RFLP test is conducted:

1. DNA from blood or other tissue is collected from the crime scene and the suspected sources. A larger sample size is required than with the PCR test.
2. The DNA of each sample is chemically cut into fragments using restriction enzymes.
3. Each sample's resulting DNA fragments are placed in a quantity of gel and separated into bands by running an electric current through the gel, a process called electrophoresis.
4. The patterns of bands, still visible at this point, are transferred to nylon membranes.

5. Radioactive DNA probes are applied to the membranes and bind to matching DNA sequences. Excess, unattached DNA probes are washed away.
6. X-ray film is placed next to the membranes. The film is developed, revealing a pattern of bands where the radioactive probe has bound to the DNA fragments. This DNA profile is the genetic "fingerprint."
7. The final DNA fingerprints are patterns of light and dark bands that look like supermarket bar codes. The DNA fingerprints of the crime-scene samples are compared to DNA fingerprints of the suspected sources.

Almost no one disputes the power of DNA analysis. Having a forensic scientist take the witness stand and tell the jury that evidence found at the crime scene connects the defendant to the crime by a million-to-one or a billion-to-one odds is strong testimony. Yet the truth is that no one regulates DNA testing. In 1991, Congress tried to pass the DNA Identification Act, which would have set standards for lab testing and guidelines for presenting evidence. But Congress failed, and today there is no regulation regarding how evidence is collected, preserved, or tested.

In her testimony, Dr. Cotton said that five drops of blood discovered outside of Mrs. Simpson's home did not come from either victim. However, she said there were 170-million-to-one odds that they did come from O.J. Simpson. Then came the most significant point in her testimony: Blood found on the socks in Simpson's bedroom contained a DNA match of Nicole Brown Simpson. When asked how many other people, white or black, could have this type of DNA, Dr. Cotton said that the odds of someone else having it were less than one in 9-7 billion—pretty dramatic testimony considering that there are only about 5.5 billion humans on the Earth.

While there is widespread acceptance of DNA and its usefulness, there remain major concerns regarding the astronomical percentages that many of the genetic-testing laboratories employ.

The defense took a twofold approach to attacking the

blood and DNA results. First, the defense lawyers accused
police of stealing blood samples taken from Simpson and
planting them on his clothing; we will get to this later. But it
was their second plan of attack, in which they claimed that the
positive DNA results came from contaminated samples, that I
thought was off-base and misleading. You can take blood or
any human tissue, throw it into the sewer, retrieve it, and it
will not produce a false positive. It may no longer produce a
definitive result, but it would not create a false positive.

On the other hand, there was a question of contamination
within the lab itself. The issue, as Michael Baden explained to
me, was whether Simpson's own blood contaminated the test
sample, which would have then showed a false positive. This
could have happened, he argued, if the lab technicians had
accidentally sprayed or dripped Simpson's blood sample into
the test sample.

Whether the defense attorneys like it or not, if the DNA
results come back a match, arguing contamination is nothing
more than blowing smoke or attempting to confuse the jury.

That's not to say that the prosecution's case was clean
or without faults. Certainly, it was not. In fact, I think the
prosecutors did something that, if not unethical, was clearly
unfair or improper. After Dr. Golden, the deputy medical
examiner, made a fool of himself and the Los Angeles coroner's
office at the preliminary hearing, prosecutors chose not to call
him as a witness during the trial.

This is unheard of. Never before have I come across a case
in which a board-certified forensic pathologist, working as a
full-time employee of a medical examiner's office, performed
an autopsy and then was not called to testify at the trial. By
keeping Dr. Golden off of the witness stand, however, the
prosecutors saved themselves from another potentially
embarrassing problem. During the preliminary hearing, Dr.
Golden had testified that *two* knives could have been used in
the slayings. This dramatically hurt the prosecution's case.

Instead, the prosecutors called Dr. Lakshmanan Sathyavagiswaran, the coroner of Los Angeles County and Dr.
Golden's boss. For nine days, Dr. Sathyavagiswaran painted a

picture of how he believed the murders occurred. It was dramatic testimony, grabbing the undivided attention of the jury and bringing tears and horror to most in the courtroom. He described each and every wound, showing photographs of each to the jury.

"Nicole died of multiple stab wounds to the neck," Dr. Sathyavagiswaran told jurors. Most graphic were the photographs that focused on the slashes to the throat that were so deep they nearly separated her head from her body.

The Los Angeles coroner laid out the following scenario: the assailant stabs Nicole Simpson four times in the neck. He also rams her head into the metal gate or fence, knocking her unconscious. It is at this point that Ronald Goldman shows up. Taking Goldman by surprise, the attacker grabs him from behind, forcing him into a small, gated area measuring six feet by four feet. The attacker then makes two parallel cuts across Goldman's neck.

"If Mr. Goldman was confronted by the assailant in this confined area, he has no means to escape, especially if he is cornered between that railing and the tree and that sapling," Dr. Sathyavagiswaran told the jury. "He has no place to escape to. He's stuck there. He was held so he couldn't move, so these controlled cuts could be made." These slashes were fatal, the doctor added, although it probably took Goldman a few minutes to actually bleed to death. It was after this, he testified, that the assailant jabbed his or her knife into Goldman to make sure he was indeed dead.

"The stab wound entered the right chest, went through the seventh rib, then the right lung and came to strike the fourth rib," Dr. Sathyavagiswaran told the jury.

With Goldman out of the picture, the attacker returns to Nicole Brown Simpson, who, Dr. Sathyavagiswaran contends, was still unconscious at this time. Under this scenario, the assailant places his foot on Nicole's back, grabs her hair with his left hand, pulling her head back and exposing her throat. With the knife in his right hand, the attacker then nearly slices the victim's neck in half.

"I would say she died within a few minutes, probably

much less than a minute," he testified. "She would have gone into rapid shock with this massive injury."

Much of the coroner's testimony was based on pure conjecture. Are there not other, equally plausible physical scenarios? Is it possible that the attacker was this tall or this small? If the assailant had been six feet two inches tall (as Simpson is), would he have been able to overpower the shorter Goldman?

But Dr. Sathyavagiswaran had another mission on the witness stand besides simply announcing the official cause of death or demonstrating just how horrible these murders were. The prosecution wanted testimony supporting its scenario regarding the time of death. It needed to show that these slayings could have occurred in the scant amount of time during which Simpson could not produce an alibi.

Under direct questioning from Los Angeles County Deputy District Attorney Brian Kelberg, Dr. Sathyavagiswaran provided the prosecutors with the ammunition they needed.

KELBERG: Doctor, what is your opinion regarding the length of time it took for these murders to have occurred?

SATHYAVAGISWARAN: I felt that the injuries sustained could have been in rapid succession.

KELBERG: How fast? A minute or so?

SATHYAVAGISWARAN: Yes. A minute is a long time. I mean, we all heat our coffee cups in the microwave oven, and you know, it takes a long time.

KELBERG: Demonstrate sixty seconds for us.

SATHYAVAGISWARAN: You take any knife and just go home and plunge it quickly and you'll see you can do fifteen thrusts in about fifteen seconds. It doesn't take that long to do a sharp-force injury with a sharp knife. [*He demonstrates this by pumping his fist up and down in a stabbing motion.*]

Under cross-examination by defense attorney Robert Shapiro, the coroner admitted that his office had made more than thirty mistakes in this case. The most important, he agreed, concerned the fact that police had not informed his department of the deaths for more than eight hours. This allowed Shapiro to hammer home the fact that the authorities could not say for sure when the deaths occurred, as well as to present the possibility of multiple attackers.

SATHYAVAGISWARAN: We can only give an estimated range [of when the victims died]. We cannot give any precision.

SHAPIRO: Based on your examination of the bod[ies], what is the time frame when these homicides took place?

SATHYAVAGISWARAN: Between 9 P.M. on June 12 and 12:45 A.M. on June 13.

SHAPIRO: Can you tell us, with a reasonable degree of medical certainty, how many people are responsible for these homicides?

SATHYAVAGISWARAN: No.

I've always had doubts about the state's scenario for the murders. In fact, based upon the evidence that I've reviewed, I do not believe it could have happened that way at all.

My first concern involves the amount of blood at the scene of the homicides. The victims were both young, healthy individuals in good physical condition and not under the influence of alcohol or drugs. Cutting their carotid arteries and jugular veins would have caused blood to spurt several feet. Add to that the fact that they were under attack. There was great terror and excitement that would have sent their blood pressures skyrocketing. This would have significantly increased the force of the blood coming up from their aortas.

Blood is not water. It doesn't simply seep into the ground and disappear. Blood is viscous. It is thick and tenacious. When blood dries, it congeals on clothes, on skin, wherever it settles. In this case, it should have been everywhere. The attacker must have been soaked in blood. If O.J. Simpson is indeed the killer of Nicole Brown Simpson and Ronald Goldman, there are many questions that the prosecution failed to answer.

Where did all the blood go?

How did O.J. peel his clothing off?

Where did the clothes go?

How did so little blood—only a few small spatters—get on the Bronco?

How come none of the blood apparently got on Simpson's hands and face?

Why was there no evidence of blood anywhere on the white carpet in Simpson's house?

Surely the police detectives checked every sink, shower, and drain in Simpson's house. If there had been blood washed down those drains, some of it would have stuck on the filters. But there was no testimony to that effect.

Before it rested its case on July 7, the prosecution did get in a few more zingers. FBI special agent William Bodziak testified that shoe prints discovered at the crime scene came from an unusual size-12, rubber-sole, Italian-made Bruno Magli shoe. The shoe size was said to match a Reebok tennis shoe found in Simpson's closet, though police made it clear that the print found at the crime scene did not match the Reebok. In addition, investigators also admitted no Bruno Maglis were ever found.

The final state witness was FBI agent Douglas Deedrick, a fiber and hair expert, who told jurors that fibers matching carpet fibers in Simpson's Bronco were found at the murder scene. More importantly, he said that hairs with characteristics similar to those of the defendant's were also discovered at the crime scene.

While most agreed that the state's case had holes, I believe it was strong enough to obtain a conviction in any other case in this country. But not in this case, and not in Los Angeles.

On August 1, 1995, as the defense was delving into the bowels of the case, Lee Bailey flew to Pittsburgh to pick my brain. He brought crime-scene photos and the autopsy reports, and we discussed the physical evidence at length.

One of the main issues for the defense team, Lee told me, was whom to call to the stand and whom not to call. A great amount of attention was being focused on whether Simpson himself would take the stand. Some members of the defense team were trying hard to convince the former football star that he should not. But many people, especially famous people, have big egos. They want to tell their side of the story. They want to stand before the men and women in the jury box and tell them in no uncertain terms that they are innocent.

O.J. Simpson was no different. While some of his lawyers were encouraging him to stay off the witness stand, friends were apparently telling him to do the opposite. They were telling him that the world wanted to see him under oath, swearing that he had nothing to do with this crime.

To demonstrate the possible pitfalls, Bailey and the other defense attorneys hired an independent trial lawyer from out of state to come to Los Angeles and conduct a mini-mock trial in Simpson's cell. For two days, the lawyer—a woman hired because her trial technique is similar to that of Marcia Clark—grilled Simpson. The demonstration did not go well for the defendant. The lawyer repeatedly tore him apart on cross-examination. She made him look guilty. His defense attorneys hoped that this would convince him that he should not take the witness stand.

Just as interesting, the lawyers had many debates about which witnesses they should call. What many people don't know is that members of the defense team voted on each and every witness. Simpson cast a vote, also.

With that in mind, there was considerable debate within the defense team about calling Dr. Baden or seeking out another forensic pathology expert. In particular, the lawyers were eyeing the chief medical examiner of Buffalo, Dr. Justin Uku, an eminently qualified witness. However, there was an additional reason some defense lawyers wanted to use him: he is black.

Simpson's lawyers thought having an African-American forensic pathologist take the stand and challenge the prosecution's suppositions would have greater impact on the jury than if the challenge came from someone like myself or Dr. Baden. It was a very understandable point—one with which I could not disagree.

"Do you mind calling or writing Dr. Uku and putting in a good word for us?" Bailey asked.

I agreed, but I clearly stated that I still thought that Dr. Baden would make their best witness. He knew the case inside and out. He was in the courtroom in Los Angeles when the coroner testified. And Dr. Baden has great courtroom skills and experience. Bailey assured me they had not ruled out using Dr. Baden and that it would be put to a vote.

Most of our focus that evening was on the state's scenario of what happened. We reviewed the blood spatters, blood locations and amounts, all of which indicated that the murders did not happen as cleanly and precisely as law enforcement was portraying.

"Keep in mind, these are stabbings," I told Bailey. "Unlike a shooting, where both parties can be standing still, stabbings are much more dynamic, much more mobile. These were two young, healthy adults, neither of whom was under the influence of alcohol or drugs. People move. They duck. They juke. They twist. They stoop. They bend. They jump. There is no room for such activity in the state's scenario." Lee had already heard many of these points from Michael Baden, which I think reinforced my point that Michael should testify.

The defense case, at this point, was simple. They wanted to show a general pattern of incompetence on the part of law enforcement in this case. With clear evidence that investigators had contaminated exhibits by placing them in the same bag with a blanket used to cover Nicole Simpson's body, this point was not difficult to make. At times, it seemed as if the Los Angeles police investigators were their own worst enemy. They provided the defense with many targets.

Since the defense could not really attack the credibility of the DNA results, they argued that Simpson's blood did indeed appear in samples recovered from the crime scene, but that he had been framed. A small portion of a vial of blood—about thirty drops—taken as a sample from Simpson was missing and unaccounted for. The defense claimed that the police had taken this and planted the blood drops on the Bronco and at the crime scene.

To bolster its claim, the defense called my good friend and colleague Dr. Fredric Rieders to testify that blood found at the gate of Nicole Brown Simpson's house, which matched O.J. Simpson's, also contained EDTA, or ethylenediaminetetraacetic acid, a chemical preservative. The same was true of the blood samples found on the socks, which matched Mrs. Simpson's blood.

Dr. Rieders's test used chemical compounds isolated and identified by the rate at which they move through liquid as well as by their molecular weight, whole and in pieces. This was the defense's key to showing that something fishy was up. If there was EDTA—and I believe Dr. Rieders's testimony that there was—then the blood did not come directly from the person. It was quite possibly taken, stored, preserved, then placed on the socks and the gate, or, in some negligent fashion, contaminated. While this did not prove that O.J. Simpson did not commit the murders, it did help to establish reasonable doubt.

Rieders's testimony led into even more startling testimony by another dear friend and respected colleague of mine, Herb MacDonell. During the first week of August, Herb took the witness stand and announced that the blood on the socks had not gotten there as a result of a natural spatter, but had been applied through "direct compression." In other words, the blood had seeped through one side of the sock onto the other side of the sock, indicating that there was no foot in the sock when the stain was deposited. The stain on each side of the sock measures one inch by one and a half inches.

As Herb was testifying, I recalled a conversation he and I had had in April when he visited me in Pittsburgh. Herb had gone to the crime scene and to the Simpson estate to see whether there was any additional evidence he could turn up. While there, he spoke with Simpson's maid. She said she knew Simpson's habits better than anyone, and that he would never leave dirty socks on the floor. While this evidence would never be admitted in court due to the hearsay rules, it made a distinct impression on Herb and me.

At 8:30 A.M. on Thursday, August 10, which is 5:30 A.M. on

the West Coast, my phone rang at home. It was Michael Baden. In four hours, he would be taking the witness stand and challenging many of the basic principles on which prosecutors were basing their case.

He wanted to bounce some of his conclusions off of me to see whether I found them to be valid and whether there were any obvious scientific holes in his theory. They were his analyses, not mine, and he was not asking for my conclusions. But he wanted me to act as a sounding board to help identify any potential flaws in his analysis and reasoning. This is something that forensic experts do all of the time. It's called double-checking yourself professionally.

I did have one specific piece of advice for Michael. The prosecutors were probably going to challenge his opinions as being less than credible, I told him. And I fully expected them to accuse him of being a hired gun for the defense. To combat this, I suggested that he mention early on and often that, just a few months earlier, he had testified for the Los Angeles District Attorney's Office.

"They obviously thought you were credible by hiring you in the first case," I said. "By merely throwing that out, I believe it should preempt any credibility attacks."

By all accounts, Michael wowed the jury. His testimony was clear, compelling, and convincing. Unlike many expert witnesses, Michael does not speak in legalese or medical jargon. He looks the jurors in the eye and tells them what he thinks and why.

SHAPIRO: You were in the courtroom and heard Dr. Sathyavagiswaran's testimony, were you not?

BADEN: Yes, I was here and I heard him.

SHAPIRO: Do you agree with his scenario on how this crime occurred? Do you believe that Nicole Brown Simpson was lying facedown unconscious when her throat was slit?

BADEN: No, I do not. While I have great respect for Dr. Sathyavagiswaran, I simply disagree with him. I think his testimony was more to produce a visual image, an awful image, than to explain the truth. In my opinion, when she received the final wound, she was eighteen inches off the ground.

SHAPIRO: What do you base your opinion on?

BADEN: The pattern of the blood spurts onto the steps of the victim's condominium. The blood on the step doesn't match. In my opinion, when the last cut was given, she was higher up.

SHAPIRO: Was she unconscious when the fatal cuts were applied?

BADEN: My opinion is that she struggled with the assailant or assailants prior to succumbing when her neck was cut. There were nine or ten cut or stab wounds on her body before she suffered the fatal injuries.

SHAPIRO: As an expert witness for the defense, did you examine the medical evidence in this case?

BADEN: Yes, I did.

. . . .

ASSISTANT DISTRICT ATTORNEY BRIAN KELBERG: Give us your professional opinion of how this autopsy was handled, and did you find evidence on your own that the Los Angeles medical examiners overlooked?

BADEN: By examining the brain, I discovered a bruise caused by a blunt-force injury. [Mrs.] Simpson had suffered a blow to the head that caused brain damage, and that's significant to a forensic pathologist. I will agree with you that these autopsies were not perfect. There were numerous mistakes. But I don't want to trash Dr. Golden. Dr. Golden did a fine job as far as I'm concerned. His autopsy is better than most autopsies and better than the autopsy of President Kennedy.

Michael's bombshell came when he described visiting the Los Angeles police crime laboratory less than two weeks after the homicides took place. Michael told jurors that he had examined nearly all of the physical and medical evidence collected by authorities, including the bloodied socks found in Simpson's bedroom. There was only one difference between his findings and the prosecution's: he saw no evidence of blood on the socks. This was big. Keep in mind that Los Angeles authorities did not report finding the bloodstains on the socks until August—more than six weeks after the socks were recovered. This played directly into the defense's theory that the blood on the socks had been planted to frame Simpson.

That evening, after completing his first day of testimony, Michael and I again talked by telephone. I gave him kudos for his first day on the witness stand, especially for his comment on the JFK autopsy.

"You were excellent," I said. "You spoke slowly and clearly. You used language that the jurors could understand. And you spoke with force and authority."

My only advice was for him to remain as calm and relaxed as possible. "Don't let the prosecutors agitate you," I said. "Stay as pleasant as possible. Let the prosecutors rant and rave. It will work to your benefit and their detriment."

Michael has a relaxed and comfortable demeanor anyway. Every commentator, even those who strongly believe O.J. was guilty, stated that Dr. Baden had been a significantly positive witness for the defense.

The next day, under continued cross-examination by prosecutor Kelberg, Michael made several key points for the defense team:

- That the report of Goldman's stomach contents indicates he died sometime after 10:15 P.M.
- That, based on evidence of defensive wounds on the victims' hands, both victims struggled with their killer or killers
- That Goldman's knuckles were bruised, indicating that he struck his assailant

KELBERG: Isn't it illogical to think that Nicole Brown and Ronald Goldman died in a ferocious struggle as you contend and more logical to conclude that it all happened quickly?

BADEN: Murders and struggles are not logical. If they were logical, there would be fewer of them.

KELBERG: Isn't it true that no human being can eat enough food to support your theory on time of death based on the stomach contents?

BADEN: You don't have grown children.

KELBERG: But why can we not reconstruct the crime scene exactly and know the time of death by examining the stomach contents?

BADEN: Human beings are not able to be studied like worms. We can't do controlled studies of feeding people and then killing them. We can't do controlled studies of cutting people's necks.

KELBERG: You have been particularly critical of the quality of crime-scene photographs taken in this case. Isn't it true that you have not raised that issue in many previous trials in which you have testified?

BADEN: Mr. Kelberg, you are misinformed.

Michael's wry sense of humor served him well at the trial. When Kelberg continued to question his position on the time of death in the stabbings, he replied, "Stab wounds don't cause death. Bleeding causes death."

But as compelling as Michael was, I must say that his performance came in second. The star of the entire show, if there was one, had to be Dr. Henry Lee. Even the *New York Times* wrote that Henry dazzled jurors with his courtroom demeanor and humor: "Dr. Lee, perhaps the nation's pre-eminent forensic scientist, dominated the courtroom as he disclosed the results of his scientific sleuthing in a vivid show-and-tell exhibition. The lawyers at the prosecution table could only sit there and sweat."

As an example, he could not remember at one point which of two very different looking Caucasian defense attorneys had gone with him to conduct crime lab experiments. "You all look alike," he joked to a packed courtroom and national television audience.

However, entertainment was only a means of educating the

jury. During more than four days on the witness stand, Henry provided backbone to the defense team's claim that there was more than one attacker. In dramatic fashion, Henry announced that in his examination of the crime scene, he found "imprints" on the sidewalk where the homicides occurred that appeared to be shoe prints. There were several of these imprints with identical markings. But not all of the imprints were on the ground. One was found on Ronald Goldman's blue jeans, which was consistent with the attacker kicking his or her second victim.

LEE: I cannot definitively say that is definitely a shoe print. It could be.

BARRY SCHECK: Could it be the Bruno Magli shoe?

LEE: No.

SCHECK: Have you ever seen a single assailant wear two pairs of shoes?

LEE: No.

PROSECUTOR HANK GOLDBERG: Could the imprint be from the police officers shown in this photograph mistakenly walking through the blood?

LEE: I don't think these two officers deposited these shoe prints. I don't think their shoes are parallel designs.

GOLDBERG: But can you eliminate the possibility that the imprints were made by police officers?

LEE: I cannot eliminate.

Henry also poked a hole in the prosecution's assertion that the murders took place in blitzkrieg fashion. Instead, he said, the evidence pointed to a protracted struggle. For instance, he said, there was a knife cut in Goldman's boot indicating he may have tried kicking back, a hole in the dirt at the crime scene that could have been dug out in a struggle, dirt caked on top of and in the cracks of Goldman's boots, and blood drops that had been smeared.

"I cannot tell you exactly how long, but it was not a short struggle," Henry told the jurors.

At the same time, Henry slammed law enforcement for

how they handled the evidence. He said that he found the bloodied socks packaged together in the same envelope, meaning they contaminated each other.

Under cross-examination, prosecutors asked him why he was shown in photographs examining evidence without using gloves, a hairnet, or a lab jacket.

"They didn't offer me those things," Henry responded. "Doesn't matter what I wear. Space suit, body armor—evidence still contaminated."

Henry also blasted Los Angeles officials for treating him "in a very mean, hostile fashion" when he traveled there to review the evidence. The policy of nearly every medical examiner's office in this country is to allow colleagues hired by the defendant's or plaintiff's lawyers to review and even test evidence.

So disgusted was Henry at the conduct of the Los Angeles authorities that he had once called me about leaving the case several months prior to his testimony. I told him that he should stay on for two reasons. First, he was allowing the prosecution and police to achieve their goal—intimidation of defense witnesses. Second, if he quit it would send a message to the news media and the general public that he must have believed Simpson was guilty. Fortunately for Simpson, Henry agreed to stay on and testify in the case.

During the Labor Day weekend, Henry and I had dinner in New Haven. Henry was still very upset. Throughout his career, his integrity had never been called into question. Everyone—prosecutors, defense attorneys, civil litigators, and judges—had always had nothing but the highest regard for Henry, who is nothing if not objective, logical, dispassionate, and precise.

Now, for the first time, there was criticism and second-guessing. For forensic experts like Michael Baden and myself, such attacks are common. We almost expect the opposing side in a lawsuit or criminal case to attempt to undermine our credibility. But to Henry, it was devastating. He wished he had never become involved in the Simpson case.

"One week we are testifying for the prosecution and we

are fine," Henry told me. "The next week, we are testifying for the defense and we become the great evil. Yet we testify to the same thing—the scientific truth."

"People ask me if O.J. did it," Henry continued. "I tell them I don't know. Some evidence points to him. Some evidence points the other way. But the news media and the public in this case made up its mind before all of the evidence was in. That put a lot of pressure on us. When we didn't go along with their opinion, we became enemy number one."

Henry said that he felt the prosecution and defense lawyers were very well prepared. And he felt that the prosecutors had treated him fairly on the witness stand. But it was what went on outside the courtroom that really got to him. "If the Los Angeles Police Department spent as much time investigating homicides as they spent investigating us," he said, "they would solve every murder."

Herb MacDonell and Michael Baden had told me the very same thing—that Los Angeles authorities involved in the Simpson prosecution had gone to extraordinary lengths to look into their pasts, trying to dig up dirt in an attempt to discredit the experts on the witness stand. "I was especially dismayed by the tactics of Marcia Clark," Herb later confided in me. "She told people she was going to destroy me. She later said it was all a joke."

Herb told me that investigators for the Los Angeles police and prosecutors had called Milton College in Wisconsin, where he taught between 1951 and 1954. "They asked questions about whether I had ever gotten into trouble, whether I had ever molested any students, whether I had ever used or sold drugs—stuff like that," Herb said. "With all the background checks they were doing on us, it was like we were running for political office."

Herb does believe that Marcia Clark grew to like him near the end of his testimony. "I think she finally came to the conclusion that I was honest," he said. "It came at a point when [defense attorney] Peter Neufeld was questioning me about how the gloves had supposedly shrunk 15 percent. I quickly interjected that the estimate was 10 to 15 percent. At that very second, Marcia Clark looked up at me and smiled. I think she knew at that moment that I was being completely honest and accurate."

Henry's appearance on the witness stand had coincided with the recent discovery by the defense team of tape-recorded interviews in which Los Angeles police detective Mark Fuhrman used racial slurs dozens of times—directly contradicting his own testimony early in the trial that he had not used such language over the past ten years. On these tapes, Fuhrman discusses beating criminal suspects and planting evidence against defendants.

Amazingly, Judge Ito ruled that the defense lawyers could play only two examples of Fuhrman using the word "nigger" in the interviews. They could not play any of the clips of the detective elaborating on framing suspects. In making his ruling, the judge said the tapes were more prejudicial than probative.

I must say that I found Judge Ito's decision outrageous. Here was a key witness for the prosecution who found a key piece of evidence against the defendant. Yet the defense attorneys were prohibited from playing testimony to the jury that proved that this detective had a propensity for fabricating evidence. To those people who believe that the police can do no wrong, I must remind them that in 1995, the Los Angeles District Attorney's Office dropped charges against three individuals charged in three separate homicides after it was learned that police investigators had tampered with evidence or fabricated evidence in order to obtain a conviction.

California authorities claimed they would conduct a thorough investigation into the statements made by Detective Fuhrman. However, we know how these so-called internal probes go. There was a lot of hype at the time of the announcement, but the proposed inquiry quickly fizzled out. Unfortunately for the people of Los Angeles, police misconduct and ineptitude will continue to be a problem in their community.

At any rate, with Judge Ito's ruling keeping the tapes out of evidence and away from the ears of the jury, the defense was confronted with a problem—how to support its theory that Simpson was the victim of a racist frame-up. The defense used the only avenue available to it: witnesses.

In one day, defense attorneys called two women, Kathleen Bell and Natalie Singer, to the witness stand. Both claimed they had brief social encounters with an off-duty Detective Fuhrman. Neither said it was pleasant. Both said he repeatedly used racial epithets. Both said he voiced hatred toward interracial couples. They said he talked about using his position as a police officer to beat black people and fabricate evidence against minorities.

"'Cops are God,'" Bell quoted Fuhrman as saying.

More damaging was the testimony of Laura Hart McKinney, the North Carolina professor to whom Fuhrman had made the racist statements during ten years of interviews for a movie script on which she was working. She had fought hard in court to keep the tapes out of the hands of the defense attorneys. But a North Carolina judge had ordered them turned over anyway.

McKinney told the jurors that Fuhrman had lied to them when he claimed he had not uttered racial slurs in ten years. In fact, she said, she had him on tape using "the N word" forty-two times, including during a few interviews since Simpson's arrest. It was powerful testimony. The jurors took extensive notes.

The next day, defense attorneys subpoenaed Detective Mark Fuhrman to testify. In one of the most dramatic moments of the trial, they asked the investigator if he had ever used "the N word" in the past ten years. He refused to answer, citing his Fifth Amendment right not to incriminate himself in possible crimes. The defense attorneys asked Fuhrman if he had perjured himself earlier in the trial. Again, the detective took the Fifth.

While it was a devastating moment for the public perception of the prosecution and the Los Angeles Police Department, the jurors would never hear a word of it. They were not present during this questioning, and the appellate courts ruled that the jury could not be told about it. The defense understandably saw this as a serious blow to its case. Defense attorneys wanted the jury to see and hear Fuhrman refuse to answer questions about whether he had planted evidence. They wanted the jury to see and hear Fuhrman declining to answer questions regarding his racist statements that had been captured forever on tape.

Personally, I thought the jury should have been permitted to hear this evidence directly from Fuhrman's lips. That being said, I'm not sure that the jury didn't get wind of it. I know they were sequestered throughout the entire trial. However, they were allowed conjugal visits on weekends, and no one is going to convince me that there was no pillow talk about what was going on. I am willing to bet that spouses of some of the jurors told them what had happened in court when the jury was not present.

There were, of course, a slew of other witnesses called by the defense. Each offered a little nugget of information meant to poke a hole in the state's case. For example:

- Stephen Valerie, a UCLA graduate student, sat next to Simpson on the American Airlines flight from Los Angeles to Chicago. He testified that he looked at Simpson's hands for an NFL Super Bowl ring and saw no evidence of cuts, as prosecutors had contended must have been there. (Neither did he see a Super Bowl ring, but that's because Simpson's team had never won an NFL championship.)
- Jim Merrill, a Hertz employee who picked up Simpson at Chicago's O'Hare International Airport, said he saw no cuts on the football star's hands and that Simpson was cheerful and appeared happy. By contrast, Merrill testified, on Simpson's return to the airport, he was frantic and cried while making three phone calls to friends.
- Raymond Kildruff, a vice president for Hertz, took Simpson to the airport to catch a flight from Chicago back to Los Angeles the morning after the slayings. He said Simpson did have a bloody bandage on his left hand at that time.
- Juanita Moore, O.J.'s barber, told the jury that Simpson

had dandruff. An expert witness testified for the prosecution that hairs found at the crime scene were from a black man but showed no sign of dandruff.

In all, the defense called fifty-three witnesses. Throughout this time, however, the main question on everyone's mind was whether the defendant himself would take the stand. The public certainly wanted to hear from him, and no doubt the prosecutors wanted their own chance to examine him. The only words we had heard out of his mouth were an occasional "Yes, Your Honor," and one "Too tight," when he tried to put the gloves on his hands.

Despite all of the speculation by legal pundits, the defense team kept Simpson's intentions secret. Finally, on September 25, as the defense was closing its case, Judge Ito asked whether the defendant was waiving his right to testify on his own behalf. Cochran responded that Simpson wished to address the court on this matter. Even though the jury was not in the room, Marcia Clark objected. She said it would be allowing Simpson to testify without taking the witness stand or being subject to cross-examination.

"This is a very obvious defense bid to get material admitted that is not admitted in court," Clark argued. "Please don't do this, Your Honor. I beg you."

Judge Ito took Clark's plea as an affront to his ability to keep control over his courtroom and insisted that all he was interested in was knowing whether Simpson was going to forgo his right to testify. With that, Simpson rose in his chair.

SIMPSON: Good morning, Your Honor. As much as I would like to address some of the misrepresentations about myself and my Nicole, and our life together, I am mindful of the mood and the stamina of this jury. I have confidence, a lot more it seems than Miss Clark has, of their integrity and that they will find as the record stands now, that I did not, could not and would not have committed this crime. I have four kids. Two kids I haven't seen in a year. They ask me every week, "Dad, how much longer before this trial is over?"

ITO: Mr. Simpson, you do understand your right to testify as a witness and you chose to rest your case at this . . . [*Simpson nods in agreement.*] All right. Thank you very much, sir.

CLARK: Since he would like to make these statements to the Court, I would like the opportunity to examine him about them. May he take a seat in the blue chair and we'll have a discussion?

ITO: Thank you.

On Tuesday, September 27, closing arguments began. Because the burden of proving the case rests with the prosecution, it gets to argue first and last.

Marcia Clark and Christopher Darden went over every single piece of evidence. They talked about the timeline and Simpson's lack of an alibi. They reminded the jury of the 911 phone calls Nicole had made to police and the evidence of spousal abuse, including large photographic blowups that highlighted bruises around Nicole's eyes and on her cheeks. The arguments ranged from the serious (DNA evidence) to the ridiculous (Kato Kaelin, O.J. Simpson's house guest and an aspiring actor).

In my opinion, however, the two most interesting aspects of Clark's final statements dealt with Detective Fuhrman and the miscues involving the scientific and medical evidence. These were the two areas, I believe, in which the prosecution had the most to lose. In discussing Fuhrman, for instance, Clark made the following points: "Did he lie when he testified here in this courtroom saying that he did not use racial epithets in the last ten years? Yes.

"Is he a racist? Yes.

"Is he the worst the LAPD has to offer? Yes.

"Do we wish that this person was never hired by LAPD? Yes.

"Should LAPD have ever hired him? No.

"Should such a person be a police officer? No.

"In fact, do we wish there was no such person on the planet? Yes.

"But the fact that Mark Fuhrman is a racist and lied about it on the witness stand does not mean that we haven't proven the defendant guilty beyond a reasonable doubt. And it would be a tragedy if, with such overwhelming evidence, you found the defendant not guilty in spite of all that because of the racist attitudes of one police officer."

When it came to the sloppiness of Los Angeles forensic experts, Clark took a similar tack: "The defense lawyers throw out questions about whether LAPD has some bad police officers. Does the scientific division have some sloppy criminalists? Does the coroner's office have some sloppy coroners? The answer to all of these questions is, Sure, yes, they do. That's not news to you. I am sure it wasn't a big surprise. We should look into quality control; things should be done better, things could always be done better. There is no question about that, but we are not here to vote on that today."

In response, defense attorneys Johnnie Cochran and Barry Scheck hammered home the key points that favored Simpson's innocence. Like a prize boxer, Cochran jabbed at the hot spots, sounding more like a Southern Baptist evangelist than a trial lawyer and invoking more Bible verses than legal citations. He also used rhyme and reason.

"Remember these words: If it doesn't fit, you must acquit," Cochran told the jury, referring to the glove demonstration that was so devastating to the prosecution's case. He continued to challenge the prosecution's theory, specifically the position that Simpson donned a disguise the night of the murders.

"If I put this knit cap on, who am I?" Cochran asked, displaying his flair for courtroom theatrics by putting on a dark, knitted ski cap like the one prosecutors had claimed the defendant wore. "I'm Johnnie Cochran with a knit cap on. From two blocks away, O.J. Simpson is O.J. Simpson."

He jumped on Detective Fuhrman with both feet, calling him a racist bigot who planted evidence to frame black defendants. He even went so far as to compare Fuhrman to Adolf Hitler.

In the end, most legal experts gave both sides high marks. However, Fred Goldman was not among them. The day of Cochran's closing argument, the victim's father rushed out of court, down the elevators, and to the hundreds of microphones waiting outside. With lips trembling, eyes tearing, Goldman lashed out at Cochran.

"This man is sick," he said. "This man is a horror walking around amongst us. We have seen a man who perhaps is the worst kind of racist himself. He is someone who shoves racism in front of everything, someone who compares a person who speaks racist comments to Hitler, a person who murdered millions of people. This man is the worst kind of human being imaginable."

Goldman proceeded to point out that Cochran had surrounded himself with muscle-bound bodyguards in bow ties supplied by Nation of Islam leader Louis Farrakhan, a known racist and anti-Semite himself.

Two points need to be made here. First, I am a Jew and the father of four children around Ron Goldman's age. It is not difficult for me to empathize with Goldman and his family. The loss they suffered is immeasurable. However, I was not particularly insulted by Cochran's comparison of Detective Fuhrman to Hitler. While the reference to the Holocaust may have been tactless and the comparison itself a gross hyperbole, the fact is that both men were ugly, vicious racists. Both men were in positions of power. In fact, Fuhrman even boasted to people about gathering all of the black people and burning them. That's called genocide. Tragically, it was a theory that Hitler carried out, killing six million innocent people simply because they were Jewish.

I was, on the other hand, greatly disappointed by Cochran's decision to use bodyguards supplied by Farrakhan. I understand that Cochran and his office had received numerous death threats. That was a serious and understandable concern. As a major celebrity and hero to the black community, however, Cochran could have hired bodyguards from any number of groups. Personally, I believe Cochran hurt himself by hiring the Nation of Islam. Furthermore, I think he unintentionally insulted his colleagues Alan Dershowitz, Barry Scheck, Peter Neufeld, and Robert Shapiro—all of whom are Jewish. Hopefully, this was simply an unintentional mistake, a move that he did not think through at the time.

On Friday, September 29, the case of *California v. Orenthal James Simpson* was placed into the hands of the jury. One year and three days after jury selection began, the case was coming to a conclusion. The jury had heard from eleven defense attorneys and nine prosecutors. The state had called 58 witnesses, who took twenty-three weeks to tell their story. The defense case included 53 witnesses, who took ten weeks. Prosecutors introduced 723 pieces of evidence, compared to 392 exhibits for Simpson's side. There were more than sixteen thousand objections made, of which nine thousand were overruled. The jurors had been sequestered for 266 days and nights and paid only $1,330 each for their service. The state had spent $3.6 million to investigate and prosecute Simpson. Another $3 million had been spent on food, shelter, and security for the jurors.

Most experienced lawyers and courtroom observers, myself included, believed that the jury deliberations would last for at least several days. After all, there was so much evidence and so many theories to discuss. If I were a betting man, I would have put my money on this trial ending in a mistrial with a hung jury. But as we all know, after less than three hours of actual deliberations, the jury announced they had reached a verdict.

As if employed by the television networks, Judge Ito postponed making the verdict public until 10 A.M. the next day. In all fairness, however, several of the lawyers had made quick trips out of town and the judge wanted to give them time to get back. This delay did one thing: it allowed time and opportunity for a great deal of speculation concerning the imminent verdict by legal pundits on national and local television and radio. Prominent trial lawyers, district attorneys, and law school professors were interviewed for their thoughts on the case. Interestingly, most were predicting a guilty verdict. They based this opinion on two facts.

First, the jury had asked Judge Ito to read back the testimony of the limousine driver who took Simpson to the airport on the night of the slayings. The jurors only wanted to hear the direct testimony and not the cross-examination by defense attorneys. Some lawyers believed that members of the jury were trying to nail down the timeline, and considered the limo driver to have been a key witness for the prosecution.

Secondly, none of the jurors would look at Simpson when they reported in open court that they had reached a decision.

I, on the other hand, interpreted these events differently. That evening and the next morning, I told several reporters from local and national radio and TV shows that I disagreed with many of my fellow legal analysts and now predicted unequivocally that Simpson would be acquitted of the charges.

At 1 P.M. Eastern Standard Time, the nation stopped working. We planned our lunch breaks to be near TV sets. It was like a Super Bowl or World Series. People were betting on how it would turn out. Restaurants were offering free orange juice and Bloody Marys to customers who came to watch the verdict announced live. No doubt about it, the case of *California vs. Orenthal James Simpson* had become pop culture.

The words will go down in history: "We, the jury in the above entitled action, find the defendant, Orenthal James Simpson, not guilty of the crime of murder. . . . "

The trial of the century was over, and the overwhelming response was negative. The moment that the jury announced its decision, many were calling for jury reforms. Some wanted non-unanimous jury verdicts in criminal cases. Others sought sanctions against lawyers who openly ask jurors to ignore the law. And there were those who wanted cameras eliminated from the courtroom.

However, I doubt the case will leave any great legal legacy. Why? Because what most people fail to understand about this case is that it was not the norm. In fact, it was a complete and fantastic anomaly, an aberration. And for that reason, we should not judge the criminal justice system based on this case.

That being said, there was a lot we learned from the Simpson trial. First, it educated many to the rules of law, such as "innocent until proven guilty" and "beyond a reasonable doubt." From Michael Baden, Henry Lee, Herb MacDonell, and Fredric Rieders, the average person received a lesson in the forensic sciences and pathology. The public learned how DNA works and how crime scenes are, or should be, investigated.

The case certainly exposed the tragedy of spousal abuse as well. There can be no doubt that Simpson badly mistreated Nicole during their marriage. And while there was no evidence that he had physically abused her since 1989, his jealousy was well documented. We can only hope that this verdict encourages women to come forward to get help in situations where they have been abused.

But perhaps the greatest lesson to have been learned in this case had to do with what can legitimately be expected from our legal system. In debating what led the jury to reach its decision, legal experts questioned whether it was the Fuhrman factor, commonly referred to as "the race card," or the prosecution's failure to present enough reliable violence. I believe these people are missing the point:

It wasn't "or"—it was "and."

To be sure, the jurors must have been aware of the racism that was prevalent throughout the case, but the fact is that the defense, using such witnesses as Baden and Lee, created a great deal of doubt in the state's evidence. Those two elements worked together to bring about a verdict of acquittal. Either by itself most likely would have led to a hung jury.

Personally, I believe the prosecutors made a huge mistake early on by not exposing Fuhrman as a racist. The prosecutors and his fellow detectives had worked with him for years. They had to know his bigoted beliefs and vicious propensities. A person doesn't make these racial statements to strangers, as was unveiled at trial, and not say similar things to co-workers. Indeed, we have come to learn that the U.S.

Department of Justice had previously investigated Fuhrman for possible civil rights violations.

Assuming that prosecutors knew about some of the prior statements and acts by Fuhrman, I think they committed a fatal error by making him a key witness. For instance, they could simply have decided not to use the glove as evidence, thereby keeping Fuhrman off the witness stand. That would have taken the race card away from defense attorneys.

What lasting impact this case will have on our society remains unclear, although some interesting feedback has already been registered. Americans were divided in their opinion of Simpson's guilt along racial lines: 70 percent of white people polled believed he was guilty while 70 percent of African-Americans felt he was innocent. This division was obvious the day the verdict was announced. Groups of black people were shown cheering as white people were viewed in shock and crying.

An interesting commentary on this phenomenon was later provided by another former Buffalo Bills football player, Jack Kemp. The Republican politician was on NBC's *Meet the Press* the Sunday after the trial discussing the case. On the program, he made the following statement:

"I know a lot of whites were upset, even angry when they saw blacks cheering the verdict. What many whites don't understand is that they were not cheering that a man got away with murder. Instead, they were cheering for a legal principle. They were cheering because the criminal justice system finally held that a black man accused of a crime is indeed innocent until proven guilty."

If you think this case is over, think again. Both the Brown and Goldman families have filed civil lawsuits against Simpson. I would not be surprised to see the Brown family withdraw their lawsuit. After all, now that Simpson has been acquitted of all criminal charges, he probably will gain complete custody of his children. If the Browns pursue a hostile legal action against him, they should be concerned that Simpson will refuse to give them visitation rights to their grandchildren.

On the other hand, the Goldman family has nothing to

lose. I predict they will do anything and everything in their power to make Simpson's life miserable. They will challenge him at every turn. And keep one thing in mind: now that the criminal trial is over, Simpson cannot avoid testifying. With criminal charges no longer possible, Simpson cannot invoke his Fifth Amendment right protecting himself against self-incrimination.

Considering Simpson's ego and the Goldman family's anger and resolve, I would have to say that the most dramatic moments in this case are yet to come. And then all the millions of Americans who had become addicted to the O.J. Simpson trial will jump off the wagon and become hooked once more.

TWO

THE MYSTERIOUS DEATH
OF VINCENT FOSTER

I f Abraham Lincoln's noble conviction that all men are created equal is valid, then in theory all men are equal in death as well. The truth of the matter is, however, that the deaths of some people command more attention. They are the people with money, societal influence, or political power, who, by the very act of dying, raise eyebrows. But whereas their high stations may have offered them certain advantages in life, they are often not so blessed once placed beneath the ground.

Such was the case with Vincent Foster. As deputy White House counsel, former partner in an Arkansas law firm with Hillary Clinton, longtime personal friend of Bill Clinton, and personal lawyer of record for both the President and First Lady, Foster was a man of significance. At the White House, he was known as the manager of personal affairs for the First Family, and the keeper of its secrets. He was the only person, for example, who knew all there was to know about the Clintons' role in the Whitewater land development project.

And so, when his body was found on the afternoon of Tuesday, July 20, 1993, at a public park just minutes away from downtown Washington, D.C., his death should immediately have been the object of the utmost scrutiny. Unfortunately, it was not. As a result, theories of murder, political conspiracy, and cover-up have abounded ever since.

My first contact with the Foster case occurred nearly a year after his death. I was at my office when a reporter from the Associated Press called. An article had appeared that morning in the *New York Post* questioning the premise that Foster had committed suicide and focusing on the position of the gun in Foster's hand. The AP reporter was interested in my analysis of the scenario.

According to the Park Police, a .38 Colt revolver was clutched in Foster's right hand when his body was discovered. His fingers were wrapped around the back of the pistol's hand grip, and his thumb was caught behind the trigger. His right arm was lying down by his side. The *New York Post* article suggested that this was impossible, that if it had indeed been a suicide, the gun would have been thrown several feet away by the involuntary spasm of his arm and hand at the moment of discharge.

I told the AP reporter that none of these findings automatically ruled out suicide. In many such instances, I explained, the victim can have an instantaneous, spasmodic reflex, which is entirely involuntary, and the hand will clutch the object it is holding very firmly. Often, I said, the fingers will actually tighten around the weapon. Moreover, depending on how firmly Foster's thumb was jammed behind the trigger, even a major muscular spasm may have failed to dislodge it.

The next day, articles in the *New York Post* and other major daily newspapers reported that the White House was being bombarded by telephone calls from representatives of the media seeking information on Foster's death. One or two of these papers stated that the White House was "referring" reporters to Dr. Cyril Wecht of Pittsburgh!

That afternoon, I received calls from several friends who had either seen this reference or had heard my name mentioned on the radio. Apparently, Rush Limbaugh had told his massive listening audience that the White House was having me handle the press for them. Limbaugh described me as a left-leaning, liberal pathologist. How he could claim to know anything about my political ideology, I have no idea. I wonder, for instance, if Limbaugh knew that while I may be a registered Democrat, I was the forensic pathologist who testified for the Massachusetts state attorney against Senator Edward Kennedy's lawyers in 1969 in an attempt to have the body of Mary Jo Kopechne exhumed and autopsied. Of course, he never mentioned that.

I did find it amusing that I was now an unofficial, informal, unpaid consultant to the White House—surely the pinnacle of my career! This was a fascinating and humorous thought, to be sure. Little did I know that in the months ahead, my involvement with White House concerns was to grow deeper and considerably more serious.

At this point, all I knew about the Whitewater investigation and the Foster death was what I had read in the newspapers or heard on television. Some columnists and political analysts were speculating that the entire controversy could lead to the political demise of President Clinton. Others were just as adamant that Whitewater was much ado about nothing. But Foster's death itself was what interested me, and so I began to look into the case a bit.

Vincent Foster's six months in the nation's capital had not gone as planned. He had supervised the nomination of Zoe Baird, the White House's first choice for attorney general, which was aborted after it was learned that she had not paid taxes for her child's nanny. He had come under fire after issuing a legal opinion that Hillary Clinton's health care task force was not an official government group and therefore did not have to open its meetings to the public. And he was once again embarrassed when seven employees in the White House's travel office were fired amid hints of financial shenanigans. Making matters worse, the situation took on an odor of cronyism when friends of the Clintons were chosen as replacements.

Then came Whitewater. A complex real estate deal that led to the failure of Madison Guaranty, an Arkansas savings and loan institution, the Whitewater scandal has dogged President

Clinton and other members of his administration ever since he took office. For one thing, there are the allegations that money earned from the deal was diverted into Clinton's political war chest. More damaging, however, are the accusations that the President and his followers used their newly obtained positions to keep federal banking regulators from conducting a thorough investigation into the whole debacle.

As has been mentioned, no one knew more about the Clintons' role in Whitewater than Vincent Foster. He was their personal lawyer. Ostensibly, he knew everything, and the pressure to do something about it was building.

Criticism soon began appearing in the news media, particularly on the editorial page of the *Wall Street Journal*, taking Foster to task for exhibiting elitism and incompetence. According to friends and co-workers, this negative scrutiny took a toll on Foster's emotional stability. He found it difficult to eat or sleep. His sense of humor disappeared. Staying focused at work was a major chore.

In the week prior to his death, Foster secretly contacted his personal physician in Little Rock, apparently seeking help in fighting depression. He also begged the doctor to keep the request completely confidential, fearing that public disclosure of the fact that he was being treated for depression would place his high-level security clearance in jeopardy. The physician agreed and prescribed an antidepressant. Later, his wife would confirm that he had, indeed, been under treatment for depression just before his death.

On the last day of his life, Foster reported to work just as he had every day since his boss and grade school friend moved into 1600 Pennsylvania Avenue. He spent that morning alone in his office with the door closed. There, he paid his family's bills, wrote some thank-you notes, and wrapped up a few odds and ends from his father's estate—something he had long promised his wife he would do.

For lunch, Foster ate a hamburger and french fries while sitting on the couch in his office. About 1 P.M., he grabbed his suit coat and walked out of the office, telling his secretary, "I'll be back." She thought it odd that he left his briefcase behind.

About 4 P.M., a witness noticed a car that was later identified as Foster's parked in a lot at Fort Marcy, a small military memorial park located in suburban Virginia just off the George Washington Parkway and next to the Potomac River. A suit coat was neatly folded on the passenger's seat. It was not until sometime between 5:30 and 6 P.M., however, that Foster's body was discovered.

A man in a white van, whose identity has been kept secret by the investigating agencies at his request, had reportedly stopped at the park to urinate when he spotted the body. At first, he told police, he thought the man was sleeping and started to walk away. But then he noticed that the man's face was swollen. Stepping closer, he saw blood around the man's face. The eyes were partially closed and glazed.

When the authorities arrived, they found Foster's body resting on a slope beside a Civil War cannon. The pistol was still in his hands, but his blood-spattered glasses were found more than eight feet away. Detectives could find no witnesses, no one who had seen anything or heard any shots fired. It should be noted that very few people ever visit Fort Marcy Park, and that the nearest building, the home of Saudi Arabia's ambassador, is located several hundred yards away. Oddly, the man who found Foster's body originally told the police that he had not seen a gun in Foster's hand. In later questioning, however, he admitted that the foliage around the body may have hidden the weapon from his sight.

As soon as the body was identified, official Washington was sent into a state of pandemonium. A massive and expansive investigation ensued. Of course, that did not guarantee competence or accuracy. In fact, just the opposite occurred.

A few weeks after the *New York Post* and Rush Limbaugh got me involved in the case, I received a call from a colleague, Dr. Julian Bailes, a prominent Pittsburgh neurosurgeon. He said that he had been contacted by friends in Washington who had asked him to review the medical circumstances of Foster's death. His contacts were Republicans on the Banking Committee of the U.S. House of Representatives, which was examining the medical and investigative reports in the Foster case as part of its investigation into the Whitewater deal.

With my permission, Dr. Bailes gave my name and number to lawyers for the committee. In brief conversations with the congressional staff attorneys, Dr. Bailes and I were told that we would be contacted in short order and flown to Washington.

Several weeks passed, however, and that call never came. One reason may have been that special prosecutor Robert Fiske, who was appointed by U.S. Attorney General Janet Reno to investigate the Whitewater land deal, had named a panel of four pathologists to review the investigative records in the Foster case. My thought was that the committee members wanted to see what the panel of experts came up with first.

On July 1, 1994, nearly a year after Foster's death, the case appeared dose to being put to rest. That day, Mr. Fiske issued an extensive report concluding that Foster had committed suicide and that his death had nothing to do with the Whitewater investigation. According to the fifty-eight-page report, which drew on interviews with more than 125 witnesses, including members of Foster's immediate family, there was no doubt that the deputy White House counsel killed himself due to depression and general anxiety. Much of this conclusion was based on the findings by the panel of forensic pathologists that the original autopsy report was correct.

Far from hushing talk of a conspiracy and governmental cover-up, however, such allegations, particularly from the right wing, only grew stronger. Radio and television talk shows were filled with speculation about how Vincent Foster really died and why. The prevailing theory was that Foster had been killed at an apartment rented or owned by First Lady Hillary Clinton, with whom he was allegedly having an affair, and that his body had been carried to Fort Marcy Park. So widespread was this allegation that stocks on Wall Street reportedly plummeted as a result.

Despite Fiske's report—and keep in mind that Fiske was

widely respected as a Republican—GOP members of Congress were gearing up for what were sure to be explosive ethics hearings on Whitewater. As the minority party at the time, the Republicans were hoping to embarrass the President, which, in turn, would hurt Democrats across the country at the polls in November.

Not having heard from our contact on the House Banking Committee for several weeks, I surmised that my involvement in this matter was concluded and that my impact had been minimal at best.

I was wrong.

Later that month, I received a late-night phone call from Dr. Peter Fallon, a dentist in Florida who had been a student at the University of Pittsburgh School of Dentistry, where I have lectured for many years. He told me he was doing some work in the field of forensic odontology, and I was delighted to learn that I had helped to motivate him in that direction. Eventually, Dr. Fallon got to the point of his call: his daughter was a staff lawyer for Republicans on the Senate Banking Committee, which was still investigating Whitewater and Foster's death.

"Would you be interested, as a special favor to me, in speaking with my daughter or another attorney working for the committee?" Dr. Fallon asked.

"Of course," I said.

"They may want to call you right away, because things are happening so rapidly. Would that be okay?"

"No problem at all," I responded. "If they need to call me tonight, that would be fine."

Dr. Fallon said he would contact his daughter immediately and that I should expect a telephone call sometime soon.

About an hour and a half later, shortly before midnight, the phone rang again. This time it was Roman Darmer, chief counsel for the Republican senators on the Banking Committee. We talked for an hour that night about the case and about my previous contact with House Republicans. The conversation ended with his promising to fax me the next day the original autopsy report, the crime lab report, and the findings of the four independent pathologists who had reviewed the case for Fiske. At this point, all the political intrigue must have been getting to me, because my adrenaline level was pretty high.

I arrived at my office the next morning to find a stack of documents that had been faxed from the Capitol, marked "urgent." I wasted no time in reviewing them.

First was the original autopsy report by the Fairfax, Virginia, forensic pathologist, Dr. James Beyer. He was acting under the supervision of Dr. Donald Haut, the district's medical examiner. At only two pages, the autopsy report itself was amazingly short. It began with the usual fact sheet on the deceased:

Age: 48
Race: White
Length: 76½ inches
Weight: 197 lbs.
Eyes: Hazel
Hair: Graying black

In a diagram of Foster's head, the bullet was shown entering through the inside of his mouth. Gunpowder debris was found on the soft tissues of his mouth, which clearly indicated that the barrel of the gun was inside Foster's mouth when it was fired. The exit wound was depicted in the middle of the back of the head, approximately three inches from the top of the skull. The autopsy found no other trauma to Foster's body, strongly suggesting that there had been no struggle. In addition, none of Foster's teeth were broken, meaning that it is unlikely anyone had forced the pistol into his mouth.

Accompanying the autopsy report was a synopsis of the facts and evidence put together by Mr. Darmer. It was dated that day and read as follows:

Death in Ft. Marcy National Park in Virginia over Potomac River. GSW [gunshot wound] to roof of mouth, 3 inches below crown. Star shaped wound—.38 caliber, Colt Revolver.

Sitting on incline berm with head higher (approximately 45 degrees). Bullet not recovered. Gun found in right hand—both hands down at sides. Powder residue found on right index finger and web of hand. Powder residue also found on left index finger. Gun powder found on shirt and undershirt. No visible dirt on outside of shirt (according to witnesses). Index finger found on trigger with thumb wedged between trigger guard and handle of gun. [While most of Darmer's report would remain consistent with what I later learned about the crime scene, the index finger and thumb positions described in this last sentence are not and, in fact, show up nowhere else in the investigative record.]

No other injuries—lots of blood found behind the head on earth and on top part of back of shirt.

Trace amount of anti-depressant, Trazadone (prescribed by his doctor)—no alcohol or other drugs.

Blond hairs (different from his brown hair) and carpet fibers (various colors) found on pants and T-shirt, but not on shirt.

Wife has auburn hair.

[Bullet] Tract upwards and backwards.

Gun was family owned.

Body found at 6:00 p.m.

Autopsy done at 7:21 a.m. next day. No forensic pathologist at scene.

At my request, Mr. Darmer had also sent me copies of the crime lab investigative reports. They were filled with many insights that, at the time, had not been released, including the following:

- The gun contained two different serial numbers, indicating that it was assembled with parts from two separate guns. Records for those serial numbers show that the gun was originally purchased in 1913.

- When shown the pistol, Foster's sister, Sharon Bowman, said it looked very similar to the gun their father had kept in his bedside table.
- The crime lab performed several tests on the gun and found that it was operable, and that the gunpowder from the revolver's cartridge was physically and chemically similar to powder recovered on Foster's shirt.
- Officials did discover gunpowder on Foster's clothing that did not match the alleged suicide weapon. The FBI and Fiske dismissed this, however, claiming that the shirt had been accidentally contaminated by other gunpowder residue at the crime lab.
- There were no fingerprints found on the gun. One print was located on the inner surface of the gun's grip, but the FBI crime lab determined it was not Foster's print.
- Foster's clothes did not contain any obvious soil stains. However, the crime lab did find small particles of mica on his pants and shoes. Mica is a substance that is consistent with the soil in the area where Foster's body was discovered.
- On April 4, 1994, nine months after the shooting, sixteen FBI agents used high-tech equipment to search the park for the missing bullet, bone fragments from Foster's skull, and the presence of blood beneath the soil. The FBI even developed a map showing the likely path and direction of the bullet after it exited Foster's skull. The agents did find twelve slugs in the park. However, tests showed that none had been fired from Foster's revolver.

After carefully reviewing all of the materials dealing with the medical and physical evidence in this case, I called Roman Darmer back to offer my own analysis of what had happened.

"Vincent Foster almost certainly died from a self-inflicted wound to the head," I told him. "All of the evidence points toward suicide and away from homicide. And all of the evidence points toward him shooting himself at the park.

There is no evidence that he died elsewhere and that his body was dumped at the park.

"That being said, there are many problems with this case," I continued. "First, why in the world were the Park Police in charge of this high-profile homicide investigation when the FBI certainly could have and should have had jurisdiction? The FBI has the expertise in this kind of case, not the Park Police.

"Secondly, why was the medical examiner not immediately called to the scene to examine the body and the scene of death, and collect and preserve evidence properly? Why did it take more than twelve hours to do the autopsy? This is investigative sloppiness and incompetence. If the medical examiner had been there, any questions of the body having been moved would have been eliminated.

"As for the autopsy itself, it was incomplete and insufficiently detailed. It was only two pages long when it should have been a document of great detail. The fact that the medical examiner fortuitously arrived at the correct manner of death does not mean the autopsy or the medicolegal investigation was adequate. In this case, it most certainly was not.

"Let me add one more thing," I said. "Just because I believe Vincent Foster committed suicide and did it in Fort Marcy Park does not mean that I believe that should be the end of the investigation. There are many questions about his death that remain unanswered. But the most important question is this: Why did he commit suicide? Was it simply because he was depressed or is there a more sinister reason? Did he take any secrets with him to the grave that the public or Congress need to know about?"

At the end of our lengthy conversation, Mr. Darmer thanked me for my assistance and promised that he would pass on my analysis to the Republican senators on the Banking Committee. Interestingly, when the Whitewater hearings took place in the House and Senate Banking Committees in the summer and fall of 1995, Republicans in both branches of Congress said they were satisfied that Foster had killed himself and that there was no conspiracy or cover-up.

Still, the doubts persisted. In articles appearing in Pittsburgh's *Tribune-Review* and a handful of other papers, questions about the death of Vincent Foster continued to be raised. They included the following:

- Why were there no fingerprints on the gun found in Foster's hand?
- Who is the source of the blond hair strands found on his body?
- Where did the multicolored carpet fibers found on his clothing come from?
- Why didn't Foster leave some kind of good-bye note for his wife and three children?
- Why did the coroner's report say that Foster's body had been x-rayed when it had not?

All of these are very intriguing questions, but they do not necessarily amount to much. Just prior to the Whitewater hearings, my friend Henry Lee traveled to Washington to examine the crime scene. In conversations I have had with him since, I have learned a few things that tend to put some of these questions to rest. First, contrary to the public claim that the soles of Foster's shoes were clean, Henry, using higher magnification lenses, identified grass and mineral deposits on them. Secondly, Henry conducted a shooting experiment using pigskins in which he found that, in some instances, bullet fragments either did not exit or did not travel far; in other words, pieces of the missing bullet may have been lost in Foster's blood-matted hair or in the dirt at the scene. As for questions raised about blood spatters found on Foster's glasses, Henry's conclusion was that these were 100 percent consistent with a suicide scenario.

When one considers the murder theory, other evidentiary weaknesses pop up as well. For instance, Foster, at six feet four inches and almost two hundred pounds, was a large, physically fit man. Yet there was no sign of physical struggle, either on his body or at the scene where he was found. Neither is there any evidence that Foster was in any way drugged or otherwise incapacitated prior to the shooting. How, exactly, do those who claim Foster was murdered believe the murder occurred?

Then there is the fact that suicide in this case actually makes sense. Foster was depressed. His physicians said so and his wife later said so. Why? We can only speculate. As a lawyer with an impeccable reputation for honesty and fairness who had never encountered failure, he now found himself in the middle of a national scandal. This must have been personally and psychologically devastating to him. To Vincent Foster, this must have been a life he was not prepared for and could not deal with. Combine these circumstances with a biochemical predisposition to depression, and suicide may have seemed an attractive alternative. Tragically, every experienced forensic pathologist has handled suicides that have involved even less apparent motivation.

Despite such a cogent argument for suicide, however, and despite the fact that every investigative body that's looked into Foster's death has labeled it a suicide, many Republican members of Congress and right-wing media commentators persist in their dubious claim that foul play was involved. As far as I can tell, these folks are just playing politics, trying to turn the whole incident into the Democratic Party's equivalent of Watergate. The reason they focus on Foster's death rather than the Whitewater deal is the simple fact that the majority of Americans don't understand or care about real estate or savings and loan institutions. They care about death and sex and scandal. And however scant the facts may be, those who would have the Clinton administration go down in ignominy can be expected to do their best to keep the innuendo alive in the public mind. For innuendos, they know, often speak louder than facts.

THREE

WHAT REALLY
HAPPENED AT WACO

Lies, lies, nothing but lies. That's all Dick DeGuerin was hearing, and he no longer had any patience for it. He needed some answers. He needed some facts. He needed the truth.

A prominent Texas trial attorney, DeGuerin was accustomed to publicity. He had defended murderers and rapists, drug dealers and child molesters. But never had he received as much media attention as this case had generated. And never had there been so much hatred directed toward one of his clients.

It was during the first week of May 1993 that DeGuerin called my office in Pittsburgh. I was familiar with his name from newspaper and TV interviews.

"I have a little case in which I'm in dire need of input from an expert in your field," he began. "Maybe you've heard of my latest client?"

"Of course," I responded. "The whole world knows of David Koresh."

DeGuerin had represented Koresh in life, and he continued to represent the notorious cult leader now that he was dead. DeGuerin had spent many hours with the man who called himself the "Messiah," a few of them in recent weeks at the Branch

Davidian compound in Waco as hundreds of federal agents from the Bureau of Alcohol, Tobacco and Firearms (ATF) and the Federal Bureau of Investigation (FBI) watched and listened, their guns loaded and pointed in Koresh's direction.

"I need someone to fly to Waco as soon as possible to help me with this investigation," he said. "I'd like for you to come. If you can't, I was wondering if there is someone else you can recommend."

When a case like this comes your way, whether you're a lawyer, an investigator, or a forensic pathologist, you do not back away or recommend someone else. Without hesitation, I told DeGuerin I would rearrange my schedule and make immediate travel plans.

Like most Americans, I had been following the Waco saga ever since the government's disastrous February 28 raid on the Branch Davidian compound. Four ATF agents had died and sixteen others had been wounded when the Branch Davidians, apparently tipped off to the raid, unexpectedly opened fire on the approaching agents. In an ensuing gun battle, an unknown number of cult members were killed or wounded, including Koresh himself, who claimed to have been shot in the abdomen.

For a while after that, authorities had reason to hope for a peaceful resolution to the conflict. Koresh and his right-hand man, Steve Schneider, maintained frequent phone contact with negotiators and met regularly with DeGuerin and other attorneys in an apparent good-faith effort to negotiate their release. Within five days, twenty-one children and two adults were let go, and within the next two weeks, twelve more adults were released. Still, ninety-five people, including seventeen children, remained inside.

Moreover, it soon became clear that Koresh was more interested in playing games with the authorities than in engaging in honest diplomacy. First, he failed to keep his side of a promise to surrender after local radio and TV stations broadcast an hour-long taped message by him. His reason? God had told him to wait. Then, on March 20, he demanded that he be allowed to preach to his flock while awaiting trial.

But when the FBI sent Koresh a letter two days later agreeing to this demand, he simply wadded it up into a ball and threw it away. In early April, Koresh agreed to surrender after the cult celebrated Passover. Not surprisingly, however, that holiday came and went with no resolution. Finally, Koresh vowed to emerge after he'd completed a manuscript he said he was writing on the Seven Seals of the Book of Revelations. As it turned out, there was no such manuscript.

Federal agents tried everything to force the Davidians out into the open, including psychological warfare. First, they shined powerful spotlights on the compound. Then they began blaring recordings round-the-clock of everything from Nancy Sinatra and Andy Williams to Tibetan chants and rabbits being slaughtered. Far from breaking the cultists down, however, these tactics only seemed to stiffen their resolve.

By the middle of April, tension was running high. At one point, Koresh became abusive on the phone. A couple of days later, he sent the FBI a letter in which he predicted there would be an earthquake and that a dam would burst. Many authorities viewed this cryptic statement as a threat. Soon, Koresh was refusing to take phone calls even from DeGuerin.

Meanwhile, the FBI had developed a plan to break down the compound's walls with tanks and force the cultists' evacuation with CS, a potent tear gas. There was much hesitation, but finally, when reports of children being beaten and rapidly deteriorating sanitary conditions reached the Justice Department, Attorney General Janet Reno approved the plan. On April 18, she called President Clinton to inform him of her decision. Assured that it was the only way to go, the President gave her his blessing.

Before dawn on April 19, the FBI stood ready with 170 agents and a fleet of armored personnel carriers and M60 tanks that had been converted into combat engineering vehicles. Just before 6 A.M., the FBI's chief negotiator called the compound and reached Schneider. In a statement that was simultaneously broadcast to the Davidians over a PA system, the negotiator said: "There's going to be tear gas injected into the compound. This is not an assault. Do not fire. The idea is to get you out of the compound." When Schneider threw the phone out the window in disgust, the troops moved in. Inside the compound, the gas masks went on.

Almost as soon as the tanks began punching holes in the walls, say authorities, the cult members began firing on them with automatic weapons. For the next thirty minutes, gas was pumped into the building. Then they stopped. Two minutes later, when no one had come out, the gassing resumed. By noon, eighteen bottles of tear gas had been injected into the compound, and still no one had emerged. It was shortly after that when authorities noticed the smoke.

At first it was just a gray plume sneaking out of one of the building's edges, but it soon became apparent that the compound was on fire. In fact, there appeared to be as many as four separate fires burning. At this point, people finally began to emerge. But either they were not fast enough or they were not all permitted to leave, for within minutes the entire ranch had erupted into a huge inferno. In the end, only nine members made it to safety. Eighty-six people, including the seventeen remaining children, died in the flames.

From my brief conversation with DeGuerin, I knew that there were several major questions to be answered. For one, the FBI was claiming that Koresh had died from a gunshot wound to the head, while Texas officials were saying publicly that this was absolutely not true. Had Koresh been shot at all? If so, was the bullet fired from close range or long distance? Was it possible that the bullet wound was inflicted after Koresh's death in the fire?

A separate matter were the public allegations by government agents that horrible crimes of physical and sexual abuse against children had been committed inside the compound. According to reports, girls as young as eleven and twelve had been forced to have sexual intercourse with Koresh, while infants had been slapped and beaten. DeGuerin, however, told me that he had seen no evidence of such abuse on his trips inside the compound during the siege.

DeGuerin said he was not even sure that the body Texas officials were claiming to be that of David Koresh was really his. There was strong speculation that Koresh had even survived and escaped the fire through a series of underground tunnels built by his Branch Davidians. Although there was no direct evidence for such a strange scenario, he said, he just couldn't be sure.

"I have no way of knowing what to believe," he said. "That's why I need experts like you down here to tell me what is real and what is not."

DeGuerin told me that he had been asked by Koresh's mother, Bonnie Haldeman of Chandler, Texas, to continue to investigate the case. He said he was working with Jack Zimmerman, another well-known Texas trial attorney, who was representing the family of Steve Schneider, who along with his wife, Judy, had also presumably died in the blaze.

"The main thing we need from you," DeGuerin told me, "is to conduct repeat autopsy examinations of Koresh and the Schneiders. We want to make sure they are proper identifications and we need to know the cause of death."

I told DeGuerin that I was ready to travel to Waco immediately. However, there were some complications. Because of apparent miscommunication between the Tarrant County Medical Examiner's Office and the Texas justice of the peace supervising the evidence in the case (including the bodies), I was not able to gain official permission to conduct examinations until early May—a full three weeks after the tragedy. Eventually, however, I found myself en route to Waco.

From my conversations with DeGuerin and from having read several articles on the subject, I was able to piece together a historical profile of Koresh and understand a little bit more the kind of man he was.

David Koresh was born Vernon Wayne Howell in Houston, Texas, on August 17, 1959. His mother was only fourteen years old and was unmarried. His father married another woman just weeks after he was born. Raised in Dallas by his grandmother, Howell dropped out of school in the tenth grade, then worked as an auto mechanic and began playing guitar in a rock and roll band.

At age twenty, Howell followed in his mother's and grandmother's footsteps and joined the Seventh-Day Adventist Church in Tyler, Texas. Seventh-Day Adventists live by a strict moral code. The use of tobacco products and alcohol is prohibited, the Ten Commandments govern daily life, and premarital fornication is considered a definite no-no.

Howell seemed genuinely eager to learn about God and to live by solid moral values. Every time the church doors were open, he was there. He attended every Bible study, and other church members readily welcomed him into their flock. However, discontent with Howell arose when he made it known to several women in the church that he was sexually attracted to them. News reports say that he would use verses from scripture to try to convince women that they should have sex with him. During this same period, Howell became more and more resentful of the church's authority over him.

In 1983, less than four years after he joined the church, Koresh was involved in a showdown with the elders. One Sabbath, he walked to the pulpit and launched into a lengthy tirade against them. They let it go, but when he did it again the very next week, the elders of the church told him to leave and never come back.

Upon his official rejection by the church, Howell turned to the Branch Davidians, a group created sixty years earlier by Victor Houteff, another disenchanted Adventist who had parted ways with the church after declaring himself a prophet. When Howell joined the religious sect, it was under the leadership of a man named George Roden. Together, followers would sit around and talk about God, the Bible, and government control for hours upon hours.

In 1984, Howell married Rachael Jones, the fourteen-year-old daughter of a high-ranking member of the Branch Davidian cult. He told the girl's father that God was giving him Rachael to meet his needs. During their nine-year marriage, Rachael gave birth to two of Koresh's children. (Cyrus was eight and Star was six when they died in the Waco fire; their bodies were discovered huddled next to the body of their mother.)

Like Koresh, many of the original members of the Branch Davidians were dissatisfied former members of the Adventist Church. In 1987, Howell capitalized on this common bond to wrest control of the cult away from its established leader and declare himself the group's overseer and provider of God's word. Over the years, he would variously describe himself as Jesus Christ, the Lamb of God, and the "chosen one." But in interviews with the news media, he would back away from such grandiose claims and say only that he was a prophet sent personally by God.

In 1990, Vernon Howell officially changed his name to David Koresh, an amalgamation of the names of two biblical kings. As a leader, he had incredible charisma and magnetism. Those who belonged to his sect have been quoted admiring his extensive knowledge of the Bible. More important, he was tremendously successful in attracting new recruits. His boyish smile, curly hair, and dimples disarmed people looking for the meaning of life. If recruits became converts, they were invited to the seventy-seven-acre Branch Davidian compound, which had been completely paid for by the first followers. Koresh called this compound, appropriately enough, Ranch Apocalypse.

One of Koresh's first recruits was Steve Schneider, who, together with his wife, Judy, hailed from Green Bay, Wisconsin. Ten years Koresh's senior, Schneider had a degree in religious studies from the University of Hawaii and had taken additional courses at Seventh-Day Adventist schools in Michigan and England. A staunch disciple, he was quickly promoted to chief lieutenant. Apparently, the respect was mutual. In fact, so convinced was Schneider that Koresh was God's chosen one that he allowed Koresh to sleep with Judy and claim her as his own wife. In fact, Koresh fathered a daughter by Judy named Mayanah. She was two years old when she and her mother died in the fire.

Upon my arrival in Waco, I was met at the airport by one of DeGuerin's associates, who immediately drove me to the Tarrant County Medical Examiner's Office. From what I could tell, the pathologist had done an excellent job despite the intense pressure generated by the circumstances of this incredible drama. The autopsies were thorough and accurate. Nevertheless, the families of the deceased wanted my opinion, and so I went to work.

All three bodies were badly charred, their faces scorched beyond recognition. Most of the soft, fleshy tissue had been burned away, so that what we were dealing with, essentially, were bones.

But then, one can tell a lot from bones.

By referring to the dental and anthropological charts prepared by other forensic scientists, I was able to make enough positive comparisons with the remains to conclude with reasonable certainty that the body in front of me was, in fact, that of the thirty-three-year-old David Koresh. Having resolved that matter to the satisfaction of both myself and Mr. DeGuerin, I turned my attention to the wounds.

In Koresh's skull were the clear marks of a gunshot wound. The entrance was located in the mid-forehead area, about an inch above the brow. The bullet had exited in the back of the head, near the top. By lining up the wounds, I could tell that the bullet trajectory was most likely upward. While this position did not absolutely rule out suicide, the highly unnatural bending of the wrist that would have been required to self-inflict such a wound strongly suggested that someone else had fired the shot. Because the body was so badly burned, however, I was unable to determine how close the gun was when it was fired. This was crucial, since federal agents claimed that Koresh had either shot himself or had instructed one of his followers to shoot him. Several supporters of Koresh, on the other hand, said that the bullet came from outside the building, from the gun of an ATF or FBI agent. Unfortunately, without being able to determine the presence or absence of powder-burn marks, it would be impossible to tell.

As I continued my examination, I spotted evidence of a second bullet wound in the front of the left hip area. Officials told me they had corroborating testimony that this wound was indeed the one that Koresh had said had been inflicted during the original shoot-out with ATF agents. Although this wound, if treated, would not have been fatal, I immediately realized that if the bullet had entered Koresh an inch or two closer to the center line of the body, it probably would have struck a loop of his bowel. Left untreated, this very likely would have resulted in peritonitis, which in turn can lead to septic shock and death. I find it interesting to think that if this scenario had played out, all those innocent people would most likely still be alive today.

From toxicology tests performed on the remains, I could tell that Koresh was most likely alive when the fire started. The carbon monoxide level in the tissue samples was rather high, indicating that he had inhaled fumes from the fire before he died. Moreover, I knew that he could not have lived long enough after sustaining a gunshot wound to the brain to have inhaled that quantity of carbon monoxide.

The second examination I conducted was on the body of forty-three-year-old Steve Schneider, whose identity I also was able to confirm through comparisons with dental records and X rays. Although severe charring and fragmentation of the skull prevented me from being absolutely sure of the number and positions of his wounds, the location of a bony defect in the occipital region of his skull strongly suggested the possibility that one shot had been fired into the back of his head. If so, Schneider's death would not appear to have been a suicide either. Still, because of the poor state of his remains, I could not be certain. Like Koresh's toxicology tests, Schneider's showed a fairly high level of carbon monoxide, indicating that he, too, was alive when the fire began.

Finally, the body of forty-one-year-old Judy Schneider was brought out and placed on the examination table. Like the two previous bodies, this one had very little fleshy tissue remaining. Quite unlike the others, however, it did not have a head. Sometime during the shooting and the subsequent fire, I was told, her head had been separated from her body and the authorities had been unable to recover it.

Because of this, I was unable to determine a precise cause of death.

According to investigative reports, the bodies of Koresh and Steve Schneider were found near each other in a room located near the compound's kitchen that functioned as the communications center. Mrs. Schneider's body was found with the bodies of several other females, including her daughter, Mayanah. All were wearing Star of David necklaces around their necks, a sign of their dedication to their leader.

After I'd concluded my examinations, a senior producer with ABC's *Good Morning America* offered to drive me to the Branch Davidian compound, which was located several miles outside of town. Although it was now three weeks since the fire, dozens of people were standing around or sitting in their cars around the compound's fringes. I was amazed that this scene of human tragedy had already become a tourist attraction. In fact, there were vendors alongside the roadway selling bottles of dirt and ash from the compound. Others hawked T-shirts and baseball caps proclaiming I SURVIVED WACO or I SURVIVED KORESH. Even for America, the scene was unbelievable.

In the direction of the compound, the only sign of life was a herd of cattle grazing in the distance. The landscape was as startling as it was stark. Most of the compound had been bulldozed, leaving only rubble. Trees, grass, everything green was gone. In its place was a blackened strip of land between what used to be the compound's buildings and the area where federal investigators had camped out.

As I walked around the compound, I noticed several burned-out cars and a sixty-four-passenger bus that had been used as an air-raid bunker and was now partially buried in the debris. The site was completely colorless except for little orange and red flags that dotted the landscape like flowers. Each marked a spot where a body or weapon had been found. The Star of David flag that had once flown over the compound was gone. In its place was the Texas state flag, which flew at half-mast. Beneath that was the official flag of the Bureau of Alcohol, Tobacco and Firearms. On it were four stars—one for each of the ATF agents who died in the February 28 shoot-out.

Back in Pittsburgh, I was interviewed by dozens of TV, radio, and newspaper reporters over the next few days. On May 17, the *Washington Post* ran an article that highlighted my three principal findings: that Koresh had died from a gunshot wound to the head, that the wound was "not typical" of a suicide, and that Koresh was alive when the fire started.

In all likelihood, I speculated, the bullet had come from a gun held by someone who was in the room with him—not from outside the building, as so many were claiming. As for federal officials' claims that Steve Schneider was the trigger-man, I could offer no proof to support that conclusion. The same scenario applied to Schneider himself, I told them, although the incompleteness of his remains made the determination of manner of death even more difficult. As for Judy Schneider, I added, as long as her head was missing I could not really say how she died.

In the finger-pointing battle that followed the Waco incident, my conclusions were often cited as evidence that the government did not kill the residents of the Branch Davidian compound. But I can only agree with that conclusion halfway. While there is no evidence to suggest that any of the three people whose bodies I examined was killed by federal agents, I can't say that the blood of the eighty-six other men, women, and children who died is not on the hands of the ATF and the FBI. For several reasons, this was a tragedy that never should have occurred.

First, if federal agents believed that Koresh was illegally stockpiling weapons at the compound, there were far more peaceful and intelligent means of dealing with this activity. Witnesses said that Koresh made trips into town several times a week. How difficult would it have been for a trained agent to arrest him while he was unarmed and alone?

Secondly, the ATF had an undercover agent inside the compound who warned them prior to the February 28 raid that Koresh knew they were coming. What emergency demanded that the warrants be served that day? Might not the entire siege have been avoided by waiting for a more opportune moment?

Finally, why did federal agents have to go on the offensive on April 19, 1993—only fifty-one days after the siege began? Koresh and his followers eventually would have run out of food. Based on my conversations with DeGuerin and Zimmerman, both of whom had visited Koresh inside the compound during the siege, I'm of the impression that Koresh eventually would have surrendered peacefully. At the very least, he would have allowed several more of the women and children to leave prior to armed conflict.

There are many additional questions that remain to be answered. For instance, did anyone die as a direct result of the tanks banging holes in the compound walls? And what impact did the CS gas that was pumped into the compound for six hours have on the cult members? Could it have immobilized them when the fire broke out? Did it hinder their ability to escape?

To be sure, the Waco incident was not without its impact on the federal government. The ATF later dismissed several of the agents involved, and the director himself was forced into early retirement. Even so, this agency remains one with serious problems. Around the same time Congress was looking into the Waco affair, another committee was conducting hearings on the so-called Ruby Ridge incident, in which a deputy U.S. marshal and two members of white supremacist Randy Weaver's family were killed at an Idaho cabin. It was later learned that the FBI had shot at the Weavers unprovoked. As a result, the FBI was forced to change its policy to one that permits agents to shoot to kill only if their own lives are in danger.

Of course, Waco has had other consequences as well. The tragedy would resurface in horrifying fashion on April 19, 1995—exactly two years after the disaster in Waco—when a truck bomb exploded in front of the federal building in Oklahoma City, killing 170 people, including dozens of children. It was the worst act of terrorism ever committed on U.S. soil.

More significantly, early evidence in the bombing pointed to right-wing militia members who viewed the Waco showdown as a symbol of tyranny by the federal government against the American people. To the alleged perpetrators of the bombing, the government had simply gotten too big and too intrusive.

Indeed, Waco should never have happened and could easily have been prevented. Koresh may have been a crazy man, but everyone is entitled to his or her own religious beliefs. I do believe that Koresh deserves some if not most of the blame for this horrible tragedy. However, Koresh is dead, and so are many innocent men, women, and children.

The federal government and its investigative agencies, on the other hand, are alive and well, and can and should be better scrutinized. An agency with a reputation of going in with guns blazing, the ATF in Waco was simply out of control. Keep in mind that the legendary Elliott Ness and his "Untouchables" were Treasury agents, direct predecessors of today's ATF. And because of the genuine public distrust of this agency, it is important to document and review every move that was made in Waco.

We cannot and must not let this kind of horrible event happen again. If we do, it will do nothing but fuel speculation about wild government conspiracies and distaste of our own elected leaders.

FOUR

A SHOOT-OUT IN CLEVELAND

Working on the Waco case and following its aftermath in the news, I was reminded of the fact that bloody confrontations between armed zealots and overexcitable law enforcement officers are nothing new to our society. From the Whiskey Rebellion of 1794 to John Brown's 1859 standoff in Harpers Ferry to the siege of the Oglala Sioux at Wounded Knee in 1973, American history is replete with tragic examples of such altercations. But perhaps no era produced more of these incidents than the 1960s, when political divisions were many and passions ran high. My profession, for one, seemed to be right in the thick of it.

In the summer of 1968, the United States was in the midst of great racial upheaval. Martin Luther King, Jr., had been murdered that spring, and in neighborhoods large and small, radical black organizations were rapidly forming and growing in numbers. Confrontations with the police were not infrequent.

In Cleveland, Ohio, the violence erupted around dusk on July 23. As members of a tow truck crew attempted to recover an abandoned 1958 Cadillac in the city's predominantly black, low-income community of Glenville, shots were fired at them from the porch of a nearby house. The driver was hit four times and seriously injured. His partner, also wounded, called for help on the tow truck's CB radio.

Within seconds, police had begun arriving at the scene, and thirty minutes later more than a hundred officers had saturated the neighborhood. Inside three apartments, what appeared to be a group of heavily armed black men continued to spray bullets on those outside. For four hours, the gunfire was furious. Then, at midnight, the shooting stopped. All eyes were focused on 12312 Auburndale Avenue, the apartment building that had been at the center of the attack. Suddenly, the front door opened and out stepped a tall, bare-chested black man with a cigarette hanging from his lower lip. He was unarmed.

"How many of my men are dead?" he coolly inquired of the men wearing badges and pointing pistols and shotguns at his head. When no one answered, he continued in a boisterous tone. "They died in a good cause. If my carbine hadn't jammed, I would have killed you all."

The man was Fred Ahmed Evans, the thirty-seven-year-old leader of a small but vocal group of black nationalists. To young blacks, he was a man of great courage, willing to stand up to and speak out against the white establishment. He had become a symbol for those who believed that black people could not or would not get any justice in a system run by white people. But to most white people, he was a troublemaker, a deviant, a criminal. And to police, he was a dangerous, violent militant who had now become a cop killer.

Evans had received national headlines only two years earlier, when he told a reporter from the *Wall Street Journal* that the streets of America's cities would flow with blood from a race war. "The beast will be eliminated," he had repeated on numerous occasions. In the months leading up to the shootout, Evans had predicted a black-white confrontation. Now, it appeared, his prediction had come true.

On the morning following the shoot-out, the headline of Cleveland's daily paper, the *Plain Dealer*, announced MASSACRE OF POLICE. In truth, the casualties were even, with three police officers and three black nationalists dead. (A bystander had also been killed and fourteen others wounded.) But according to the news story, Evans and his followers had been heavily armed and waiting to ambush the men in blue.

At any rate, the incident sparked major rioting, which continued for four days after Evans and his crew were taken into custody. During that time, four more people were killed, bringing the death toll to eleven.

These were indeed rough times for all races in America. Blacks had seen the foremost leader of their time murdered in April, and just a month prior to the Cleveland incident, Senator Robert Kennedy had been assassinated. For all minorities, the deaths of these two men constituted a huge setback for the advancement of civil rights. The result was resentment, fear, and anger on the part of many young blacks. At the encouragement of certain leaders, some adopted a more militant stance. In the process, they began collecting all kinds of weapons. Throughout 1968 and 1969, the newspapers and television news shows were filled with reports of racial violence, many of which were sparked by black militants looking to pick fights with police or with white society in general.

In the forty days following the July 23 shoot-out in Cleveland, two dozen other cities across the United States experienced racial uprisings. In St. Paul, Minnesota, two off-duty patrolmen took a gun away from a black youth at a dance party and were quickly surrounded by teenagers throwing rocks and bottles. Two nights of violence ensued, resulting in twelve arrests and fifty-two injuries. In Newport News, Virginia, a white police officer fatally shot a black man who'd beaten another patrolman unconscious and taken his handgun. This incident sparked several days of rioting that resulted in $2 million in property damages. Among the many other sites of racial violence that summer were Gary, Indiana; Holdboro, North Carolina; Peoria, Illinois; York, Pennsylvania; Little Rock, Arkansas; Seattle; and Memphis.

It was very difficult for many non-black people, myself included, to understand and tolerate this new trend toward mindless, unprovoked violence. Society viewed people like

Evans as deviants, unwanted as neighbors, let alone as community leaders. This new form of rebellion seemed to contradict everything Dr. King had preached. In fact, a month before the Glenville shoot-out, U.S. Supreme Court Justice Thurgood Marshall publicly lashed out at black militants, claiming that they were hurting the civil rights cause more than they were helping it.

"Anarchy is anarchy," Justice Marshall, the first black to sit on the nation's highest court, said in a speech in New Orleans. "It makes no difference who practices it. It is bad. It is punishable, and it should be punished."

I think it was very important for black leaders to speak out on this issue. White leaders trying to address these situations simply did not have the credibility needed within the black community. Besides, few, if any, whites knew what it was like to be black, living in a world of poverty and crime. Life there seemed bleak and hopeless.

All that being said, I do not think it was right for Evans's group, or any other group, to collect guns with the intent of practicing anarchy. Evans and radicals like him were preaching hatred and separatism, not equality and unity. They were undermining everything for which Dr. King had fought.

But my personal and political views are always differentiated in my mind from my concept of justice. No matter how much we may disagree with some radically thinking group of activists, these "social rebels" have a right to express their views in the marketplace of ideas. Too many times, we are intolerant of others who do not share our values or vision of what America should be.

For this reason, I approach every case with an open mind. No matter what types of people are involved, no matter what crimes they have been accused of, no matter what their views of life are, they are protected by the Sixth Amendment of the U.S. Constitution. They deserve fair trials, and they are entitled to due process. To that extent, I have learned never to prejudge any case.

Moreover, the police in American cities and elsewhere have a long history of brutality toward black political groups.

In 1968, many police officers still viewed themselves as the "thin blue line" separating the white society they were there to protect from the black community they were there to patrol.

For example, two weeks prior to the Glenville incident, eight members of the Paterson, New Jersey, police department threw tear gas into a meeting of the Southern Christian Leadership Conference, a leading civil rights advocacy group at the time. They then physically attacked several black people leaving the meeting and inflicted a great amount of damage to black-owned businesses in the neighborhood. The actions by the officers, who were later indicted by a federal grand jury on civil rights violations, came amid five days of racial uprisings, rioting, and firebombing. In the end, many young blacks were convinced that police officers hated them and that the justice system did nothing to protect black citizens against police brutality.

About a week after the Glenville shoot-out, two lawyers from Cleveland called my office in Pittsburgh for an appointment. As part of their representation of Evans, they had contacted NAACP and Urban League officials across the East Coast seeking an independent forensic pathologist— someone with credibility who did not blindly hew to the law enforcement line when the facts mandated otherwise. Their search led to me.

Even though I had been the chief forensic pathologist in the Allegheny County Coroner's Office for less than three years, I had gained a reputation for fairness and accuracy, especially in the black community. A year prior to this case, for example, a black man had been found hanging in his jail cell in Pittsburgh. The police had called it a suicide, but members of the black community and the inmate's family were claiming he was the victim of police brutality.

After conducting a thorough autopsy and investigating the man's jail cell, I called the immediate family and their minister into my office. Based on the available evidence, I told them, I had to agree with the police. At first, they were upset and unsure whether to accept my findings or to call me a part of the white conspiracy. Then I did something that few medical examiners or coroners would ever do: I urged them to contact an independent forensic pathologist. I even offered to make all of my reports and samples available to the person of their choice, and to do a second autopsy if necessary.

The family took me up on my offer. A few days later, a very sharp young pathologist from Howard University Medical School visited my office and spent hours examining everything I had. In the end, he agreed with all of my conclusions. To me, this was no big deal, but to black leaders in Pittsburgh, it demonstrated that I was not a pawn of the police. More importantly, it showed that I was willing to open my office doors to inspection and criticism.

Now, these two lawyers wanted me to rush up to Cleveland to review the physical and medical evidence of their case. At first, I hesitated; between the recent birth of my daughter, my duties in the coroner's office, and my private consultations on the Robert Kennedy assassination and other cases, I was busier that summer than I'd ever been. But the Glenville incident interested and troubled me, so I agreed to look into it. Two days later, I caught a flight to Cleveland.

Charles R. Fleming, one of Evans's lawyers, met me at the airport. On the way to the coroner's office, he asked me if I'd like to drive by the scene of the shoot-out. Without hesitation, I said yes.

The neighborhood known as Glenville lies in the northeast corner of Cleveland. In 1968, it consisted of two square miles of short, narrow streets lined with two- and three-story apartment buildings and an occasional deli, clothing store, or laundromat. About eighty thousand people lived there at the time, more than one-fourth of them in poverty. As we drove through this neighborhood, Mr. Fleming pointed out 12312 Auburndale Avenue, the location of the hideout where Evans and the other black nationalists had lived, as well as the spot about two hundred yards down the street where the tow truck had been parked. Once again, he expressed his doubt that the incident had happened the way police said it had.

While I had no reason to disagree, I was painfully aware that he had a tough row to hoe.

As we drove toward the coroner's office in downtown Cleveland, I was blunt with my host. "No matter what the evidence shows, the odds are going to be against you and your client," I warned him. "He's not a very popular guy. What he did and what he stood for—namely, the use of violence—is not accepted in any white circles and not very many black circles."

Fleming agreed, but he also wanted me to have a little background on the suspect before I reviewed the case. Evans, he told me, was a former U.S. Army sergeant who had served in the Korean War as a Ranger, a group of elite, specially trained commando soldiers known today as the Green Berets. He spent most of the year he was in Korea behind enemy lines and was highly honored for his service. Later, however, he was court-martialed and given an honorable discharge after he slugged an officer for making a racist remark.

In the years that followed, Evans moved to Cleveland, full of anger and leaning toward violence. But according to Stanley Tolliver, Evans's other lawyer, the Reverend Dr. King visited Cleveland in 1967 and managed to convince Evans that violence was not the answer to the plight of blacks, and that by working peacefully within the confines of society, black people could achieve equality. For a while, Evans tried to do this. At one point, he opened a community workshop in an abandoned neighborhood tavern to teach young black people how to make African-style clothes and artifacts. But the landlady, a white woman, changed her mind and revoked the lease, leaving Evans without the place he had promised his supporters. Then, when King was slain in 1968, everything changed.

"If Dr. King had not died," Tolliver said, "there never would have been a Glenville shoot-out. When Dr. King was murdered, Fred took it personally. He blamed it on 'the beast' and declared war on the police."

It was at this point, Tolliver said, that Evans started buying guns, mostly rifles. But while the police would announce publicly that Evans had purchased thirteen high-powered guns in the weeks prior to the shoot-out, they did not mention that all the guns were bought at local department stores. Nor did they publicize the fact that Evans had followed Cleveland city ordinances and registered each weapon with the police department.

"The police and the news media made Evans out to be a black Frankenstein from day one," Tolliver said. "Yet Fred had no criminal record."

In fact, despite the rage that King's murder invoked in him, it was Evans who walked the streets of Cleveland in the hours following King's death, helping Mayor Carl B. Stokes, the city's first black elected executive, keep the peace. And despite Evans's belief that Stokes was not doing enough to improve conditions for blacks, he never spoke a negative word about the mayor.

The same could not be said for Stokes, who was known to frequently criticize Evans and his supporters as radicals who were hurting the cause of black people. On one occasion, the mayor was quoted in the newspaper as calling Evans a "punk" who needed to learn respect for authority. Yet it was also Stokes who arranged for Evans to receive several thousand dollars in city tax money to develop social and employment programs for underprivileged inner-city minorities. Accusations that Evans used that money to buy illegal weapons for his followers were never substantiated.

At the coroner's office, I started by reviewing the official autopsy records, including clothing, microscopic slides, X rays, photographs, and transparencies. The first autopsy I reviewed was that of James Chapman, a twenty-two-year-old black male. He was a small man, about five feet eight inches and only 135 pounds. From the photographs and the autopsy report, it was clear Chapman had died from a gunshot wound to the head that caused massive destruction of the skull and brain. Two other bullets had grazed his right shoulder and right arm, but neither wound was serious.

Chapman, a filing clerk who was allegedly killed while driving a police officer into the line of fire in an attempt to recover wounded officers, was being labeled a hero. But as I reviewed the autopsy report, several problems with the scenario of his shooting popped up. First, the pathologist who did the autopsy had called the entrance wound on Chapman's right forehead an exit wound. I pointed this out to the coroner's staff, who said they would check it out. Then, as I examined the close-up shots of the large, gaping bullet entrance wound, I noticed substantial amounts of black powder deposits on the skin all around the bullet wound.

"What does this mean?" Fleming asked.

"The police officers are lying," I responded. "This young man was killed execution-style from very close range. And from what I understand about the circumstances, it might not have been one of your clients who pulled the trigger."

This news completely shocked the attorney. He had suspected the officers had incited the shoot-out, but this evidence stunned even him.

The second autopsy protocol I reviewed was that of Patrolman Louis Golonka of the Cleveland Police Department. A lean, thirty-three-year-old white man, Golonka stood five feet ten inches and weighed 148 pounds. By examining the photographs and the autopsy report, I was able to tell that Officer Golonka had been hit numerous times with shotgun pellets in the neck, chest, abdomen, arms, and legs. The bullets that caused his death were the ones that entered the chest and abdomen and pierced the lungs and heart, causing massive internal bleeding. There was a lot of blood in the chest cavity, the sac surrounding the heart, the windpipe, and the lungs.

Patrolman Willard Wolff was next. Unlike his colleague, Wolff was well-nourished. At age thirty, he stood five feet ten inches tall and weighed 220 pounds. On the left side of his face near his nose, Wolff had a large entrance wound.

Finally, I studied the autopsy report of Lieutenant Leroy Crantz Jones, a forty-seven-year-old veteran of the Cleveland Police Department who stood six feet tall and weighed 177 pounds. The photographs showed that he had been shot once in the left side of the neck, twice in the left side of the chest, and twice in the lower right abdomen. The bullets to the neck and abdomen were the fatal blasts. The wound to the neck had fractured several of Lieutenant Jones's cervical vertebrae, while the two bullets to the abdomen perforated the small intestines and the large bowel, lacerated the kidney, and produced massive internal bleeding.

While I was able to spend the entire day at the coroner's office reviewing the autopsy records, I asked if I could make copies of each report to take back to Pittsburgh to examine more closely in my own office. Although the officials said that would be no problem, my next request raised some eyebrows.

"Where are the toxicology reports?" I asked.

Usually, these are part of the autopsy records, but I hadn't noticed them. Toxicology reports indicate the various foreign chemical levels in a person's body at the time of death. The significance of a toxicology examination is obvious in cases where poisoning, smoke inhalation, drug overdose, or alcohol may be the cause of death. In this case, however, the cause of death was certain: gunshot wounds. There were no allegations that anyone had been injected with some deadly drug or smoked out of their apartment.

Because of this, I thought the toxicology reports had perhaps been excluded from the postmortem protocol simply because they did not show anything significant. Or maybe they had been left out accidentally. In any case, I did not suspect there would be any relevant information in these additional files. At the same time, it was my duty to look at all the evidence and information available to me before arriving at my final conclusions.

Slowly, somewhat reluctantly, the coroner's assistants retrieved copies of the toxicology reports of each of the seven victims. Nothing particularly interesting jumped out at me until I came to the reports of two of the three police officers. While none of the victims showed any evidence of illicit drugs in his blood or body tissues, Patrolmen Golonka and Wolff had significantly high blood-alcohol levels. When a person dies, the alcohol level in his or her blood and urine remains essentially unchanged until decomposition begins, thus offering an accurate reading of his or her state of intoxication at the time of death.

According to the official report I now read, the alcohol level in Officer Golonka's blood was 0.19 percent and the alcohol in his urine 0.20 percent. If I was stunned at these values, I was totally shocked when I looked at Patrolman Wolff's toxicology report; his blood alcohol was recorded as 0.25 and the urine-alcohol level as 0.30.

There were two aspects of this finding that were completely outrageous. First, the alcohol levels were considerably above those allowed when operating a motor vehicle. In 1968, the legal limit for drinking while driving in Ohio was 0.15, and that was higher than in most states. Today, the blood-alcohol level for driving legally without being deemed under the influence is 0.10, and, in a few states, 0.08. In several European countries, such as Norway, it is 0.05.

But the significance of the 0.19 and 0.25 percent blood-alcohol levels was even worse than their face values. Keep in mind that both of these officers had been on duty for six to eight hours. That means one of two things: either they had been drinking heavily prior to going on duty or they had been drinking on the job just before the shoot-out began.

The alcohol level in the average person dissipates at a rate of about 0.015 to 0.020 of a percentage point per hour. In other words, if the officers had done their drinking prior to coming on duty, their blood-alcohol levels would likely have been at least a tenth of a percent higher than what was found at the time of their deaths, or at least 0.29 and 0.35. Four shots of hundred-proof whiskey will give the average-size man a blood-alcohol level of 0.10, and one shot of whiskey is equal to twelve ounces of beer or four to six ounces of wine.

The second incredible point about these alcohol levels was that no one outside the coroner's office knew about them. Because they were not included in the official autopsy reports, the defense attorneys were completely unaware of them. Neither had the alcohol levels been reported in the local press or publicized in any manner by the coroner's office.

This was extremely troubling to me. At the time, the

coroner's office in Cleveland had a reputation as one of the best and most sophisticated medicolegal investigative offices in the country. Its forensic pathologists were highly trained and well-qualified. Such an office should not inadvertently or negligently confuse entrance and exit wounds. And when blood-alcohol levels are as high as those found in the two police officers, they should not be left out of the autopsy protocols given to defense attorneys and made available to the news media. In my opinion, this was not mere sloppiness, incompetence, or negligence by the coroner's staff. I suspected it was much worse—deliberate, willful, and cleverly orchestrated deception.

As I left the coroner's office, I informed a stunned Fleming of my discovery. I detailed each finding and my interpretation of its significance and legal relevance.

"This puts the case in an entirely different light," Fleming said. "Are you prepared to testify to this in court?"

"You supply the subpoena," I replied, "and I will supply the testimony."

The trial against Evans started on March 24. He was charged with seven counts of murder: the deaths of the three police officers, the witness Chapman, and three of his own followers. Ohio, like many states, has a conspiracy law that allows people involved in a crime to be charged with crimes committed by fellow conspirators. The law reads: "Whoever aids, abets, or procures another to commit an offense may be prosecuted and punished as if he were the principal offender." In other words, even though it was the police who had shot and killed three of Evans's followers, Evans could be held responsible for their deaths.

The first ten days of the trial were consumed by jury selection. During this phase, which is called voir dire, the defense attorneys, prosecutors, and judge are allowed to ask questions of potential jurors. If a juror is predisposed toward any one side or has already made up his or her mind in the case, the lawyers may ask the judge to excuse that person from the case. These are known as "cause challenges." Both the prosecution and defense also are given a small number of "peremptory challenges," which they can use to remove a potential juror from the case without reason. This allows both sides to feel comfortable that someone who may be biased against them will not be deciding the fate of the defendant.

It was during jury selection that racism reared its ugly head for the first time—and it wouldn't be the last, either. Prosecutors used all of their peremptory challenges to remove every black person from the jury pool. The age-old legal concept that a person be tried by a jury of their peers apparently did not apply to Fred Ahmed Evans in Cleveland, Ohio. Before any evidence was even heard, it was obvious that Evans was not likely to receive a fair trial. (Seventeen years later, the U.S. Supreme Court would rule that prosecutors could no longer use their peremptory challenges to remove possible jurors based on race.)

During opening arguments, Cuyahoga County District Attorney John T. Corrigan told the all-white jury of seven men and five women that what happened on July 23 in Glenville was nothing short of a planned massacre of police. He painted Evans as a person who hated and wished to kill all white people.

Defense attorney Tolliver, on the other hand, told a different story. He said that Evans was not even home when the shooting began and that it was the police who had started the gunfight. Furthermore, Tolliver added, not only did the police shoot and kill three black nationalists, but they may have shot one another and undoubtedly did shoot and kill an innocent bystander, James Chapman, one of the people Evans was charged with killing. Tolliver contended that the tow truck did not spark the shooting. Instead, he argued, the shooting was already under way and the tow truck crew simply had the misfortune of being at the wrong place at the wrong time.

This news shocked the courtroom and brought immediate objections from the prosecution. When asked what evidence he had to support his position, Tolliver said he would be calling a forensic scientist who would lay the groundwork for such an argument. The judge allowed the case to continue.

The first witness called by the prosecutors was the only

person who claimed he was an eyewitness to Evans's firing a weapon. William H. McMillan, the police tow truck driver who was seriously wounded by one of four bullets that struck him, told the jury that he saw Evans pointing a gun at him. Earlier, McMillan had told reporters that he believed the abandoned car down the street from Evans's apartment was a decoy planted by the black nationalists. He said Evans lured the police into the ambush by reporting the car, then waited for it to be picked up. In Cleveland, police operate a tow truck service to haul away abandoned cars and trucks.

However, a nurse at the hospital where McMillan was treated testified that she had asked McMillan several times the night of the shooting and the day after who it was that shot him. The nurse said McMillan didn't have a clue. "He didn't know what happened to him or who shot him," the nurse told the jury. As for the decoy theory, it also was debunked. Most abandoned vehicles were not picked up by the city for several days after being reported, and there was no evidence that anything more sinister had happened here.

To establish Evans's state of mind as a radical racist who hated all white people, prosecutors called Sergeant John J. Ungvary, a thirty-year veteran of the Cleveland Police Department and director of its Subversives Squad, known for its conspiracy theories and investigations of alleged Communists. On the witness stand, Sergeant Ungvary testified that Evans had told him just weeks before the shoot-out that a "revolution" was "inevitable."

"Sooner or later, there's going to be open warfare between whites and blacks, and the beasts will be eliminated," Sergeant Ungvary quoted Evans as saying.

To support Sergeant Ungvary's position, prosecutors called to the witness stand Walter Lee Washington, Jr. At age seventeen, Washington described himself as a member of the Black Panther Party, a group he said was nothing more than a "social club." Washington told the jury that on the morning of July 23, just ten hours before the shooting, a meeting was held at Evans's apartment in which Evans announced that the time for a shoot-out with police was at hand.

WASHINGTON: Fred showed us how to load and unload a rifle and what to do if it jammed.

CORRIGAN: What was the purpose of the meeting?

WASHINGTON: To tell us when the pop is going to jump off.

CORRIGAN: What do you mean?

WASHINGTON: When there was to be a revolution.

There was only one problem with Washington's testimony: he was completely untrustworthy. On January 23, six months after the Glenville shoot-out and two months prior to trial, Washington had been arrested for stabbing to death a sixty-eight-year-old man. Four months earlier, in September, the man had been stabbed eleven times after discovering that Washington and four of his friends had set fire to a church, a fruit and vegetable market, and an abandoned building.

When police arrested Washington, they accused him and his cohorts of terrorizing Glenville residents and merchants. Washington was charged with murder, arson, and theft. However, after he agreed to testify against Evans, all charges against him were dropped and he was released from jail. As part of the deal, prosecutors also had Washington accepted by the U.S. Army as an active-duty soldier.

The use of informants completely baffles me. I understand the traditional need for informants. They tell police where the gun is located or where the body is buried. They are supposed to act as an aid to detectives in an investigation. However, that no longer seems to be their role. More and more, police and prosecutors have started using informants on the witness stand.

Today, there are two kinds of snitches. The first are paid in cash and are used by police mainly as the basis for obtaining search warrants or as a source of information on where to find illegal drugs or other criminal activity. But the days of detectives paying twenty-dollar tips to informants is long gone. In 1994, federal law enforcement agencies such as the FBI, the DEA, the IRS, and Customs paid more than $120 million to criminals turned informants. These types of informants, in other words, are no longer small-time criminals or helpful, honest citizens. They are often professional snitches and hardened criminals themselves.

The second kind of informant is what we had in the Evans case. When police arrest someone, there is usually only one way for that person to avoid a long prison term: cooperate with the police and become an informant. The problem is that informants like this will say almost anything just to cut a deal.

Take Walter Washington as an example. Here was a guy facing life imprisonment at best, and quite possibly the death penalty. His days of freedom were over. Suddenly, he is approached by law enforcement officials about testifying against Evans. If he says the right thing, the police promise to see to it that the charges against him are dropped. The incentive to lie is obviously overwhelming. Yet in case after case, prosecutors put these characters up as witnesses, judges allow them to testify, and juries usually believe them. Sadly, there are dozens of cases on record in which informants have come forward years, even decades, later to admit they completely fabricated their testimony. In several of those cases, the people against whom they'd testified were sentenced to death. The decision to use Washington as a witness showed how desperate prosecutors were to get a conviction against Evans.

Over the next four weeks, the government swore in eighty-six witnesses and introduced 350 exhibits to prove their contention that the Glenville shoot-out was a deliberate, planned attack on police. Officer after officer told the same story. It was as if they were reading a prepared script. They claimed that an informant had told them early in the day that Evans was preparing for a showdown with police and had recently purchased a large cache of guns. At 2:15 P.M., they said, top police officials called Mayor Stokes, who was out of town on business, to tell him the news.

"Be very careful," Stokes had supposedly warned them. "Do not aggravate the situation."

But instead of heeding the mayor's warning, police assigned several unmarked police cars to patrol Evans's neighborhood for the ostensible purpose of surveillance. Police officials said it was 8:25 P.M. when the tow truck arrived and the shooting began. They claimed Officer Golonka was wounded at 8:35 P.M. and pronounced dead at Forest City Hospital at 8:40 P.M.

When the defense attorneys' turn to present their case came, they questioned the time frame laid out by prosecutors and police. One key defense witness was Joseph Turpin, a neighbor of Evans who worked as a guard at the county workhouse. According to Turpin, Evans was at Turpin's front door at 8 P.M. And another witness said that Evans did not arrive at the shoot-out until after 11 P.M.

Finally, my day on the witness stand arrived. After introducing me to the jury and listing my qualifications and credentials, Mr. Tolliver started the questioning by asking me to describe the wound to James Chapman's head:

WECHT: The bullet wound was a large gaping defect. It caused a large area of destruction on the right side of the forehead region. In the photographs, you can see the underlying brain.

TOLLIVER: Was there any powder in the wound?

WECHT: If you look at the skin on the forehead, which is located above the eye and below the area that the bullet penetrated, you will see black deposits on the skin. That deposit is powder.

TOLLIVER: Doctor, can you tell us what caused the powder residue in the wound?

WECHT: I think this was a gunshot wound of entrance, as opposed to exit. The significant amount of black powder deposited on the skin indicates that this shot was fired from very close range. I would say it was fired from just a couple of inches or so away. In my opinion, the gun was no more than six inches from this man's head when it was fired.

TOLLIVER: On what do you base that opinion?

WECHT: The opinion is based largely upon the large powder residue you see in these photographs. [In] a wound from a bullet fired from a distance of more than eighteen inches or two feet, you would have some kind of stippling pattern . . . where little burning particles [of carbon] hit the skin. There is no stippling pattern with this bullet wound, but there is an abundance of black powder residue. If you look at the other wounds in the other victims, you will not see this kind of powder residue.

TOLLIVER: When did you reach this conclusion?

WECHT: I came to this opinion when I visited the Cuyahoga Coroner's Office and looked at the microscopic slides. That's when I discovered the powder residue.

TOLLIVER: Now, Doctor, Cleveland police pathologists have previously testified that the powder burns you have described came from a "dirty bullet" wiping itself off as it went through the wound. Do you agree with that finding?

[*After I discovered the black powder residue, Cuyahoga County pathologists were forced to come up with an explanation. Thus, they developed the "dirty bullet wiping itself off" theory, one of the biggest pieces of nonsense I've encountered since the single-bullet theory.*]

WECHT: No, I do not. All bullets are a little dirty after they have been fired, but not like this. I have no idea what they mean when they say "dirty bullet." Was it greasy or [did it] have dirt on it? In this case, we are talking about a definite black powder residue on this man's head. That could not be caused by a dirty bullet wiping itself off. That is silly.

This line of questioning by Tolliver established several major points for his defense of Evans. First, it let the jury know that the local pathologist had messed up by mistaking an entrance wound for an exit wound. Second, it allowed me to make a good case that the bullet that killed James Chapman was fired from no more than six inches away. If Evans and his group were across the street in their apartment shooting at police and Chapman was on the same side of the street as the police, there could only be one logical conclusion: Fred Ahmed Evans did not shoot and kill Chapman. Police officers, on the other hand, could have.

The questioning continued:

TOLLIVER: Were fragments of the bullet found in the wound?

WECHT: The X-ray reports, which I have reviewed, indicate there were bullet fragments found within the wound.

TOLLIVER: Doctor, is there a test called neutron activation analysis, and can you explain that test in connection with fragments from bullets?

WECHT: The neutron activation analysis is a very fancy name for a test that incorporates principles that we have learned in recent years from the use of neutrons— [concepts] that have emerged from the development of atomic power. It is a procedure that requires very elaborate equipment. There are only two places I know of that do it—a laboratory in California and another in Canada.

Here's how it works: [scientists] take a fragment from a spent bullet and bombard it with high-speed neutrons to get a pattern, a very specific pattern. This test is absolutely scientifically irrefutable. Through neutron activation analysis, they are able to determine whether or not the little particle came from a larger object. . . . By taking a fragment of metal, they can tell which bullet it came from. They can then match it up and determine whether or not it was a particular kind of ammunition and a particular batch of ammunition.

TOLLIVER: Doctor, were there sufficient amounts of fragments in the wound of Mr. Chapman to make such a test?

WECHT: Yes. The X rays indicated that there were fragments of bullets inside the brain.

TOLLIVER: Can you tell us whether that test was performed to determine what kind of bullet killed Mr. Chapman?

WECHT: No. I saw nothing to indicate that the test had been performed or even requested.

TOLLIVER: If requested, you are saying that the facilities to make such a test are available?

WECHT: Oh, yes. They are readily available through a large firm in California which is part-governmental, part-private. The cost is nominal and readily available to any official governmental or scientific source.

This line of questioning was intended for one purpose only—to show the jury that neither the police nor the local coroner's office had done an adequate job of investigating the case. Either they were negligent in not being aware of neutron activation analysis or they were afraid of what the results would show had such a study been performed by outside experts.

The direct examination then moved into its third stage—introducing and discussing the high levels of alcohol in the bodies of the dead police officers:

> TOLLIVER: Doctor, by examining the laboratory reports and specimens made available to you, were you able to determine if there was any alcohol found in Patrolman Golonka's body?
>
> WECHT: Yes. There was 0.19 percent in the blood and 0.20 percent in the urine.
>
> TOLLIVER: Do you have an opinion on whether he was able to function and carry out his normal duties as a police officer with that amount of alcohol in his blood and urine?
>
> WECHT: I think it is unwise to even suggest that anybody performing any duty, but particularly a police officer performing official police duties, is able to perform with a blood-alcohol level of 0.19 percent. This is very high.
>
> TOLLIVER: And sir, calling your attention to the laboratory findings of Patrolman Wolff, did you find there was alcohol in his blood and urine?
>
> WECHT: Yes. Mr. Wolff had 0.25 percent alcohol in his blood and 0.30 percent alcohol in his urine.
>
> TOLLIVER: How significant are these findings?
>
> WECHT: Well, it's quite high. . . . It would definitely alter his ability to function, both in his muscular and motor coordination—that is, balance and movement—and in his ability to perceive and . . . appreciate the significance of his surroundings with regard to himself, the people he is

dealing with, and the nature and scope of the activities he is involved in.

This level of alcohol in the blood would markedly impede an individual's ability to perform. It would markedly alter his ability to handle situations which would require any kind of sensory perception and judgment.

The revelation that two of the officers killed were drunk at the time the shoot-out began completely opened the door for Fleming and Tolliver to argue their case: namely, that the officers were so out of control that they started the gunfight with the black nationalists and ended up shooting themselves and an innocent bystander in the process. Once the attorneys had achieved that goal, they rested their case.

As for the prosecution, an underlying tone of racism seemed to permeate its case. Both of the prosecutors, Corrigan and Assistant District Attorney Charles R. Laurie, repeatedly referred to the two defense attorneys, who were black, as "boys"—a term with blatantly derogatory and demeaning connotations. Under subpoena by the defense lawyers, tape recordings of the two-way radio traffic between the police officers at the scene of the shoot-out were played in open court. Over and over again, the officers were heard using the word "nigger" when referring to blacks.

While cross-examining one black witness, Laurie started screaming, "You hate white people, don't you? Wasn't my color the people that put up the money for these [social] programs?" And in describing James Chapman at one point, Laurie said, "He was a decent citizen and he wasn't even a white citizen." But perhaps the most inflammatory reference of all came during Laurie's closing statement to the jury, in which he told the jurors that they had "a duty as Americans to stand up and be counted."

"Let's wake up, America," Laurie preached. "From an acorn grows a mighty tree. A spoonful of ink in a gallon of water gives you a tainted color."

One would think, based on this blatant display of racism and the overwhelming lack of sound evidence against Evans, that no sane group of individuals would find for the prosecution. Well, that jury must not have been sane, because on May 12, after sixteen hours of deliberation, it found Evans guilty of murder on all seven counts. After the verdict was read, each juror was asked if that was his or her verdict. Each responded that it was.

Prior to sentencing, Cuyahoga County Common Pleas Court Judge George J. McMonagle asked Evans if he had anything to say.

"I am not a murderer," Evans told the packed courtroom. "I had knowledge of what I was doing when I became a black nationalist. I joined because I wanted to help my people. I don't think there is any doubt that the people of my race have every right in the world and have every reason in the world to resist and reach out and become what they were created— men, not symbols, not half anything, but whole, as I am now whole. I fully understand the ways of life as they are now, and the truth of the matter is I have no regret. That is to say I have no malice toward anyone, white people or anyone else, just the reality of the matter that counts."

In response, Judge McMonagle told Evans that no man had the right to make his own laws. "Now you have caused, really, a dreadful and awesome state actually to exist in our community and our nation," the judge said. "You know, before we had this Glenville incident that has been adjudicated as [having been] caused really by you, there was never any open display anywhere of firearms by youngsters. Now, boys of the same age as your followers and who are, however, college students, they now feel that apparently it is the proper thing to do and the legal thing to do, to have a show of rifles, shotguns, bandoleers. Basically, these children are emulating the example that you set as a part of this incident which is now coming to a conclusion. You have caused a horrible wound on the minds and souls of our community."

And with that, the judge sentenced Fred Ahmed Evans to die in the electric chair. Guards surrounded the prisoner, put chains around his arms, hands, and legs, and led him from the courtroom. Evans's case was on appeal in 1972 when the

U.S. Supreme Court struck down all death-penalty statutes in the country. His sentence, like those of many thousands of others in place in 1972, was automatically commuted to life in prison. But it made no difference for Fred Evans. In 1978, he died of cancer.

FIVE

BLACK PANTHERS
AND FLYING BULLETS

The 1960s were turbulent times for America, and the field of forensic medicine was certainly no exception. From the investigations of the Kennedy assassinations to the examination of cases involving racial violence and alleged police brutality, this was the era in which our profession first took center stage and was placed under the public spotlight as never before. As medicolegal investigators grew more visible, their abilities and techniques came to be better understood and appreciated by the general public.

But with this heightened visibility also came a greater social responsibility. To establish ourselves as impartial scientists interested only in the truth without bias toward race, politics, or any other societal pressures or influences—this was the goal to which we aspired. Regardless of our personal opinions, we recognized the importance of searching for and reporting evidence as impartially as possible.

Just a year after the incident in Glenville, another highly charged racial conflict would test this professional commitment. This time it involved the Black Panthers, the former militant black rights organization. Formed in 1966 to patrol the black ghettos of Oakland, California, and protect its residents from police brutality, the Panthers soon burgeoned into an organized political party with branches in several major cities across the country. By 1969, Chicago had one of the largest chapters, boasting about five hundred members—at that time, one-fifth of the organization's national membership. The organization's chairman and founder was Bobby Seale, whose disruption of the previous year's Democratic National Convention as a member of the so-called Chicago Seven had earned him a national reputation.

Politically, the Panthers were a Marxist revolutionary group that encouraged blacks to arm themselves and take control of their own lives. They declared as their enemy the "white establishment," which in many cases meant law enforcement. Due in part to the increasing poverty of America's inner cities and the growing despair and hopelessness of their residents, many young black men and women were attracted to the Panthers' message. And as the rhetoric of violence began to influence them, confrontations with police became common.

One such confrontation occurred in the early morning hours of December 4, 1969. Just a month earlier I had been elected coroner, and I remember hearing the news on the radio as I drove to the office. According to the report, a group of armed police officers had shown up to serve a search warrant at a rented apartment on Chicago's west side as nine members of the Black Panther Party slept inside. When the Panthers opened fire on the officers, the officers stormed the apartment. In the end, two Panthers were dead, including one of the group's leaders, and two others were injured. In addition, two police officers sustained minor injuries.

Within twenty-four hours, however, Black Panther leaders were crying foul—or, to be precise, murder. The police—more than two dozen of them, they claimed—had come to their headquarters that morning for one reason and one reason only: to eliminate two leaders of their political movement. The search warrant, they said, was just a charade. Already, this sounded eerily familiar.

In view of the Panthers' violent reputation, the story told by police seemed completely acceptable. Many of the Panthers were convicts, angry young men looking for an opportunity to punish authority figures for what they viewed as societal inequities. Like a majority of Americans, I viewed the Black Panthers as a left-wing group of radicals and revolutionaries who were doing nothing positive to help the cause of African Americans. In fact, I believed they were damaging the civil rights movement and the accomplishments of the late Martin Luther King, Jr., and the Southern Christian Leadership Conference.

From my work in the Glenville shoot-out case, however, I also knew that police officers did not always do their duty "to protect and to serve" all the citizenry in an honest and unbiased fashion. Indeed, it was my work in the prior case that led lawyers representing the Panthers to call my office in Pittsburgh a few weeks after the shooting to request an emergency meeting. Because of my heavy work schedule at the time, I told them that I'd be unable to fly to Chicago. However, they were more than welcome to come to Pittsburgh. The lawyers agreed, and said they would bring medical and police reports for me to study.

The next morning, Chicago attorney Francis Andrew arrived with Dr. Victor Levine, a former deputy chief pathologist at the Cook County Coroner's Office in Chicago. Victor and I had been friends for a few years and had worked together within the American Academy of Forensic Sciences. At sixty-five, he was nearly three decades my senior. He was also as honest as the day is long, and I respected his integrity immensely.

On the day of the shooting, I learned, the bodies of Black Panthers Mark Clark and Fred Hampton had been taken to the coroner's office for examination. The autopsy findings confirmed the story told by police—that it was Hampton and the other Panthers who started shooting first and that the police returned fire only to protect themselves. Dissatisfied with this official version of events, the family of Fred Hampton asked their lawyers to seek an independent autopsy. That very day, Victor and some of his associates performed a second autopsy at the funeral home handling Hampton's arrangements. It was Victor who had suggested to the Panthers' lawyers that I be consulted.

My visitors from Chicago gave me both Hampton autopsies to review. The official report, signed by Cook County Coroner Andrew J. Toman, showed three bullet wounds to Hampton's body. The first shot, according to the report, was the one that killed him. It entered the top of his head above the left temple and emerged near his right eyebrow. A second bullet entered the back of Hampton's neck and exited from the front of his head. However, because there was no apparent wound on the front of Hampton's head to correspond with this shot, the report concluded, the bullet must have emerged from his eye socket without doing much damage. A third bullet barely grazed his arm.

Before I'd even looked at the second autopsy, a red flag was waving. The idea that a bullet could exit through an eye socket without causing any noticeable damage was completely absurd. All three of the bullets that wounded Hampton came from a .30-caliber weapon, and a bullet that size leaves a pretty good-sized hole in anything it strikes. And considering the fact that this bullet would have had to course through bones before exiting, it would have caused extensive damage to Hampton's face.

The autopsy performed by Victor and the other independent pathologists was much more detailed—and reached notably different conclusions. According to this report, the first bullet entered the skull about two inches above the middle of Hampton's *right* eyebrow or temple—not the left. The trajectory of the bullet was downward and toward the center of the body. According to this report, there was no exit wound for the first bullet, which apparently lodged at the base of the skull just behind the nose. The second bullet, they said, entered just below the right ear at an almost identical trajectory as that of the first bullet, and emerged from the front of Hampton's neck just to the left of his larynx. The downward trajectory of both bullets was at about a forty-five-degree angle.

If these trajectories were correct, then Hampton was not standing up facing the officers when he was shot; rather, he was lying on his back, and the officer who shot him was standing directly above him and slightly to his right.

"So what do you think?" asked Dr. Levine.

"This is astonishing," I said. "What's the coroner's story behind the first bullet? It obviously didn't exit."

"I have been told by a senior member of the pathology team that did the examination that they removed the bullet and sent it to the crime lab," Victor explained. "However, Toman continues to tell the press that the bullet *did* exit. I have no idea what's going on there."

I made a mental note of what Toman had said for possible future reference, and then continued to study the autopsy reports. The independent pathologists duly noted the third bullet wound to Hampton's right forearm, but they also found a fourth wound that the Cook County Coroner's Office had completely missed. Although this, too, was only a superficial wound—a graze on his left shoulder—that held little significance in figuring out what happened that morning, it told me that the official autopsy and examination of Hampton's body was neither thorough nor accurate.

I next turned to the toxicology findings. According to the report, the coroner's office had dissected the stomach looking for contents, but had found nothing helpful. However, buried in the report prepared by Victor and the independent pathologists was a finding that Hampton's blood samples contained incredibly high levels of Seconal, or secobarbital—4.5 milligrams per deciliter, in fact, or about four times the amount considered to be toxic and potentially lethal.

Seconal, a prescription drug for which there is a significant street market, is a barbiturate, known among drug abusers as a "downer." As a central nervous system (CNS) depressant, it generally gives its users a relaxed, tranquil feeling. However, anything that depresses or relaxes the brain also slows down the heart and lungs, which, of course, lowers the pulse rate and blood pressure. Thus, there is a fine line of physiological safety involved in the use of CNS depressants. Quite simply, the more barbiturates a person takes, the more the CNS is depressed and the more the heart relaxes. The more one's heart rate and respiration slow down, the less oxygen gets to the brain. As this happens, the brain becomes more depressed, and a vicious, deadly cycle ensues. Eventually, the system becomes so depressed that the heart and lungs go into a state of arrest, and death occurs.

Neither Victor nor Mr. Andrew was aware of the clinical significance of the Seconal level in Hampton's blood sample. In addition, Victor told me that the pathologists at the coroner's office were lying when they claimed they had opened Hampton's stomach.

"When we examined the stomach, there was no evidence that it had ever been cut," he said.

"They made a mistake and then lied on their autopsy report to cover it up," I speculated. "This Seconal level is very important evidence that's been overlooked. If this toxicology report is true, then Fred Hampton was in a very deep sleep or even in a stuporous state at the time the police raided his apartment. If that's the case, then there's no way he could have been shooting a gun, let alone initiating a gunfight. And if this is true, then the police have been lying from the beginning and this whole operation may have been nothing more than a political assassination."

Amazed by my findings, Mr. Andrew asked if I would accompany him to Chicago to take a look at the scene of the incident. Although I was still very busy, I was also quite intrigued at this point. I immediately agreed.

A few days later, I found myself on a flight from Pittsburgh to O'Hare International Airport. To prepare myself for my work, I reread every police report available on the Hampton case and all the press clippings from the days following the shooting. The police version was simple: They had come there peacefully to serve a warrant. The Black Panthers started shooting at them, so they shot back.

According to this version of events, the incident had begun when a special division of the Chicago Police Department assigned to the Cook County State Attorney's Office received a tip from an informant within the Black Panthers organization that the group had been collecting "a large cache of shotguns and other weapons." Using this information, the prosecutor obtained a search warrant to seize all illegal arms in the possession of the Panthers. But the special police squad did not serve the warrant on December 3, when they received it. Instead, they told reporters, they waited until early the next morning, when the Panthers would be caught off guard and there would be less danger of a violent response.

At 4:44 A.M. on December 4, approximately fifteen plainclothes officers, armed with shotguns, pistols, a submachine gun, and a sawed-off shotgun, arrived at 2337 West Monroe Street, located in a predominantly poor, black neighborhood two miles west of downtown Chicago. When they arrived, police said, they found the two-story brick flat ready to be defended from an outside attack. Mattresses were propped up against or fastened across windows, and dressers and other furniture barricaded the doors.

According to Sergeant Dan Groth, who was in charge of the case, he and four other officers went to the front door of the apartment building, while other officers surrounded the building and searched for a rear entrance. After knocking at the outside door and getting no answer, the officers stepped into a foyer where they found two more doors. The door on the right led upstairs to a second apartment, while the one on the left led into the hallway of the apartment occupied by the Panthers. Sergeant Groth said he politely knocked at the second door, announcing he was a police officer carrying a search warrant. When again there was no answer, the officers broke down the door. Before them was a third door and, to the right, a hallway.

Sergeant Groth said he again announced who he was and stated his intentions. But in the place of a response came a shotgun blast that blew a huge hole through the door. The officers returned fire and began to charge into the apartment. At the same time, officers stationed at the back of the apartment building burst through the back door and also started firing. According to Sergeant Groth, the gunfire from the Panthers was fast and furious. "There must have been six or seven of them firing," he said.

On two separate occasions, the officers claimed, they shouted at the Panthers to cease fire. Both times, they said, the Panthers responded by yelling, "Shoot it out." The gunfight, according to Sergeant Groth, lasted about ten to twelve minutes. "If two hundred shots were exchanged, that was nothing," he said.

When the shooting stopped, two men were dead and six others wounded, including two police officers. One officer had been "nicked" by a flying bullet, while the other had been cut by flying glass. Neither man was seriously injured. Inside the house, however, the situation was a bit bloodier. Mark Clark was found in the living room near the door, a shotgun beside him. In a bedroom down the hall, Fred Hampton was found lying on a mattress soaked with blood. Police said that a .45-caliber automatic and a shotgun were on the floor near the bed. The officers said he had used both weapons in the attack.

The officers also announced that they had seized a large assortment of weapons in their raid—seven rifles, an army carbine, a shotgun that had been stolen from a police car, five revolvers, three automatic pistols, and thousands of rounds of ammunition. As for the seven surviving Panthers, they were arrested and charged with illegal possession of firearms and attempted murder.

"The immediate, violent, and criminal reaction of the occupants in shooting at announced police officers emphasizes the extreme viciousness of the Black Panther Party," Cook County State Attorney Edward V. Hanrahan told reporters later that day. "So does their refusal to cease firing at police officers when urged to do so several times."

Because of the public's dislike for and distrust of the Black Panthers, as well as a general belief that the police always told the truth, the official version was quickly accepted by most people. To be sure, there were a few skeptics, including a reporter here or there, but nobody of prominence was seriously challenging the credibility of the police or the state attorney.

As I've already stated, I was no fan of the Black Panthers either. I did not understand them, nor did I approve of their politics or their methods. But no matter what we think of any given organization, one thing is certain: we cannot allow the police or the government to decide which political movements are going to fail by eliminating various leaders execution-style. That is not what our country is about.

The more I read about Fred Hampton, the more interested I became. During his days at Chicago's Proviso East High School, he had been an A student, as well as a member of the football, basketball, and baseball teams. He was also active in Junior Achievement and dreamed of becoming a lawyer. And at the age of seventeen, he became politically active, getting himself elected president of the NAACP's Youth Council. Within two years, however, having decided that the NAACP was moving too slowly to achieve racial equality, Hampton quit and joined the Black Panthers. He rose quickly through the ranks and, in 1968, became the Illinois chairman, widely recognized as the third most powerful person in the party nationally.

What had transformed this obviously intelligent young man from a hardworking NAACP officer into a radical separatist? I found at least part of the answer in a videotaped speech he had given a year earlier.

"My involvement at Proviso East at present can be explained by going back to the summer of 1966, when I decided the only way to deal with that institution of racism [the NAACP] was to organize the masses of young blacks to form a power bloc to deal with these bigoted whites and apathetic Negroes," he said. "Because of our constantly struggling and a few decisive victories, we now have over one thousand members in the Maywood area dedicated to the intelligent, human, and legal philosophy of self-defense by any means necessary. Some people in Maywood would contend that our actions are of an extreme nature, but I know of no other intelligent way to act in an extreme situation other than extreme."

Based on this brief speech, one thing was very clear to me: Fred Hampton was not the mindless, criminal thug that police had made him out to be. Even if one disagreed with his actions, which I did, it was clear that his motives were purely political and not criminal.

Arriving in Chicago, I had no idea what to expect. In light of the fact that it had been only a few days since the incident, I thought the apartment itself would probably be roped off by police and kept under tight security. Monroe Street runs east to west through the center of downtown Chicago, and 2337 West Monroe is, as mentioned earlier, about two miles from the business district. The two-story, twin apartment building looked similar to all the other residences on that block. As Dr. Levine and I walked up to the apartment, we were greeted by a security guard; surprisingly, he did not work for the police, but rather for the Panthers. I could not believe it—the police had not secured the crime scene. It seemed they had come to do their business and had promptly left without giving much thought to collecting and protecting evidence. The FBI would later seal off the building, but that was not until December 17, after an estimated twenty-five thousand members of the press, the Black Panther Party, and curious onlookers had walked the premises, likely collecting souvenirs that would have made excellent pieces of evidence.

As I climbed the short stairway to the outer front door, other Panthers who were there told me how "the pigs have murdered" their leader. Entering the foyer leading into the Panthers' five-room, two-bedroom apartment, I noticed that the lock on the door had been forced open.

"The pigs did that," a Panther pointed out.

The apartment inside was very dark. There was junk all over the place—clothes, shoes, boxes, food cartons, wood, plaster, glass. As we approached the first room in the house, the living room, I noticed that the door was partially off its hinges. There was a large hole, most likely from a shotgun blast, and a smaller hole, probably from a .38-caliber weapon, in the door. There was also a small blood splatter on the door as well.

After examining the two holes and seeing how the wood had splintered from each, I could easily tell that the shotgun blast had originated from inside the apartment, and that a .38 had been fired from outside the room. There was very little doubt that these were the first two shots fired. If it was the

Panthers who shot first and the officers who responded, then it would be awfully difficult for the Panthers to win any case in court. I scanned the walls next to the door where the police had entered, searching for additional bullet holes, but I found none.

The living room was small. There was a double-sized mattress in one corner and a twin-sized mattress in the other. It was obvious that this room had been converted into sleeping quarters. In the wall above the double bed, the plaster had been riddled with bullets. I counted forty in the wall, but there were probably more.

As I walked down the hall, I noticed that the first door on the left, which led into a bedroom, had two dozen bullet holes in it. Inside, there were two twin beds, a chair, and a portable heater. The bathroom was directly across the hall. Amazingly, neither the bathroom door nor the wall contained any bullet holes. This meant that all twenty-four bullets that had gone through the bedroom door had been fired inward by police and that none had been fired outward by the Panthers. If the Panthers had fired weapons from inside the bedroom, the bullets would have landed somewhere—either in the bodies of the police officers, the bathroom door, or the wall. The absence of these bullet holes told the story of a one-sided gunfight.

Even though a key element in this case was the question of which of the Panthers fired guns at police, none of the Panthers, including Fred Hampton, had been tested for gunpowder residue on his hands or body. Such testing is basic "police investigation 101," and it made me wonder whether the lack of a proper investigation was intentional.

The next room on the right was the dining room, which contained no table or chairs, only a double bed. Across the hall on the left was the second bedroom, the place where Fred Hampton and his eighteen-year-old girlfriend, Deborah Johnson, had been when the shooting started. Johnson, who was eight months pregnant with their child when the incident occurred, was not injured in the raid. Next to the bed was a book called *Toward an African Revolution*. It, too, had been sprayed with pellets from a shotgun.

As I examined more closely the bed where Hampton and Johnson had been lying, I noticed a huge bloodstain covering the mattress. My mind quickly flashed back to the crime-scene photographs that Mr. Andrew and Dr. Levine had shown me, specifically the one of Hampton's mattress. I remembered that the bloodstain in the photo was not nearly this large. Someone who was bleeding must have lain on the bed during the couple of days following the shooting, because this bloodstain was not from Fred Hampton. At this point, I was beginning to wonder what other evidence had been destroyed or altered.

The more I examined each room and the bullet holes in each door and wall, the more I felt the story given by police was total fiction. I am not a ballistics expert, but I have been involved in thousands of cases in which bullet trajectories were at issue. This experience caused me to reflect on what the Chicago police officers had said about the raid—that six or seven Black Panthers were shooting multiple bullets at them. The only problem with this scenario was that I had found only one indication of a bullet being fired from the inside out. If the Panthers had done all this shooting, what had happened to their bullets? Did they vanish in thin air? There simply was no way the Panthers fired as many bullets that night as the police officers said they did. Not being a ballistics expert, however, I kept this opinion to myself.

"So what do you think, Dr. Wecht?" Mr. Andrew inquired.

"I think you may have a case here," I replied. "But you need a real expert in firearms, ballistics, and trajectories. You need Herb MacDonell." Later, I learned that Professor MacDonell had previously been to the scene and had already noted all the physical details associated with the shoot-out.

Professor Herbert MacDonell, who had worked with me on the Glenville shoot-out case, is a good friend of mine and one of the best criminalists in the country. Based in Corning, New York, Herb had collaborated with me on several cases. We would later work together on the Jean Harris murder case and keep in close contact during his work on the O.J. Simpson case.

"If anyone can tell you, and be able to prove who fired first and what really happened here, it is Herb," I told Mr. Andrew.

My next stop was the Cook County Coroner's Office, where I viewed the official copies of the autopsy reports. Just like the copies Dr. Levine had shown me, these reports claimed that pathologists had opened the stomach of Fred Hampton and looked at the contents—a claim we knew was a complete lie. The pathologists also lied to me about the first bullet wound, repeating that they had not recovered a bullet from Hampton's head. In the weeks that followed, the Chicago Crime Lab would admit this was not true and that the coroner's office had indeed turned the bullet over to police.

With my business in Chicago completed, I traveled home to Pittsburgh. That very day, Mr. Andrew and other lawyers representing the Black Panthers were on the phone with Herb MacDonell, and within twenty-four hours, he was on a plane to Chicago. Amazingly, Herb was able to trace the path of every single bullet fired in the apartment during the raid, and was able to tell where each shot had originated. The depth and detail of his conclusions astounded even me.

As I had suspected, the two bullet holes in the door leading to the living room were the key. Using string, straws, and long, wooden dowels, Herb was able to show that, based on the angle and the path of the shot fired from the shotgun used by Panther Mark Clark inside the living room, the door was almost completely open at the time. Using the same technique, Herb traced the path of the bullet shot by police through this same living room door and into a wall in the living room. The trajectory of this shot showed that the door was only slightly open when the officer fired his weapon.

As far as I could tell, the mystery had been solved: the police had shot first, as they were starting to open the door. After the door was opened further, Clark had shot back, missing the officers but hitting the door. But Herb had even more incredible news. After tracing every bullet path, he had discovered that the shotgun blast by Clark was the only fire returned by the Panthers that morning. Every other shot had come from police. This proved what I had suspected—that Fred Hampton had been murdered.

Despite the overwhelming evidence gathered by Herb MacDonell, Dr. Victor Levine, and myself, the Black Panther case was litigated for twelve years. Eventually, the original attempted murder charges brought against the seven Black Panthers were dropped, and State Attorney Hanrahan and the fifteen officers involved in the raid were charged with obstruction of justice. Even though they were later acquitted, their credibility was forever blown. Hanrahan, for example, lost his re-election bid in 1972; the Black Panther case was the main campaign issue. And in a subsequent civil case brought by the survivors accusing the authorities of violating their civil rights, the prosecutor and police officers were hit for a $1.8 million judgment for their actions, which the city had to pay.

This case demonstrated to me how easily the coroners and medical examiners in many cities can be improperly influenced by politics. In Chicago in 1969, the coroner's office was completely politically oriented and professionally inept. Ironically, a few years later, I would be asked to testify before a special committee in Chicago that was established to reform the coroner's office and recommend an appointed medical examiner system.

As the old law enforcement saying goes, even in the most carefully thought-out crimes, a criminal will make a mistake. I suppose it is no different when police officers become criminals. Still, I have always wondered what would have happened if the officers in this case had been a little smarter, perhaps setting the Panthers' house on fire as they were leaving, thereby destroying all the evidence that would later be used against them. Would this case ever have been exposed at all?

SIX

THE OAKLAND EARTHQUAKE AND THE NEGLIGENCE OF MEN

Marc Zambetti was excited about the changes taking place in his life, the biggest being his recent move from New York to San Francisco. Grandson of the founder of the Stella D'oro Biscuit Company, Zambetti had been in the family business for four years, and although he enjoyed it, he had wanted to move away from the family and try life on his own for a while. Realizing the twenty-seven-year-old needed some room, the family offered to make him sales manager at its San Leandro facility. Zambetti eagerly accepted the offer and moved to the Bay area in August 1989.

Two months later, on October 17, 1989, Zambetti was driving his BMW sedan home from work on the lower deck of the Cypress Street Viaduct when it hit. The Loma Prieta earthquake shook the San Francisco Bay area for only fifteen seconds, but that was long enough. As cars and trucks in front of and behind Zambetti bounced from side to side, the bridge crumbled around him. Huge chunks of concrete fell, killing many of the vehicles' occupants instantly. Finally, the entire upper structure came crashing down, smashing the BMW and trapping Zambetti inside. Ironically, Zambetti had told a coworker just the day before how disappointed he was that he'd not yet experienced an earthquake.

The Loma Prieta quake, named after a mountain that sits near the tremor's epicenter about eighty-five miles from San Francisco, registered 7.1 on the Richter scale. When those fifteen seconds were over, sixty-seven people were dead, three thousand others were injured, and fourteen thousand were left homeless. It was the worst earthquake to hit California since 1906.

Forty-two of those killed were passengers in cars on the Cypress Street Viaduct. On that same stretch of highway, another fifty-six people were seriously injured, as more than 115 cars and trucks were trapped beneath 1.25 miles of rubble.

Three days later, rescue workers digging through the wreckage found Marc Zambetti's lifeless body inside his car.

The car directly in front of Zambetti's was a 1987 burgundy Olds Cutlass driven by John Levanitis. He was twenty-six years old and lived in San Leandro. A big guy—six feet five inches tall and 265 pounds—Levanitis was crushed when an entire section of the upper deck came down on top of him. His body was found three days after the quake.

Just a block ahead of Zambetti and Levanitis was a tan 1988 Pontiac Bonneville driven by the Reverend Walter James Butler, a sixty-one-year-old Baptist minister and father of four who made extra money working as a glazier. He had installed some windows that day and was driving to his home in the East Bay just across the Golden Gate Bridge when falling concrete smashed into his car. Rescuers took two days to find Butler's body.

Michelle Marie Richard was a passenger in a car on that same roadway. At age eighteen, Michelle had big plans for the near future. Just five months earlier, she had given birth to James Henry Brown. Engaged to her high school sweetheart, she was earning a high school diploma at a local school. Upon graduation, Ms. Richard planned to enter a training program to become a nurse. But by the time rescue workers found her car, nearly two days after the earthquake, those plans were irrelevant.

In legal terms, Richard and Butler, Levanitis and Zambetti had all died as the result of an "act of God." After all, who would try to blame their death on anyone or anything other than a natural disaster? That's what I thought, too. However, I am now of the opinion that these four people and as many as five others who died in their vehicles on the Cypress Street Viaduct should still be alive today—and would be if state and local emergency management officials had done their jobs quickly and efficiently.

After reviewing extensive medical and police reports, I have come to the conclusion that these nine people lived long enough in the rubble that they could have been or should have been rescued. I also believe that many of them suffered great pain in the hours after the collapse of the structure.

I was nowhere near the San Francisco Bay area when the earthquake hit. I was at my home in Pittsburgh preparing to watch the World Series game that day between the Oakland A's and the San Francisco Giants on television. It was 5:04 P.M. West Coast time, about twenty minutes before the game was scheduled to start, when the earthquake occurred. The entire world was able to see the ground shake and Candlestick Park in San Francisco begin to sway as cameras from ABC-TV captured the event live. I still remember listening to ABC's baseball play-by-play announcer Al Michael describe what was happening.

My first thought concerned the sixty thousand people seated and standing in the ballpark. Immediately, baseball players like Jose Canseco, Ricky Henderson, and Dave Stewart of the A's and Will Clark and Robbie Thompson of the Giants ran out of their dugout and onto the field, where it was safer. Only when news crews from the various television stations put helicopters in the air to survey the damage did those of us outside the Bay area realize how bad it was. Bridges had collapsed, buildings had fallen, and whole city blocks were on fire. Property damages would total more than $10 billion.

Despite the tragic loss of life and the extensive damage, experts interviewed that night on television dismissed any

Accused of murdering Nicole Brown Simpson (*top left*) and Ronald Goldman (*top right*), O.J. Simpson (*center*) is surrounded in court by defense attorneys Johnnie Cochran, Jr. (*right*) and Robert Blasier (*left*). Dr. Wecht's analysis of the forensic evidence reveals the strengths and weaknesses of both the prosecution and defense arguments.

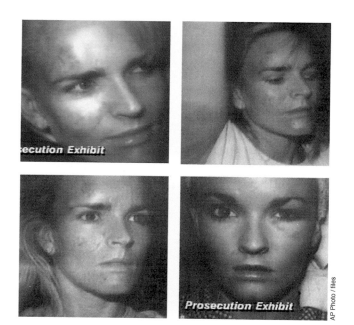

Above: These photographs of a battered Nicole Brown Simpson were used by the prosecution in an attempt to establish a history of spouse abuse as well as a motive for murder. *Below:* O.J. with "Dream Team" lawyer Robert Shapiro during his arraignment in Los Angeles Criminal Court, where he entered a not-guilty plea.

Members of O.J. Simpson's "Dream Team" presented their views of the trial at a forensic science seminar organized by Dr. Wecht shortly after the verdict was announced. Barry Sheck (above left), Dr. Henry Lee (above right), and F. Lee Bailey (below).

Above: Vincent Foster, White House attorney and close friend of President and Mrs. Clinton, was found dead, clutching a pistol in his right hand, in a park outside the capital. Rumors of foul play and cover-up led to Dr. Wecht's involvement in the case. *Below:* After viewing what is purported to be a video of an alien autopsy, Dr. Wecht, though doubtful, was unable to rule out the possibility that this seemingly "humanoid" creature was in fact an alien.

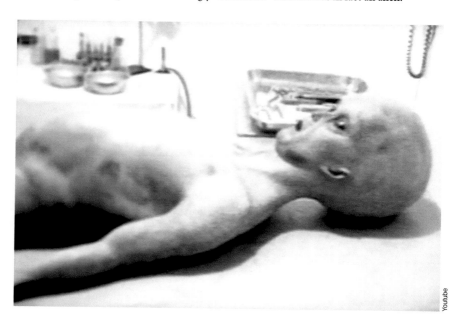

Above: A view of the Nimitz Freeway in Oakland shows the devastating effects of the 1989 earthquake. *Below:* Rescue attempts in San Francisco's Marina District. Dr. Wecht cites evidence that many deaths could have been avoided.

Above: David Koresh, self-proclaimed messiah and leader of the Branch Davidians. A government raid on the cult's Waco, Texas compound ended in tragedy when eighty-six cult members, including seventeen children, perished in flames. *Below:* An army tank patrols the perimeter of the Branch Davidian compound during the 127-day siege.

Above: The Branch Davidian compound burns. Only the water tower remained standing after the conflagration. Workers continued to search for bodies in the underground tunnels for days afterward. *Below:* Authorities used an earth mover to search through the charred remains of the compound.

Above: Dr. Wecht at the Allegheny County Coroner's Office, using a microscope to examine tissue slides—an essential step in determining cause of death. *Below:* Dr. Wecht's expertise has made him a highly valued consultant around the globe. Here, Dr. Wecht is shown with his colleague Dr. Michael Baden as they examine the exhumed skull of Della Maga, a maid whose murder brought the Philippines and Singapore close to a severing of diplomatic relations.

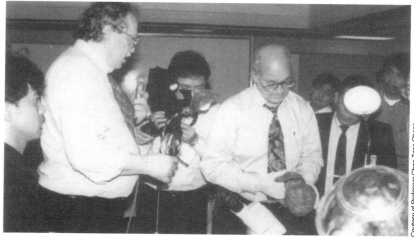

thoughts that this was the "big one." While a tremor recording 7.1 on the Richter scale was a biggie, they said the "big one" will be much larger and do considerably more damage.

Only once have I experienced an earthquake, and it was relatively small, quick, and harmless. I was testifying in an international drug-smuggling murder case in San Diego in the mid 1980s. Back at my hotel, in the middle of the night, I got out of bed to get a drink of water. As I walked across the floor, I suddenly felt dizzy, as if the floor had moved under my feet. At the time, I dismissed it as a result of my being excessively tired and getting out of bed too fast. Only the next morning, when I went down for breakfast, did I learn that I had survived a tremor that measured 4.5 on the Richter scale.

Much of the focus that first night following the Loma Prieta quake was on the Cypress Street Viaduct, and rightly so. Rush hour traffic on the bridge was bumper-to-bumper. In the seconds after the earthquake shook the foundation of the two-layer bridge, concrete from the upper level came crashing down on cars stranded in traffic below.

I watched on television as rescue workers arrived on the scene to dig people out of the tomb of concrete rubble and twisted steel. Some of the cars were smashed to only four inches in height. Workers found a child alive in the back seat of a car while his parents lay dead in the front seat.

About five hundred firefighters, volunteer rescue workers, and some ironworkers from a nearby factory immediately tried to start digging through the rubble to find anyone who might be alive. A handful of people who were heard crying for help were located and taken to safety.

However, about 11 P.M., less than six hours after the quake, city and county officials ordered the search-and-rescue efforts ended for the night.

"There may be a guy out there who is going to write his story for *Reader's Digest* [about being found in the rubble] after three days, but I doubt it," an emergency rescue physician told reporters that night. "You can't drop that much concrete on a car and have people get out."

The next day, police officials made similar statements.

"They are not alive," Oakland police sergeant Jim Hahn
told reporters after rescue workers searched for a few hours
Wednesday but found no one alive. The search was halted by
officials in the early evening hours. "Look at it," Sergeant
Hahn said to reporters as he escorted them around the quake
damage. "Look at the totality of it. You can't survive. You
can't survive. You can see how much we got done today.
Zip."

But amid all the news stories of death and tragedy came a
tale of hope and courage more than three days after the quake
had struck. A fifty-seven-year-old man, Buck Helm, was found
alive in his silver Chevy Sprint under the rubble. As the rescue
workers searched from car to car, they heard a faint voice
and saw some movement below them. Using jackhammers
and, eventually, a Jaws of Life power tool to cut apart the car
body and pry it open, rescue workers and emergency medical
technicians were able to remove Mr. Helm from his car and
take him to the hospital. He was suffering from a crushed chest
and kidney failure.

The news media proclaimed as heroes the rescue workers
who found Helm below the tons of concrete. And that they
were. Unfortunately, four days later, Helm died at a local
hospital. Too much time had passed before he was freed and
given medical treatment.

Finding this one person alive seventy-two hours after the
quake raised an interesting question: Just how intense could
the search have been if it had taken the authorities three days
to find a living person? However, I dismissed any doubts I had
about the rescue efforts after rationalizing that this was the Bay
area, a place that lives with earthquakes on a regular basis, a
community expecting the "big one" to hit at any time. Surely,
I thought, emergency crews there were well-organized and
properly staffed to handle such a tragedy.

How wrong I was.

Nearly two years later, toward the end of the summer of
1991, I was working in my office at St. Francis Central Hospital
in downtown Pittsburgh when my secretary informed me that

Lance Williams, a reporter with the *San Francisco Examiner,* was on the telephone holding for me.

As a matter of courtesy, I routinely accept all calls from reporters when I'm in the office; if they call when I'm out, I make sure to return their calls. Most of the time, the reporters are interested in obtaining information about a homicide case on which I have been consulted. Sometimes I can give them what they want, sometimes I cannot, depending on the status of the case and my role in it.

But Mr. Williams was working on a story of a different kind—one that greatly intrigued me. He was part of a team of investigative reporters looking into just how well prepared emergency rescue officials were for the Loma Prieta earthquake two years earlier. A worthwhile probe, I agreed, but how do I fit in?

That's when he told me he had obtained the autopsy reports of the forty-two people who died in the Cypress Street Viaduct collapse. In the weeks following the tragedy, he had gone to the coroner's office seeking to obtain copies of those autopsies.

"In the past, any time I requested copies of official autopsy findings, they would turn them over to me without any question or hassle," Mr. Williams told me. "But with these, they started stonewalling, saying I didn't have a right to see them."

As any public official should know, if you tell a news reporter that he or she cannot have something—especially an official public document—that will do nothing but pique their interest and cause them to fight even harder to get it. It raises their suspicions and makes them wonder what is in those documents that the public official does not want them to see. That is exactly what happened in this case.

Mr. Williams explained to me that for eighteen months the Alameda County Coroner's Office had resisted his attempts to obtain copies of the autopsy reports. Officials told him they were keeping their official reports secret to allow time for the community to heal and recover after the quake. If there were newspaper articles detailing the autopsy reports, they would only reopen these wounds and disrupt the healing process.

The *Examiner* then sued the coroner, citing the California Public Records Act, which requires that all government documents be made available to the public and the news media unless it is "clearly in the public interest" to keep them secret. The newspaper argued that it was in the public's best interest that these records be made available.

In the end, Alameda County judge Demetrios Agretelis ruled in favor of the newspaper and ordered the coroner to turn over to the reporters all documents related to the Loma Prieta earthquake and to pay the newspaper $15,000 in legal fees. The coroner's office appealed the judge's ruling, but lost.

And that's when Mr. Williams called me. He had copies of the autopsy reports, which he wanted me to review with one specific question in mind: How long could any of the people driving their cars and trucks across the lower level of the Cypress Street Viaduct have survived after the bridge collapsed? Although he could not reimburse me financially for my time and services, I could see the public safety significance of such an investigative news report, so I agreed to accept the assignment and review the autopsy reports pro bono.

A few days later, I received in the mail copies of the forty-two autopsy reports. The coroner himself had not performed or supervised the autopsies. Instead, the county contracts this service out to a private firm called the Institute of Forensic Sciences. One by one, I read through the reports. The first flaw I noticed was how incomplete the medical investigations had been.

In autopsy after autopsy, the pathologists had written down "multiple trauma" as the cause of death. That would have been fine, except they did not go on from there and identify the specific damage to the body that led to death. Instead, the areas of the body that would have given the pathologists the answers were untouched in many cases. As I read through each autopsy, I was amazed to see in case after case that no dissection of the brain had been performed in most of the victims. No toxicology tests (tests performed mainly on blood and urine to see if there are any poisons or chemicals in a person's system) were done. In very few of the cases was a carbon monoxide test requested.

As a forensic pathologist in this situation, the first thing I would want to know is when these people died. Were they killed immediately or did they live for several hours, maybe days, after the tragedy? But the coroner's office, it appears, did not share my interest in these very important questions.

Officials at the coroner's office had said the contract firm's staff were simply overwhelmed and did the best job they could under the circumstances. I can appreciate the pressure these doctors were facing. However, it's not as if this earthquake and death toll were completely unexpected. For decades, and certainly within the last few years, scientists had been warning about the potential for damage and fatalities if and when a tremor as large as this one hit California. For the Alameda County Coroner's Office to have been ill-prepared for this emergency is inexcusable. The rest of the world knew this was going to happen and they should have, too. And they should have been preparing for it.

As I examined the procedures followed by the pathologists, I found no uniformity, no previously established protocol. The chief pathologist should have designed a checklist of every test that needed to be performed on every victim. This was not done.

In a properly managed investigation, the procedure I recommend medical examiners follow in case of a natural disaster or a tragedy involving multiple deaths is this:

- *Separate and identify the bodies.*
- *Identify the location of each body by using photographs and written descriptions of the scene.* The goal in doing this is to document by photo and description every injury so that a reconstruction of what happened is possible.
- *Establish a protocol.* One person is needed as a liaison with the news media, a second for the families of the victims, and a third as a liaison with police and other investigative agencies.
- *Develop and follow a list of jobs to do when examining a*

body. Collect external materials, note injuries, and then proceed with the autopsies.

With regard to the last point, one should always start with close inspection of the skull and the rest of the body to identify soft-tissue injuries and fractures. In the internal exam, one needs to open the top of the head and examine the brain for evidence of injury. This is done by cutting brain tissue in one-half-inch parallel sections, allowing the identification of hemorrhages inside the cerebral tissue. Just because there is no fracture of the skull does not mean there will be no hemorrhage. Failure to dissect the brain, as happened in too many of these earthquake cases, is a big mistake.

It is also essential to obtain appropriate body fluids and tissues for toxicological analyses and to take small sections of tissues to examine microscopically in the days ahead. You look for certain white blood cells that act as the body's defense soldiers and rush to the sites of injuries. Some of these cells get there as soon as the injury occurs, while others do not come until hours later, assuming the victim is still alive. Thus, determining which white blood cells made it to the scene of the injury before death occurred is one means of scientifically ascertaining how long a person survived. Such microscopic examinations were not done, or at least not reported, in the autopsy records.

Why didn't this happen? The coroner's office in Oakland has blamed it on the heavy workload. While I understand the dilemma they faced, it is still no excuse for incomplete work in cases that were likely to be the subject of future litigation and official inquiry.

Many people may ask why it is necessary for a medical investigation to be so thorough. Aren't these people dead, and don't we already know why they died and how they died? Why is it necessary to investigate such cases further?

There are several reasons. The first is that a forensic pathologist or medical examiner is never supposed to assume anything. Because rescue workers found two bodies in a car on which thousands of pounds of concrete fell does not necessarily mean that the crashing concrete killed both people inside the car in the same fashion at the same moment. In the case of a married couple, the sequence of death could be critical insofar as the distribution of their estates is concerned.

The issue of time of death was, and remains, the most significant point of controversy in this tragedy. And this is the real reason I was asked by the *Examiner* to become involved.

One by one, I examined the autopsy reports. The first was that of Marc Zambetti. His body was not pulled from the wreckage until 2 P.M. on October 20. The quake had occurred three days earlier. The pathologist said he died of "traumatic asphyxia."

Traumatic asphyxia is a very broad, generalized term that refers to a severe compression of the chest or upper abdomen. But the medical report gave no evidence supporting this conclusion. Neither was there any evidence that Zambetti's skull had been fractured or that significant hemorrhaging within the brain had occurred. In fact, there were no injuries reported in the autopsy that would explain why he died. Even though his body was not discovered until three days after the quake, the medical records report very little decomposition.

All of this led me to one conclusion: Zambetti had survived at least six hours after the concrete blocks came down on his car. He may have lived twice that long, but we will never know. If the rescue workers had not been forced to stop searching, and if they had gotten to him within the first twelve hours, medical records show there is a good chance Zambetti would be alive today.

The next autopsy I reviewed was that of Mr. Butler, who was apparently killed when his car crashed into a falling block of concrete. Seconds later, another block fell on top of him. According to the medical reports, Mr. Butler died from "traumatic asphyxiation associated with multiple blunt injuries." The pathologist who conducted this autopsy cited the fact that Butler's ribs and sternum were fractured and that about one-third of his right lung was bruised. The pathologists noted that his body was a little more decomposed than Zambetti's and showed some signs of rigor mortis.

Still, as I searched the autopsy report, I found no indication of injuries that I would consider life-threatening. The reason a person dies when he or she receives a rib fracture or sternal fracture is that the injuries affect the heart or the lungs, which are located behind the breastplate and the rib cage. Yet in this autopsy report, the pathologist specifically stated that there was an absence of hemorrhaging in the heart and the lungs. From that information, I concluded that Mr. Butler probably lived well beyond 11 P.M. that first night, and possibly well into the next day and evening. What is tragic about this case is that he probably died from shock induced by the intense pain he suffered for several hours. He was not found until October 19, two days after the quake.

I was equally troubled by the third autopsy, that of Mr. Levanitis. The doctors said that the twenty-six-year-old San Leandro man died of "multiple blunt injuries and traumatic asphyxia." He had suffered rib fractures and some internal hemorrhaging. However, none of the injuries described would cause death. In fact, the pathologist who did the autopsy even stated that the internal body cavities were "unremarkable and basically intact." I cannot say for certain what Levanitis died of or when he died. But I know he probably survived at least twelve hours after the earthquake. If he was conscious during that time, he was in a great deal of pain.

I should not have been surprised by the fourth autopsy I examined, given the pattern established by the previous three. Nonetheless, I was just as astounded by the medical records of Michelle Marie Richard. The official cause of death for the eighteen-year-old was exactly the same as that given for Butler and Levanitis: multiple blunt-force injuries and traumatic asphyxiation. She suffered some rib and sternal fractures, but there was no evidence of internal tissue damage or of significant internal hemorrhaging.

Once again, it must be concluded that these injuries were not sufficient to have caused death and that it is very likely that Ms. Richard survived well into Wednesday morning before the pain and injuries sent her into shock. But because of the inadequate examination and documentation of all the injuries, we will never know what really caused her death.

The autopsies of five other people led me to the very same conclusion—namely, that some of these victims lived for at least six hours following the collapse, and some for possibly twelve hours or more. Many, if not all, suffered through their last hours in severe pain.

After I reported my findings to Mr. Williams, I learned that three other prominent forensic pathologists also had been asked to examine these autopsy reports. In almost every case, the other three pathologists agreed with me point by point.

Using the evidence we had developed, the *Examiner* published an extensive investigative report criticizing senior city and county emergency rescue officials for not having a standing, well-developed plan to search and save victims in just this kind of catastrophe. The article, published on October 20, 1991, was entitled "The Cypress Collapse: Did They All Have to Die?"

"The issue strikes to the heart of a critical public concern—the quality of the emergency response system in a region where another devastating earthquake is a foregone conclusion," the newspaper reported. "The emergency response system was simply unprepared to deal with a disaster of the Loma Prieta earthquake's scope." The story then went on to cite "a long list of problems and snafus afflicting the rescue efforts."

In reaction to the investigation, the California Office of Emergency Services has developed urban search-and-rescue teams trained to do what was not done properly in the Loma Prieta quake. State officials say they plan on placing these specialized rescue teams in eighteen cities throughout California.

Within days of the earthquake, the California legislature, realizing it might be held legally and financially liable for the Cypress Street Viaduct disaster, took the following steps: It approved a special recovery fund for victims and left the state attorney general in charge of evaluating the damage done to the victims and passing out the money. By April 1994, more than $71 million had been awarded to the families of the forty-two people killed and eighty-five others who were injured. The legislature also began studying the replacement of all two-level bridges in California.

What was not taken into account was the amount of pain and suffering that these victims endured. In California, unlike almost every other state in the country, once a victim dies, his or her family cannot seek damage awards for pain and suffering. This is one of the most archaic laws I have ever heard of, but it is the legal code of California.

Forensic pathology is not just utilized to solve murder mysteries. It can and should be used to examine broader issues in our society and in the public health arena. The Loma Prieta earthquake is a dramatic example of how our medical specialty can be applied in examining and improving emergency-management systems.

San Francisco is not alone in this problem. Public officials along the Mississippi River should be better prepared for the annual floods that kill so many. Emergency rescue teams along the nation's southeastern coast should be better equipped and better trained to handle the tremendous hurricanes that so frequently devastate so many coastal communities there. And northeastern cities and counties know that every year the chances are high that blizzards and severe cold weather will burst pipes, cause fires, and kill many people.

If we as a community sit down, identify such potential problems, and train ourselves to be prepared for the catastrophes we know are going to happen, then maybe people like Marc Zambetti, Walter Butler, John Levanitis, and Michelle Marie Richard will not have died in vain.

SEVEN

THE NIGHTCLUB WITH NO WAY OUT

There were two things close to Everett Neill's heart: music and Paula, his wife. A couple of evenings a week, the two would come together to the place where Everett was working. When he played the drums with Paula in the audience, the beat would calm his soul and the sight of his beautiful wife would thrill his heart. At these times, all the problems of the world left his mind. Here were exclusively the sights and sounds of friends laughing and hugging. This was where he was meant to be, a place where the world was at peace.

Everett was the drummer in a band that had developed a fairly stable and lucrative gig at one of Kentucky's most prestigious and classy nightclubs—the Beverly Hills Supper Club in Southgate, a few miles south of Cincinnati. It was the start of something that the Neills hoped and prayed would become really big.

Instead, it would end in tragedy.

On most nights, Paula, who was twenty-three, would watch her husband make music from a couch a few feet offstage. "He's in a different world when he sits in front of those drums," she told her friends. To many people, music is an expression

of love. To Paula and Everett, it was a declaration that they
would never be apart.

On May 28, 1977, as Everett and his friends played to
a packed house, Paula sat in her designated seat, watching
people in the audience and losing herself in the music. Only
a droplet of sweat from her forehead landing on her hand
brought her back to reality. For the first time, Paula noticed
how warm the room had become. Was the air conditioning
working properly? Turning to the platform, Paula saw that
Everett, who was twenty-seven, was drenched in perspiration.
Either he was really into the music this night, or the room's
ventilation wasn't working properly.

"Why is it so damn hot?" she asked a waiter. The young
man carrying drinks and appetizers shrugged his shoulders.

"Full house," he responded. "No time to chat."

Then, almost subconsciously, Paula could hear mumbling
from behind the stage. Something about smoke. Soon, however,
it all blended in with the clatter of silverware touching china
and customers ordering another round of drinks. As briefly as
she had been distracted, she closed her eyes and allowed the
music to capture her mind again. Like Everett, she found music
to be a refuge from the realities of life. It told her everything
was going to be all right.

So immersed in the music was Paula that it startled her
when the band suddenly stopped playing right in the middle
of a song. A member of the club's staff had rushed onto the
stage. A look of surprise on the faces of the band members
quickly grew into one of concern. Turning to the crowd, the
man said that everyone needed to be quiet, that he had an
emergency announcement to make.

"Do not panic," he said. "A small fire has broken out in
an adjoining room. For your own safety, we need to exit the
building."

Gasps were followed by mumbling. Paula stood up. With
all the people talking and pushing their chairs away from their
tables, she could barely hear the man on stage as he continued
to speak.

"There are exits to your right and left and to the back of

the room," he said, now almost shouting over the noise. "Please, exit slowly. Do not push or shove."

As if in shock, Paula stood silent, watching as the announcer left the stage and headed for the door. People were rushing by like cattle. Without even realizing what was going on, she was being pushed toward the exit closest to her.

That's when she discovered that she had lost sight of Everett. In the madness, she had forgotten him completely. Searching through the faces in the crowd, she felt her heart rate increase to an almost deafening pace. But the smoke was getting thicker. She could hardly see across the hallway now.

"Everett?" she yelled. "Everett?"

There was no reply. Instead, the crowd kept moving forward in a herd mentality. Before she knew it, Paula was outside. There were hundreds of people rushing around. Many, like her, were looking for loved ones.

"Everett? Everett?"

Finally, a face she recognized—a staff member at the club who worked with the entertainers.

"Where's Everett?" she demanded.

"I don't know," the man answered. "I was beside him, then I didn't see him anymore. I just don't know."

Paula screamed his name even louder. She scanned the faces in the crowd. Now she was starting to panic. She had to go back in. She had to know whether he was still in there. She had to look.

Not more than thirty feet away, Everett was asking the same questions. How could he have left his wife inside? Why had he not rushed to her immediately? Did she make it out? That's when he bumped into the same man Paula had just seen.

"Have you seen Paula?" Everett asked him.

"Yeah, she was out here looking for you," the friend said. "But I think she went back in to make sure you got out."

This was not the news he wanted to hear. Turning to the door, he watched people pushing their way out. The next thirty seconds seemed like an eternity as he investigated the face of every person who exited, hoping it would be Paula.

Finally, he headed for the entrance. To find his wife, he would have to fight his way back inside. Smoke was now billowing out of the doors and windows. Hysteria had taken over. Everywhere, there was crying. Shoving people aside, Everett entered.

Inside, flames were clearly visible. Portions of the roof were starting to cave in. The smoke was so thick, he had to grab people and stare into their faces to see if one of them was his wife. There were people lying on the floor. Some were crying for help. Others were coughing. Many were silent.

"Paula?" he called out. "Paula!"

I first learned about the fire at the Beverly Hills Supper Club the way I learn about many of the cases I've worked on during my career—through the morning paper. Early reports, however, were incomplete. Officials knew there were a considerable number of fatalities, possibly in excess of 120. But as of the next day, no exact numbers were available.

"This is the greatest tragedy in the history of Kentucky," Governor Julian Carroll was quoted as saying.

The catastrophe was being compared to some of the biggest fires in history. According to this article, the greatest number of fatalities registered in a fire in the United States was 602, at the Iroquois Theater in Chicago in 1903. The worst fire at a nightclub occurred in 1942 at the Coconut Grove in Boston, when 491 were killed. Worldwide, the most deadly blaze of all time occurred in Canton, China, in 1845, when 1,670 people died in a theater fire.

Three days after the fire, I was in the midst of an autopsy in the Allegheny County morgue when my assistant called me to the telephone. A well-known and respected plaintiff's lawyer from Cincinnati named Stanley Chesley was calling. Chesley, I knew, was an expert in class-action litigation who has been involved in complex lawsuits involving breast implants and tobacco-related deaths. As I picked up the phone, I imagined it was one of these types of cases he was calling me about.

Chesley got right to the point: He needed me to fly to

Cincinnati immediately. He had been hired by a few families
of people who had died in the Beverly Hills Supper Club fire.

"We have no idea what we're dealing with here," Chesley
stated. "But things just aren't right. Something is up, and
I need an expert like you to visit the scene as soon as
possible."

I agreed and made plans to fly to Cincinnati the next day.

On the morning of June 1, 1977, Chesley picked me up at
the airport, which is actually located in northern Kentucky.
During our short drive to the scene of the tragedy, the lawyer
gave me the latest details: 160 bodies had been recovered at
this point. Many more, it was suspected, were still in the rubble. The local medical and rescue officials were simply overwhelmed.

About two miles away from the nightclub, Chesley pointed
to a large building outside of which black hearses were lined
up. It was an armory gymnasium that had been turned into a
makeshift morgue. Big army trucks would bring dozens of black
"body bags" from the supper club for possible identification
and examination. Rescue workers from the Red Cross and
local law enforcement officials were wearing surgical masks
and rubber gloves as they moved the bodies. One by one, they
would unzip the body bags.

"This one is unidentified," a man in a green smock would
then yell out to another person with a notepad.

Some of the bodies were being kept in refrigerated trucks
that had been provided by local grocery stores. Families and
co-workers would be brought into the back of the trucks to
identify loved ones. It was a bone-chilling sight, and it brought
the entire tragedy into perspective for me.

This job of officially identifying the victims and declaring
a cause of death for each fell to Dr. Fred Stine, the Campbell
County coroner. While Dr. Stine was obviously under an
incredible amount of pressure to match names with corpses
and allow families to arrange for their burial as quickly as
possible, I did spot a potential problem: very few actual
autopsies were being performed.

At the time, I'm sure, most people probably thought that

autopsies were a needless burden for local officials and relatives. After all, wasn't it clear that these people died in the fire? Hadn't the fire caused their deaths? Didn't they perish in the flames? In answer to these very questions, I gave Stanley Chesley some advice: Don't assume everyone died from burns or smoke inhalation. Other factors that we are so far unaware of may have contributed to their deaths. But I would need to see the autopsy and toxicology reports before any of my suspicions could be confirmed. For that reason, I was extremely disappointed that Dr. Stine and local officials had decided to perform only a handful of autopsies.

As we continued south on U.S. 27 toward the nightclub, we spotted it sitting high atop a hill to the right. For the first time, I realized how large a facility it was. Chesley told me that the owners, the Schilling family, had expanded the club several times in recent years. The only way to get to the club was along a small road that wound up the side of the hill. I later learned that fire-fighting and rescue efforts had been hindered because of the narrowness of this road. At the time of my visit to the scene, less than 120 hours had elapsed since the fire had started. Yet the sprawling building was little more than a pile of rubble.

As Stanley Chesley and I walked through the charred ruins, he filled me in on the history of the facility. Over the years, the club had attracted such big-name entertainers as Dean Martin, Jerry Lewis, Dionne Warwick, the Righteous Brothers, Milton Berle, Pearl Bailey, and Abbe Lane. Built in 1937, the three-story brick building had also developed a reputation during its early days as the hottest little nightclub east of Las Vegas. In fact, the McClellan committee of the U.S. Senate once identified this area as the gambling center for fourteen states, and the Beverly Hills Supper Club as the hub of it all.

As legend has it, the plush, swanky casino and club had catered to big-time gamblers and mobsters. Old-timers told of machine gun-toting bodyguards and million-dollar poker games. That had continued until the 1960s, when a new sheriff cracked down on illegal gambling. Now, the only evidence of days gone by were several roulette wheels and a basket of poker chips that firemen had discovered in a steel vault in the club's basement.

The Beverly Hills was a place where people dressed up; blue jeans or T-shirts were out of the question. Instead, it was suits and ties for men, dresses for women. Patrons had to be prepared to pay a minimum of fifty dollars for dinner, drinks, and entertainment—a sizable chunk of change in 1977. Customers would drive to the front door, where valets would take their cars. Visitors would step into a carpeted lobby with walls covered by mirrors. The complex had three bars, a wedding chapel, and two large rooms for entertaining. The dining rooms, equipped with expensive crystal chandeliers, conveyed a sense of elegance.

"It was a place where people went to relax and have fun," Chesley told me. "It was a classy joint."

On the night of the fire, I was amazed to learn, there were as many as 3,500 patrons at the Beverly Hills. One reason for the large crowd was the scheduled appearance of singer John Davidson. He was minutes away from taking the stage when the blaze was discovered. In fact, it was in the Cabaret Room, where Davidson was scheduled to perform, that most of the deaths occurred. More than 1,200 people had packed into the room to see the show. Officials were now admitting that the large crowd may have placed the club in violation of state fire safety codes. As we would later learn, this would not be the only allegation to be lodged against the owners and operators of the club.

During our walk around the facility, we heard repeated praise of an eighteen-year-old busboy who may have saved hundreds of lives. Witnesses said that when Walter Bailey first discovered there was a fire in another part of the club, he ran into the Cabaret Room and climbed onto the stage, where two comedians who were opening for Davidson had the audience in stitches. The story Bailey told us was incredible.

"I had just finished carrying trays and was watching the show," he said, "when one of the waitresses told me there was a fire in the Zebra Room. I ran back to the showroom and asked the lady in charge if I could go to the microphone and tell everybody to get out. She didn't say anything, so I did it anyway. I walked up to the stage and took the mike away from the comedians. They just stood there, surprised. I told the crowd not to go out the front door. I told them to walk slowly out the side doors and I pointed them to the exit signs."

What surprised the teenager was that many people in the audience believed this announcement was just part of the show. It took the comedians to convince them that there actually was a fire.

"After we got out of the room, you could see the smoke coming up the halls," Bailey said. "It really spread fast. In five minutes, it was all over the building. All of the lights went out in the Cabaret Room, or else the smoke was so dense that the light couldn't be seen in there. I heard people moaning and calling for help. We went back in and started carrying people out. Most of them were down on the floor. We grabbed people by the shirts and hands or anything we could grab."

Despite Bailey's insistence that he was not a hero, witnesses said that he personally brought about twenty people out of the club.

"If that kid hadn't made the announcement," a fireman said, "there would have been a hundred fifty more dead instead of a hundred fifty survivors."

Over and over, we heard accounts of incredible heroism. But there were, of course, tragedies as well. The story of Everett and Paula Neill, a couple who died in the blaze, really broke my heart. As I flew home to Pittsburgh that evening, I had a personal feeling for what had happened that night in Kentucky. It had indeed been a horrific disaster. Now, the real work would begin.

Besides the vivid memories, Stanley Chesley had sent me home with a list of all the names, ages, and hometowns of the victims, plus autopsy reports for the ten people whose deaths had been fully examined. As for the rest, Dr. Stine had ruled that they had died of carbon monoxide poisoning. It is understandable why this would happen; to some extent, it is even logical. But experienced medical examiners and forensic pathologists know better.

The next day, I was called by several newspaper reporters who had heard that I had visited the scene. Each of them wanted to know what I had learned. Did I have any criticisms of the rescue attempts or of the investigation?

"Dr. Stine is to be commended for his efforts to get the bodies identified and back to their families," I told the *Louisville Courier-Journal*. "But we must weigh the importance of doing this against scientific needs. To say that all of the victims died of carbon monoxide poisoning is like saying a person died from burns just because his body is burned."

Meanwhile, newspapers and various state investigative agencies were turning up evidence of other possible wrongdoing. For example, there was strong evidence that several fire codes had been violated. The club's legal capacity was far exceeded on the night of the fire. The club had been warned just months earlier to add emergency warning lights and to fix their sprinkler system, but according to press reports, neither had been done.

During the next few months, hundreds of lawsuits seeking a total of $3 billion in damages were filed by lawyers representing the families of those who died in the fire. The part of the case in which the Schilling family was sued was settled for $3 million. But the biggest part of the case focused on what really caused the people trapped inside the club to die. That's where my expertise was needed.

In June 1980, I again flew to Cincinnati, this time to be interviewed by lawyers representing various defendants the plaintiffs were suing. For the better part of two days, I was deposed by more than three dozen defense attorneys who closely scrutinized my every answer.

The bottom line of my testimony was that many of the people who were overcome in the nightclub were not overcome by burns or smoke inhalation—they were overcome by invisible and odorless, but highly toxic, fumes. The scenario, as I explained it to the lawyers, was this:

The fire started and spread, unobserved, in the plenum, a small space between the building's roof and a false, lowered ceiling. In the plenum were a myriad of pipes and wires that have a special lining made of polyvinyl chloride (PVC). Under intense heat, PVC is subject to thermal degradation and produces hydrochloric acid (HCl). When HCl comes into contact with various human body parts, the results can be devastating.

Take the oropharynx, the back part of the mouth, as an example. There is a kind of trapdoor called the epiglottis that automatically closes to keep food and drink from rushing into the trachea, or windpipe. Around the epiglottis is a moist mucous membrane that covers the throat and mouth. HCl is a corrosive acid, and when it comes in contact with this mucous membrane, it causes the air passages to go into spasms, making breathing much more difficult, and sometimes even impossible. By the same token, when HCl comes into contact with the mucous membranes of the eyes, it causes tremendous irritation and tearing, even blindness.

During my deposition, I told the lawyers that I firmly believed many of the victims would have escaped the fire if they had not been incapacitated due to the effects of the HCl. They were unable to see exit signs. They struggled to breathe. Their exodus from the burning building was slowed or stopped until they were finally killed by smoke inhalation or the fire itself.

LAWYER: Dr. Wecht, how many autopsies have you performed on fire victims?

WECHT: Going back twenty years, it has been hundreds.

LAWYER: If you were writing a report on this case, what would the last paragraph be?

WECHT: The principal factors in these cases were heat, smoke, hydrochloric acid, and carbon monoxide. I think that most burns on the bodies were postmortem artifacts. That is to say that none or few of these people really burned to death in a very strict or literal sense of being consumed by flames.

LAWYER: Was heat in any way a factor?

WECHT: Heat is an additional factor to the degree that it makes air more difficult to breathe. Beyond that, people are bothered by heat at around 140 or 150 degrees Fahrenheit. At about 175 degrees, we start seeing tracheal damage. However, I have no way of knowing the temperatures as they kept rising inside the club the night of the fire.

LAWYER: Why do you believe that HCl or carbon monoxide was more of a factor of death than heat or smoke?

WECHT: From eyewitness testimony, I know that people did not react to the fire or the smoke. They had to be told that there was a fire. Even then, some of them thought it was a joke. The fact that people did not recognize the existence of the fire through smell or sight but that it definitely was going on above their heads tells me that the thermal degradation process involving these two chemicals was already taking place. Logical and deductive reasoning tells me that the HCl was in the atmosphere before the heat and smoke became major factors.

LAWYER: What are the exact effects of HCl?

WECHT: You begin to develop all kinds of problems, including shortness of breath, tightness in the chest wall, nausea, dizziness, vertigo, a loss of balance, and a general feeling of weakness.

In the end, most of the defendants in the case settled, so I was never called to testify. But at least in my mind, no courtroom drama was necessary to drive home the central point of the case—quite simply, that officials need to do more autopsies. One could have simply accepted that these victims died in the flames, but that was not the entire truth. There was much more to the story. And the families of the victims had a right to know the whole story. Furthermore, the public had to be warned about the dangers of chemicals like HCl and what could happen to them in fires.

For families like the Neills, all the money in the world would not be enough to replace what was lost. But there is great satisfaction in having laws passed that protect others. There is additional satisfaction if your lawsuit in a victim's behalf helps convince some corporation or business to change its method of operation, in turn making life a little safer for others.

EIGHT

DEATH IN THE CAUSE OF DEMOCRACY

As a ray of light peeked through the blinds, Su-jen Chen sat up. A nightmare had left her in a cold sweat. When she realized that her husband, Wen-chen Chen, was not in bed beside her, she grew more alarmed. In her dream, he had been the subject, the victim. Su-jen looked at the clock. It was 6:30 A.M. The tidiness of the blankets and pillows told her that Wen-chen had not come home the night before. A voice deep inside Su-jen told her that something was terribly wrong, that her husband was in serious danger.

Su-jen and Wen-chen Chen were visiting family and friends in Taipei—the place where they'd been born, raised, educated, and married. After a two-month visit, they were scheduled that week to return home to Pittsburgh, where Wen-chen was a mathematics professor at Carnegie Mellon University. But the day before, Wen-chen, a supporter of greater democracy in Taiwan, had been questioned for hours by government officials. Now Su-jen was worried, and with good cause.

Then, shortly before 8 A.M., police investigators called to tell Su-jen that her husband's body had been discovered at the base of a five-story library building on the campus of Taiwan University, his alma mater. It appeared he had climbed to the top of a fire escape and jumped to his death, they said. A suicide.

The day was July 3, 1981. The Kuomintang ran Taiwan with an iron fist, using the Garrison Command—Taiwan's version of SAVAK or the KGB—to defuse political opposition and subdue political dissidents. Immediately, those close to Wen-chen Chen suspected that he had died at the hands of the government. The Garrison Command admitted it had questioned Chen at length the day and night before his death, and that it had suspected him of helping to raise money in the United States for the Taiwan Independence Movement—a crime punishable by anywhere from twelve years to life in prison. However, the government police force claimed it had no involvement in Chen's death, and that he had been sent home at about 9 P.M. Instead, they attributed his "suicide" to the fact that Chen knew what he was doing was wrong and feared a lengthy incarceration.

Word of Chen's death quickly spread to the United States and throughout the world, accompanied by rumors that his life had been taken in a political assassination. Taiwanese living in the United States gathered in Pittsburgh to march and protest. Congressmen and senators, including Republican Jim Leach of Iowa (most recently known for his unrelenting inquiry into the Whitewater scandal), called for a thorough probe of Chen's death.

In late July, as pressure for full disclosure mounted, I received a call from Dr. Richard Cyert, president of CMU. Dr. Cyert told me that Dr. Morris DeGroot, who was a colleague of Chen's in the university's Statistics Department, was interested in flying to Taiwan to see what he could learn. I had never met Chen, but his death and its political circumstances did not sit well with me. And because I frequently lectured at CMU, this case took on a personal note.

"We need to know more about this case, what really happened," Dr. Cyert said. "Do you have any interest in joining Dr. DeGroot on a fact-finding mission?"

"Absolutely," I replied. "I'm very interested."

"I don't think there's much money in the budget to pay for anything more than the basic expenses," Dr. Cyert warned.

"Don't worry," I said. "This case is pro bono, a public service for the college, for Chen and his family."

Over the next few weeks, the CMU administration worked with the State Department and Taiwan officials to try to gain access to possible witnesses and evidence. Finally, in September, we received notification that the Kuomintang had agreed to allow Dr. DeGroot and me to travel to Taiwan. We would be able to conduct an independent, thorough, unobstructed investigation into Chen's death, they said.

Perhaps a little history lesson about Taiwan is necessary to understand how extraordinary this open invitation was in 1981. The population of Taiwan has been almost completely Chinese since the twelfth century. Following the 1895 Sino-Japanese War, however, the Japanese came to dominate the island, and continued to do so until 1945, when the Chinese Nationalist government of Chiang Kai-shek reassumed authority over the island. Four years later, when the Communists took over China, the Chinese Nationalists were forced to flee the mainland. Taiwan was their refuge.

For nearly four decades, the Chinese Nationalists—now called the Kuomintang political party—reserved all positions of power for themselves, even though they were in the minority. Strict oversight of all political activities was implemented. Questioning and second-guessing of government policy by the news media was completely forbidden. In fact, from 1949 until 1986, Taiwan was in an official state of martial law. The Kuomintang justified its heavy hand by claiming it was positioning itself to one day take back mainland China. Communism, they said, was Taiwan's archenemy and had to be guarded against at any cost.

What the Kuomintang did not understand was that suppression of any segment of society, especially a native majority, means oppression. The Taiwanese people quietly abided by the government's policy for many years, but in the 1970s, people started speaking out in favor of independence, free elections, and free speech. Most of the public support for the Taiwan Independence Movement came from former Taiwanese citizens living in the United States. Because the Kuomintang had no control over these people, the Garrison Command employed an extensive informant-based network to monitor the activities of the more than 500,000 Taiwanese Nationals living here. If these individuals ever returned to Taiwan, the government would arrest them and charge them with treason. This is exactly what many people believe happened to the thirty-one-year-old Wen-chen Chen.

The officers of the Garrison Command stated that during their day-long interrogation of Chen, he confessed to them that he was secretly raising money in the United States to support *The Formosa Magazine*, an underground publication that promoted political reform in Taiwan and that the authorities eventually shut down for alleged sedition. However, the government said, at the end of their interview, Chen was not charged with any crime. To the contrary, he was released and driven home. He was a free man to go anywhere he wished, they said. What he had chosen instead was to end his life.

On September 20, 1981, Dr. DeGroot and I departed Pittsburgh. During our trip, DeGroot updated me on recent conversations he had had with Chen's widow and other family members living in the United States. Su-jen and their only son, one-year-old Eric, had returned to Pittsburgh in August, about a month after Chen's death. At that time, Su-jen made it clear to DeGroot that she did not believe her husband committed suicide.

"From the moment I received the news of his death," she said, "I knew he had not killed himself."

Su-jen told DeGroot that when she first mentioned returning to Taiwan for a few months, Chen was reluctant to go. In fact, he only decided to join them a few days prior to their May 20 flight. She said he was nervous about returning home, frightened of a confrontation with authorities. However, during their first couple of weeks back in Taipei, Chen seemed very relaxed. He met old friends, bragged about his new-found life in the United States, and proudly showed off his infant son.

Wen-chen Chen had attended Taipei's prestigious Chienkuo Secondary School, where classmates referred to him as "Chen Taipan," meaning "Superstar Chen." He had breezed through his undergraduate studies at Taiwan University before moving on to the University of Michigan for a graduate degree in statistics. There, he loved to play basketball and soccer as much as he enjoyed crunching numbers on a calculator. Just a few years earlier, Chen had received permanent residency status in the United States and subsequently secured a full-time teaching position at CMU. In 1981, he and his wife had purchased their first home in Pittsburgh.

While Su-jen certainly loved and supported her husband, she did not like or appreciate his outspoken political stands. It was not that she disagreed with his positions; she simply did not like his being so publicly critical of the government.

Su-jen told DeGroot that they had planned to return to Pittsburgh on July 8 so that Chen could conduct a summer research program at CMU. However, in late June, the airline informed them that the only seats available were on a July 1 flight. That meant changing the dates on their exit visas. After contacting the appropriate authorities, the Chens, who were staying at Wen-chen's sister's house, were told to wait by the telephone for further instructions.

The call never came. Instead, at 8:30 A.M. on July 2, while returning home from playing basketball with his brother-in-law, Chen was met by officers of the Garrison Command. They wanted an interview. The term the officers used was *yueh tan,* which literally means an "appointment to talk." Theoretically, people can refuse a *yueh tan.* Chen, however, agreed. For the next twelve hours, from 9 A.M. until 9:30 P.M., the government agents questioned Chen. Su-jen had no idea what the Garrison Command said to Chen or what he told them.

As we deplaned, we were met by Director Chou, head of the Foreign Affairs Division of the Taipei Police Department. Through a translator provided by the Chen family, he explained that he was not there to hinder our work but to provide security and personal protection, including a guard posted outside our hotel doors at all times. His guards would drive us anywhere we wanted to go. If we needed anything, he said, we should just ask. Indeed, he was a most gracious host. Also there to greet us at the airport were Chen's father and brother-in-law and an escort from the American Institute, which doubles as our country's de facto embassy.

After a brief stop at our hotel to shower and change clothes, we went to the Taipei City Funeral Parlor, which served as the city's only morgue. There, we were introduced to Dr. John Fong, a Harvard-trained forensic pathologist at the National Taiwan University College of Medicine, and Dr. Shen Chun-shan, a professor at National Tsing Hua University. It was Dr. Fong and two other government physicians who had done the original autopsy on Chen.

I had spoken to Dr. Fong on the telephone from Pittsburgh and found him to be highly intelligent and forthright. Every question I posed to him was answered. I did not feel he was there as an agent of the government, but that he was truly interested in learning the truth. He did make it quite clear, however, that he did not believe the government had played a role in Chen's death.

After the appropriate introductions and the usual small talk, we were led to an examination room. A few minutes later, Chen's body was brought in. Amazingly, Taipei's morgue did not have a freezer for preservation, so Chen's body had been frozen on dry ice for the past three months. Even though the officials had tried to time the thawing of the body to coincide with our arrival, the body was still partially frozen. While this was a slight inconvenience, it did not deter me from conducting a complete examination and autopsy.

Dry ice covered the head, face, and neck completely, as well as part of the upper chest, arms, and hands, but it could be easily removed by a gentle tapping with forceps, a little prying, and the application of warm water. I had an official medical photographer present to take pictures of the body at each stage of the examination, while it was still encased in dry ice and as the dry ice was removed. As the dry ice came off,

I noted that there was no significant deterioration of Chen's body.

My first step was to examine the body externally, looking for bruises, cuts, or lacerations. The face showed no injuries of any kind. There were no abrasions or lacerations on the lips. The teeth and fingernails were in good shape as well, with no signs of loosening. Other than a few superficial injuries on the lower left forearm, there were no specific injuries on the hands, wrists, fingers, or arms. The absence of defensive injuries was, in itself, an important finding. Chen apparently did not struggle with or scratch any of the people who may have attacked him.

The original autopsy had been performed on July 6—three days after Chen's death. While it is unusual, perhaps even improper, to wait such a long time after death before doing an autopsy, I did not think this issue was significant to the mystery we were there to solve, namely how Wen-chen Chen had died.

I reopened all of the incisions made during the first autopsy to take a look for myself. In a few instances, I made my own incisions. The first thing I look for when opening a body is any evidence of hemorrhage. If there is hemorrhage within the body tissue, it is usually an indication of internal soft-tissue lacerations or a bone fracture. That is exactly what I found when I made an incision down the middle of the back, leading me to believe that the vertebral column and/or the rib cage had been traumatized. My suspicions were confirmed when I discovered that the right fourth, fifth, sixth, seventh, eighth, and ninth ribs were fractured posteriorly.

Next, I moved to the arms and legs—more specifically, the elbows and knees. To my surprise, I found no evidence of serious hemorrhaging and no fractures. The substantial injuries to Chen's back and ribs, combined with the lack of wounds to his arms, legs, hands, and head, meant that he had landed full-force on his back. He had not raised a hand or bent a knee to cushion his landing, nor had he looked down toward the ground to see the impending impact.

Later that day, Dr. DeGroot and I were taken to Taiwan's

equivalent of the FBI crime laboratory, where the toxicological analyses had been performed on Chen's blood. The tests came back negative, indicating that there were no toxic substances or drugs found in his system. An extremely small amount of alcohol was detected, but it was probably due to postmortem decomposition. There were a few tests that had not been conducted that I thought would have been helpful, but my request to take sample tissue back to Pittsburgh so that I could do my own analyses was denied.

Finally, I was allowed to examine the gross organs taken from Chen's body during the original autopsy. They had been wrapped in gauze and placed in a large bucket filled with formalin and were well-preserved. The lungs showed signs of hemorrhaging and the right kidney had several lacerations. But the remaining internal organs—the stomach, brain, liver, left kidney, tongue, heart, and spleen—appeared normal.

The next day, we were driven to Chen's father's home to examine the clothing Chen had been wearing when he died. The police had returned these six pieces of clothing in a large plastic bag. I scrutinized each item—white briefs, yellow gym shorts, light blue slacks, a brown leather belt with a metal buckle, white leather loafers, and a pale blue, short-sleeved dress shirt. Most of the articles had had portions cut out with scissors, presumably to test for bloodstains. But we found nothing particularly significant in any of these items.

Later that day, we went to an elegant private club in the center of the city to meet with General Wang, commander of the Taiwan Garrison General Headquarters, and Colonel Chou, chief of the Investigation Section of the Garrison Command Security Department. The traditional, twelve-course meal served at this penthouse restaurant was, incidentally, extraordinarily good.

It is customary in Taiwan to drink *sou shin jeu,* a rice wine similar to the Japanese sake; it is a very strong drink, but odorless and colorless. Everyone, the general included, was drinking very heavily. But because of my distaste for strong alcoholic beverages, this presented quite a social problem. Rather than create a scene by trying to explain why I wouldn't drink *sou shin jeu,* I decided to dispose of the stuff in a different manner. Each time our hosts looked away, I poured a little of my drink into a nearby glass of water. After a while, when everyone had drunk several glasses of *sou shin jeu,* I didn't have to be quite as sneaky. In the end, they never noticed what I was doing.

General Wang was an older, somewhat overweight, very distinguished gentleman who wore his fully decorated uniform. The conversation consisted of Dr. DeGroot's and my asking questions about Chen's *yueh tan* and possible government involvement in his death. Using a translator, we expressed our concerns and were quite frank with the officials. Even so, the meeting was not at all confrontational or unpleasant.

> WECHT: Why did you wish to speak to Wen-chen Chen?
>
> WANG: We wanted to interrogate Dr. Chen in connection with the Kaohsiung incident [a riot in December 1979 allegedly instigated by the Taiwan Independence Movement]. We also had information that Dr. Chen had been involved in fund-raising activities for *The Formosa Magazine.*
>
> WECHT: Why did you wait until a day or two before Chen and his family were scheduled to return home to interview him?
>
> WANG: We did not know until he visited the Exit and Reentry Processing Administration on June 30 that he wanted to leave Taiwan in early July. We had assumed we had more time, that Dr. Chen would not be leaving until late August, when most of the other professors returned to the United States to resume their teaching responsibilities. We planned on questioning him all along, but did not want to bother him while he was visiting with his family.

General Wang and his subordinates repeatedly insisted that they had no involvement in Chen's death and reiterated their belief that he had either committed suicide or had accidentally fallen from the fire escape. The officials said that

Dr. Chen had been picked up at the home of his brother-in-law at 9 A.M. and brought to the second-floor "VIP room" at the Garrison Command center.

During our meeting, which lasted more than five hours, the officials played a twenty-minute audiotaped excerpt of their interview with Chen; in that excerpt, I could not detect any trembling or fear in Chen's voice. They also showed us a copy of Chen's twelve-page statement, which he signed at the bottom of each page. Several of the key admissions contained therein were:

- That he had helped to establish foundations in the United States to raise money for *The Formosa Magazine*
- That he had transmitted those funds to Shih Ming-teh, the general manager of *The Formosa Magazine*
- That he had helped to find a translator in Pittsburgh to publish an English-language version of *The Formosa Magazine*
- That during his visit to Taiwan he had spoken to individuals about how to press for and enact political democratic reforms

It was the last of these points that General Wang and the Garrison Command took most seriously. They said they feared Chen had returned to Taiwan to publicly express his anti-government sentiments and to cause a stir among the people of Taipei. This led me to ask more pointed questions.

WECHT: Were you planning on arresting Dr. Chen?

WANG: No. There were no plans to file any charges against him. In fact, we promised to help facilitate his departure for the United States.

WECHT: Do you have any direct, physical evidence, such as letters or other documentation, proving that Chen was raising money in Pittsburgh and sending it to *The Formosa Magazine* in Taiwan?

WANG: No.

WECHT: Do you have any recordings of speeches he

may have made in the United States, or other comments Dr. Chen may have made that would prove these charges?

WANG: We did record a telephone conversation Chen had while he was in the United States with Shih in Taiwan because Shih was under criminal investigation and his phone was being monitored twenty-four hours a day. [Wang would not, however, divulge what was said in this conversation.]

WECHT: What kind of pressure was placed on Dr. Chen during his interrogation?

WANG: He spoke with us quite voluntarily. In fact, he was in a good mood when he left the interview. His suicide was as much a surprise to us as to his family.

General Wang added that Dr. Chen had not been under any kind of surveillance before or after his interview with the Garrison Command. He also pointed out that at no time during the questioning did Dr. Chen ask to make a telephone call to inform his family where he was or what was happening, even though he knew Garrison Command procedures permitted such a telephone call.

The officials said they were only able to account for Dr. Chen's whereabouts from 9 A.M., when they picked him up, until 9:30 P.M., when they told him he was free to go. They also pointed out that Dr. Chen was not being questioned the entire time, but that they broke for two hours for lunch and for two more hours for dinner. Even the transcript they showed us seemed to support their position. In it, the agent questioning Dr. Chen told him they were pleased with his cooperative attitude. The transcript shows Chen asking, "Then will I be able to go abroad again?" The interviewer answers, "Go abroad? Certainly. We will not cause trouble for you or obstruct you."

As further evidence that Dr. Chen was treated fairly, General Wang said they even escorted him home in one of the special vehicles they reserve for *yueh tan* subjects; it resembles a taxicab so that neighbors of the person being questioned will not suspect anything is going on. He also insisted that their agent walked Dr. Chen up a flight of stairs to the apartment of his brother-in-law and left him standing outside. At that point, the agent returned to his car. General Wang said they never saw or heard from Dr. Chen again.

At the end of our interview, we expressed our gratitude to General Wang and his lieutenants for their hospitality and cooperation. They did not have to meet with us at all, but to their credit, they spent several hours answering our questions. However, keep one thing in mind: there was no way for us to verify any of the statements attributed to Dr. Chen. We did not know, for example, whether the transcripts of Dr. Chen's written statement were authentic or even whether the tape recording was real. We had no choice but to accept the words of General Wang and his troops as stated without any independent corroboration.

The third and final day of our visit to Taipei was spent retracing the footsteps Dr. Chen had taken during his last hours of life. We met with several members of his family at the apartment of his brother-in-law, Chen Chung. Everyone we spoke with said Dr. Chen was not the kind of person to commit suicide. He was happy and excited about his career, his one-year-old son, and life in general. They also said that despite the Garrison Command's insistence that they had escorted Dr. Chen to his apartment, he did not return home on the night of July 2. Two small girls playing outside of the apartment said they remembered two men getting out of a car about 9:30 P.M. and walking up the stairs toward Chen Chung's apartment. However, the two girls stated they did not remember either of the men coming back down the stairs.

The next hour in Dr. Chen's life is completely unaccounted for. The next person to see him was his longtime friend and colleague, Teng Wei-hsiang, a soft-spoken gentleman who taught at a technical institute in Taipei. He and Chen had attended graduate school together at the University of Michigan. Teng said he was spending a quiet evening at home reading when Dr. Chen knocked on his door around midnight.

"What's up?" Teng asked, surprised to see his friend at such a late hour.

"Trouble," responded Dr. Chen.

"The Garrison Command?"

Chen nodded his head.

"When?"

"Yesterday," answered Chen.

Despite the obvious stress Chen was under, Teng said he appeared calm and collected. The two had a late-night snack of fried eggs, ham, grapes, and guava juice. Then Chen asked Teng for a piece of paper to write a letter. Teng retrieved a piece of Chinese-style writing paper for his friend and left him alone. But a few minutes later, realizing that Chen may have wanted American-style paper, Teng returned. Looking over his friend's shoulder, he saw the following words written in English: "To whom it may concern."

"Don't look!" Chen admonished his friend.

Teng quickly returned to his chair, allowing Chen to finish his letter. When he was done, Chen folded the letter, placed it inside an envelope, and placed the envelope inside his coat pocket. This letter was never seen again. No family member, friend, or government agency has acknowledged receiving the letter or finding it. And the police say it was not on his person when they discovered his body six hours later. To me, that meant it was not a suicide note.

After more than an hour of relaxed, idle chat, Teng said, Dr. Chen made a comment that the Garrison Command would frequently refer to thereafter as an indication that Chen was suicidal: "This is the last time we may see each other." Teng said he sat there in shock, but not because he took the comment to mean Chen was suicidal; to the contrary, Teng interpreted his friend's remark as an expression of fear that he was about to be incarcerated and separated from his family and friends for a long period of time.

Between 12:30 and 1 A.M., Teng said, Dr. Chen stood up from the table, shook Teng's hand, and said, "I'm going now." As he opened the front door, Chen cautiously looked both ways, as if he suspected someone was following him.

Then he said good-bye and left. That was the last time anyone acknowledges having seen Dr. Chen alive.

We left Teng's home and drove several blocks to Taiwan University, where Dr. Chen's body was found. After parking our cars at the college's front gate and showing our identification to the security guards, we proceeded to the research library, which is used mainly by graduate students and faculty members. The library is an old, five-story building made of gray concrete and white brick. An external stairwell scales the building's northeast corner, and a shallow, narrow ditch with brick borders on both sides runs alongside the building directly below this stairwell. Some grass has grown up to cover some of the bricks. Next to the ditch is a concrete walkway with a grassy area around it. On the brick and concrete is where Dr. Chen's body was found.

The stairwell, which was really a fire escape, had a black-painted iron railing on both sides. The stairs, which were twenty-six inches wide, were poured with concrete. One person could walk comfortably up and down the stairs, but it was not wide enough for two adults to walk side by side. There were doors at the second-, fourth-, and fifth-floor landings, but none at the third-floor level. The landing at the fifth floor—the floor from which Dr. Chen allegedly fell—was ninety inches long and thirty-four inches wide. The railing was thirty-two inches high. I noted that the railing appeared to have a fresh coat of black paint with no chipping or flaking. I was told that the rails had been painted since the July 3 incident.

Standing on the fifth-floor landing and looking over the railing, I noticed that the second-floor landing protruded about two feet further than any of the other landings; however, the grass patch covering the bricks could still be seen. As I examined the physical layout of the building, the fire escape, the second-floor landing, and the ditch below, I realized that a person voluntarily jumping from the fifth floor would, in all likelihood, have gone beyond the width of the brick ditch and concrete walk and landed on the grass. Even a person who had simply stumbled over the railing would have cleared the concrete walkway because of the momentum of the body as it fell outward and down.

However, a body picked up and dropped over the railing probably would have landed on the concrete walkway below. Several thoughts came to mind to support this notion. First, Dr. Chen was not a small person; it would have been very difficult for one or even two people to have hurled his body much farther from the building. Also, if someone wanted to make the death appear to be a suicide, dropping the body five stories onto concrete would have been an obvious choice.

As we walked around the library, we were introduced to Liu Jen-fu, the campus security guard who had found Dr. Chen's body. He said that six guards patrolled the college campus at night, but none had reported seeing or hearing anything out of the ordinary.

The university enforces a strict curfew for students, he explained. Women must be in their dorms by 11:30 P.M., and no vehicles can enter or leave the campus between 11 P.M. and 7 A.M. without special permission. Campus security records show that no cars or trucks came or went during these hours. This would imply that no vehicle carrying Dr. Chen, alive or dead, conscious or unconscious, could have entered the university grounds. However, if the occupants of a car had special permission and simply flashed their credentials, they probably would have been allowed to enter without being questioned or having a written record made of their visit.

Officer Liu said that people begin arriving at the college about 4 A.M. to walk, run, ride bicycles, and engage in other forms of exercise. In July, it starts getting light outside at 4 A.M. About 7 A.M. on July 3, he said, campus security received a call that there was a body on the ground near the Graduate School Research Library. Officer Liu was told to check it out. Twenty minutes later, he found Dr. Chen's body at the bottom of the fire escape. After determining that he was dead, and not just drunk or passed out, Liu called for backup. The officer told us Dr. Chen's body was lying in a supine position across the ditch.

That afternoon, we picked up our luggage at the hotel and were driven to the airport, where a large number of print and electronic news reporters were waiting. Their microphones and tape recorders were stacked on top of a podium. As we had a little time before our flight, we agreed to a brief press conference.

REPORTER: Do you agree with the government that Wen-chen Chen committed suicide?

WECHT: No, I disagree. I think the evidence strongly points away from suicide and toward homicide.

REPORTER: What specifically do you base your opinion upon?

WECHT: The autopsy I did on Dr. Chen and my inspection of the scene of the fall. Both provided me with evidence that I consider inconsistent with a suicide. First, his body was found close to the building in a supine position, on his back. Second, all of his injuries were limited to his ribs, sternum, and the spinal column. It simply is not within the realm of physical likelihood that Chen would climb up on the railing, jump to his death, and land so close to the building flat on his back. It's not that a jumper is trying to see how far he or she can leap, but you are trying to clear the building. There is evidence that Dr. Chen's body struck the second-floor landing. There is no way a person can jump up and out, and come back toward the building. It defies logic.

If this had been a suicide, I would have suspected other injuries to the head, neck, face, arms, or hands. If it had been a suicide, I think Dr. Chen's falling body would have landed farther away from the building, in the grassy area rather than on the concrete. If he had landed on the grassy area, his injuries would have been serious, but certainly not fatal. What the injuries to Dr. Chen are consistent with is a body that has been incapacitated in some fashion, picked up, held out over the railing, and simply dropped straight down.

Also, every person we have talked with during our trip

has told us they did not think Dr. Chen would have committed suicide. Everyone, including the officials with the Garrison Command, told us that Dr. Chen was in good spirits and gave no indication of being depressed or suicidal.

REPORTER: Is there evidence Wen-chen Chen had been knocked out or drugged or something to make him unconscious?

WECHT: I could find no head or neck injuries to support that. The official toxicology report does not mention any drugs. However, I have been denied access to body tissues that would allow me to do my own testing to determine this very question. But let me also say that there is nothing in the official autopsy report done by Dr. Fong that I disagree with. He did a competent and thorough examination.

REPORTER: Is there any evidence that there may have been a physical confrontation between Chen and someone else?

WECHT: No, although that is something I certainly looked for. I found nothing under his fingernails, such as skin from scratching an attacker, and no significant bruises on his hands, fingers, or arms from a fight. There was no visible evidence of defensive injuries or a struggle.

REPORTER: What about signs of torture?

WECHT: I found no evidence of physical torture. I found no injuries that could be distinguished from those incurred in the fall. However, let me make this point: You do not have to be the world's greatest karate expert or extremely knowledgeable in the martial arts to know that a blow to the base of the skull could render a person unconscious in a millisecond without producing any manifestation of an injury. Also, any attacker could have used chloroform to render Dr. Chen immobile.

REPORTER: Was Dr. Chen even alive when he hit the concrete?

WECHT: Yes. Because of the hemorrhaging around some of the lacerations and fractures, it is clear his cardiovascular system was still operating when he was dropped from the stairwell. However, keep in mind that death does not occur in a split second. Death is a process that extends over many seconds or even minutes, depending upon what condition or force is causing it. The extensive hemorrhaging around the fractures tells me Dr. Chen was alive when he hit the ground and may have lived for thirty minutes or more after he struck the concrete walkway.

REPORTER: What about the possibility that Wen-chen Chen's death was an accident, that he simply slipped and fell?

WECHT: I've thought about this a lot and I cannot think of a single scenario in which "accidental death" would make any sense. It defies any kind of reasonable, logical, intellectual analysis. First, you would have to ask what he was doing up there on top of a fire escape in the middle of the night. Was he sitting on the ledge and lost his balance? An examination of the crime scene and the injuries to Dr. Chen seems to rule this out. The government says no drugs were found in his body and only a very small, insignificant amount of alcohol was in his body, so we know he was not under the influence of any drug that may have caused him to slip and fall. Finally, the pattern of his injuries definitely rules out an accidental fall. If he had fallen accidentally, a natural reflex would have been to reach out his arms, hands, or legs to try to cushion the blow. That would have meant these limbs would have been fractured, and they were not. So an accidental fall is out of the question.

REPORTER: Do you believe this was a political assassination?

WECHT: It most likely was a homicide. Whenever a person is killed by someone else, it is called a homicide. In the United States and in our language, we use the phrase or term "assassination" to mean something very sinister—a planned execution. The term is usually used when referring to a murder arranged by a government or possibly organized crime. If Dr. Chen was indeed murdered because of his political beliefs, then certainly it could be described as a political assassination. Just one more question before Dr. DeGroot and I must board our plane to return home.

REPORTER: If Dr. Chen was murdered, who do you believe is responsible for his death?

WECHT: Well, that's an interesting question. I just do not have enough information or knowledge to answer that question specifically. One can say that his friends, family, or political allies would probably not have had him killed. The other side of that coin is that it would have been people opposed to Dr. Chen's political leanings. But I cannot pinpoint a person or a group of people. That must be left up to the appropriate law enforcement agency or governmental body to determine.

Upon our arrival in Pittsburgh, Dr. DeGroot and I prepared a full report of our findings and conclusions, mostly reiterating what I had already told the Taiwanese media. This report was circulated by CMU officials and was reprinted in a few forensic pathology journals.

Despite the profound differences between our findings and the official government theory of Dr. Chen's death, efforts to raise concerns about the matter in Taiwan fell upon deaf ears for several years. However, Chen's death remained a rallying point for leaders of the Taiwan Independence Movement. Throughout the mid and late 1980s, the Kuomintang slowly granted many individual rights, such as lifting limitations on freedom of the press and granting people the right to speak out against the Taiwanese government.

But only in 1986, after the Democratic Progressive Party was allowed to operate in the open, did true political reform come. Amazingly, in 1994, after the DPP had grown to become a strong political party in Taiwan, the case of Wen-chen Chen resurfaced. The country's Congress officially reopened the investigation and investigators for the national legislature flew to Pittsburgh to take a video deposition of my 1981 findings. A short while later, I learned, the official cause of death was changed from "suicide" to "undetermined."

Many people continue to believe that Wen-chen Chen suffered an unnecessary death. But his son, Eric, should realize that his father's name, his political beliefs, and his tragic death became the rallying cry that led to political freedom for the more than 20 million people who live in Taiwan. This is a great legacy for a courageous individual.

NINE

BLOOD OF A PATRIOT

Because of my involvement in the Wen-chen Chen case, I began to follow political developments in Taiwan far more closely than I otherwise would have. In the years that followed my 1981 visit to Taipei, the country went through dramatic changes. Slowly, the Kuomintang-controlled government loosened its grip on the people of Taiwan. Martial law was finally lifted in 1988. The press was given more freedom to question official government activities, and political protestors were allowed to challenge officials publicly on matters of policy. But still, there was a limit to what the government was willing to accept.

For several decades, Teng-fa Yu had been a thorn in the Kuomintang's side. He was one of the few individuals to routinely speak out against government actions. And yet for some reason, the Kuomintang did not attempt to silence him as it did the hundreds of thousands of others who dared to publicly criticize government officials and policies. Perhaps it was because he had quickly become a highly respected and even revered spokesman and unofficial leader of the native Taiwanese people.

Yu made no bones about his involvement with and

leadership role in the Democratic Progressive Party, the main political opposition to the Kuomintang. But Yu was not just a dissenter or a speechmaking activist. In his early years, he had gotten very involved in local politics and was elected a commissioner from Kaohsiung County. Later, he would become a member of the National Assembly and Electoral College, Taiwan's version of the U.S. Senate. Most of Yu's family followed him into politics as well. A son was a member of the Legislative Council (more or less analogous to the U.S. House of Representatives), a daughter-in-law had been elected Kaohsiung County commissioner, and several other relatives were activists at various levels.

"Yu was considered a great leader, generations ahead of his time," Dr. Henry Lee, my good friend and colleague, and a native of Taiwan, told me. As mentioned earlier, Dr. Lee is director of the Connecticut State Police Forensic Science Laboratory and a professor at the University of New Haven. "He was a founder and a leader in the political opposition movement. Everyone respected him, even those who did not like him."

On September 13, 1989, at the age of eighty-seven, Yu was found dead in his home. His bedroom and bathroom were smeared with blood. News media reports said Yu had either hit his head in an accidental fall or had been attacked and murdered by political opponents.

Within days of his death, friends of Yu's family called my office. A thorough investigation of the crime scene was needed, they said, as was an autopsy of Yu. Because of my strong stand in the Chen case, they told me, they knew I would not be swayed or influenced by the Taiwanese government. The official invitation for me to travel to Taiwan to investigate Yu's death came from his daughter-in-law, Chen Yueh-ying Yu, the Kaohsiung County commissioner. In a letter to me, she said she believed that her father-in-law had been assassinated and that his attackers were professional killers.

When I agreed to return to Taiwan to investigate this case, I had no idea what I was getting myself into. This time, I took my wife, Sigrid, with me. During the day-long flight, I reviewed the materials that had been sent to me. Interestingly, Dr. Jih-sung Yang, a medical investigator with the Taiwan police, had already stated publicly that he thought Yu had been murdered. Other medical experts, including those I knew at National Taiwan University, were less convinced. Some thought the evidence pointed more toward an accidental death. No autopsy had yet been performed, since all parties thought it should wait until I had arrived to participate in the procedure.

As part of the materials I reviewed, someone had written down Dr. Yang's findings from a routine external examination of Yu's body. The one-page, typed statement, written in broken but comprehensible English, read as follows:

> The cause of death were two external wounds on the left superior occipital which caused heavy blood loss for approximately three hours. Two clearly identifiable slanted cuts struck by a heavy blunt instrument. The wound is in the form of an upside-down T-shape. The first is 5 centimeters long by 0.7 centimeters deep. The second is 7 centimeters long by 0.7 centimeters deep. It appears that the instrument hit the head of the victim downward and from top to center left. The victim then tried to stand and he was hit a second time in the head upwards and from the lower part of the head towards the center left.
>
> It also appears that he was held by the arms and wrists by an assailant on each side. There are clear finger marks on his arms and wrists. The assailant on the left side hit the victim on the left scrotum with his left knee and the victim fell on his right knee. There are clear marks on his right knee. Then the assailant on the right kicked the victim on the right anterior iliac bone causing a serious wound. The assailant on the left kicked the victim again on the left anterior iliac bone, causing a blood clot.
>
> There are no other external wounds and after the blood loss and the heart failure, he was stripped according

to Taiwanese custom. This is to prevent the ghost of the victim from returning to seek revenge. The assailants then wiped their footprints off with a nearby towel and they left with the towel and the victim's clothing. They took these to make it look like an accident.

Although this report was far too speculative for my taste, I was intrigued by the scenario. From what I had heard about this case, the possibility of foul play certainly seemed present. However, I had to keep in mind that so far, I had heard only one side of this story.

As our plane landed in Taipei, I looked out the window and noticed that the airport terminal was packed with people. At three in the morning, I found this strange. Not until we had deplaned and passed through customs did I realize that these people were journalists, reporters, photographers, and cameramen from radio and TV stations, newspapers, and magazines from across Asia. They surrounded us. With pads and pens in hand and lights shining brightly, they bombarded me with questions. There I was—tired, unshaven, disheveled—participating in a major news conference, whether I wanted to or not.

"What do you expect to find?"

"Do you think Yu was murdered?"

"Did the Kuomintang do it?"

"Are the murder accusations a political ploy by Yu's family and supporters to attempt to influence the upcoming national elections?"

"What are the different ways in which you will conduct your investigation?"

I told them I could not answer many of their questions because I simply did not know the answers yet. "I am being hired by the Yu family," I responded. "I plan on visiting the scene where he died, talking to various witnesses, and performing an autopsy. Following that, I will prepare and present a report of my findings to those who have brought me here."

Thankfully, before I could be bombarded with another

round of questions, our escorts arrived and hustled us into a waiting limousine. However, they told us, we would not be able to go to our hotel room until after we had visited Chen Yueh-ying Yu's home. When we pulled up a short time later, I was surprised to see cameras flashing—the news media had been staking out her home as well! Again, Sigrid and I were escorted through the mobs of press people and Yu supporters. Inside, we were greeted by Chen Yueh-ying Yu. In the foyer of her home, I noticed what appeared to be a shrine; fruits, vegetables, flowers, plants, and various other items had been brought by neighbors and friends and arranged around a portrait of Teng-fa Yu. As I approached this shrine and faced his picture, my intuition told me to bow in respect. I did so, and only later learned that it was the appropriate thing to do.

That night, over dinner, Sigrid and I talked with the immediate family members about Yu and his career. They were quite courteous and were well-read regarding political events in the United States. They also were very firm in their commitment toward making Taiwan a more liberated country and true democracy.

Following a good night's sleep and breakfast at our gracious hotel, Sigrid and I were driven to Teng-fa Yu's home, a two-story house in a suburb of Taipei where he had lived in his retirement. Because he liked his privacy, we were told, the nearest neighbor was at least a hundred yards away. He was a widower and had not remarried, but family members gave me the impression he was "very close" to his domestic live-in servant. She had been with him hours before he died, but was not at the house when the fatal incident occurred. Both family members and the police made it clear to me that she was not a suspect.

As we pulled up to the house, I was taken completely off guard by the number of people there. There were dozens of news reporters and photographers who were covering the story. But there must have been at least five hundred more people surrounding the house as well. Police officers rushed up to our car, pushing people away from the vehicle just so we could open our doors. It was very close to a mob or riot scene. The officers cleared a path through the crowd for us to walk to the house. Had they not been there, we never would have made it inside. Only now did I comprehend the magnitude of the case.

Yu's grandson met me at the front door. A gatekeeper of sorts, he decided who could come into the house and who must stay out. Several police officers, mainly those who had originally investigated the scene the day Yu was found dead, had been invited to meet with me there. Most of the news reporters were kept out.

Yu's home was fairly large. Though he and his family were not rich, neither were they poor. They could certainly afford most modern luxuries, but Yu chose to live extremely modestly. His home had no telephone and was not air-conditioned. The first floor was divided into the foyer we walked into, a kitchen, and a laundry. The second floor was one room, large enough to accommodate two bedroom areas, a living room, a dining room, and a bathroom.

As we entered this floor, I noticed that Yu was very well-read. Thousands of newspapers from across Asia were stacked from floor to ceiling and filled at least one-third of the room. "He would read newspapers from China, Japan, and Taiwan every day," his grandson explained. "Even after his retirement, he wanted to be completely informed."

Off to one side sat Yu's modest bed and dresser. On the floor between the two were several puddles of blood. They were now dry, of course, but neither the authorities nor the family had taken steps to clean them up. Several drops of blood also were evident on the bed. I noticed that the bedposts at the foot of his mattress had sharp edges.

Throughout the room, I found bloodied finger and palm prints. Police investigators told me they matched Yu's, and I had no reason not to believe them. This trail of blood led from the bedroom into the bathroom. Both the door and the doorknob were smeared with blood. Handprints were clearly identifiable on the sink. I recalled the findings of Dr. Yang, who wrote that the assailants had wiped their bloody feet on a towel. Dr. Yang contended that the assailants then took the towel and Yu's clothes with them to make the death appear to be an accident. But when I asked the police about this, they said they saw no indications that this was the case.

Because the house was discovered to have been completely secured and locked from the inside, family members supported a scenario that could only be found in a Far East martial arts movie involving highly trained ninjas. Yu's family believed—or said they believed—that intruders had climbed up a nearby tree and swung onto his rooftop, which is flat and from which there is access to the living quarters, or through his windows.

To investigate this theory, I walked over to the two main windows on the second floor. Because it seldom gets cold in Taipei, most people keep their windows open year-round. Yu had done this as well. A small stairway led to the roof, but the trapdoor at the top of the stairs had been locked from the inside on the day Yu died. If there were intruders, I decided, they must have come in through the windows. However, I still wanted to walk around on the roof, and my hosts were only too happy to oblige.

Once we had climbed through the trapdoor and onto the roof, I walked over to the two-foot wall at the edge to look down at the crowd below. As soon as I was spotted by members of the news media, cameras started flashing; my every move was being documented. As I pointed to the nearest tree to the house, the crowd below oohed and aahed. Never in his finest hour did Sherlock Holmes receive this much attention. While I found it amusing, it was also somewhat distracting.

Forcing myself to focus on the evidence before me, I noted that the tree was a fair distance away from the house and that it was most likely not tall enough for someone—not even Steven Seagal—to swing from it into the windows of the house. For a split second, I was struck by the notion of grabbing a rope, climbing up the tree, and acrobatically swinging through the air, doing backflips through the window. That would really amuse my audience. But upon somber reflection, I decided I was too old for such a maneuver.

As we departed the house that morning, I told investigators and family members that I needed photographs of the alleged crime scene to take home with me. "It will help to refresh my memory," I said.

From Yu's house, I was driven to the city morgue. I should have been prepared, but once again I was stunned by the large number of people waiting for us outside. Again, there were so many people that it was impossible to open the car door until the police forced their way through the crowd.

At the family's request, the city had kept Yu's body in refrigeration and had not embalmed him. Dr. John Fong, whom I had met years earlier during my Wen-chen Chen investigation, was there to assist me in performing the autopsy. The autopsy, I told the onlookers, will solve this mystery. If Yu had been attacked, we will know shortly. If it was an accidental death, we will be able to determine that as well. The autopsy will end all questions.

As the body was being brought out and laid before us, a man came storming into the autopsy room, shouting at Yu's daughter-in-law and grandson, the people who had brought me to Taiwan to perform the very procedure that I was getting ready to do. I didn't have to understand a word of Taiwanese or Chinese to realize something was wrong. The tone of their voices was clear: there were serious problems.

Through an interpreter, I learned that the man was Yu's son and that he was protesting the autopsy, calling it a violation of their religious beliefs. To do an autopsy, the man said, would kill Yu's spirit. He was demanding that the procedure be halted immediately. For more than thirty minutes, the family members argued and shouted. In the middle of this argument, Yu's daughter-in-law fainted.

Finally, I was told that there would be no cutting of Yu's body.

"No cutting means no autopsy, which means no truth," I told them.

They said they understood my frustration, but that I would

be permitted to conduct an external examination of the body only and would not be allowed to make any incisions. This decision confused me. After all, this family had gone to incredible expense to fly me from Pittsburgh to Taiwan, knowing my main purpose was to conduct an autopsy. Why had this matter not been settled before my arrival? While the question may seem simple, the answer was very complicated. Not only was this a high-profile death, this was politics. As I removed Yu's dressing to examine his flesh wounds, thoughts skipped through my head. Am I being used? Is this whole thing nothing more than a political rally for the opposition movement?

The first thing I noticed was that there were several bruises and lacerations on Yu's scalp and torso. None indicated an extreme beating, but without cutting open his head to examine these wounds, I was unable to give the family a definitive answer.

In the end, I concluded that Yu had probably been drinking a bit too much in celebration of his birthday, lost his balance, and most likely hit his head on the corner of his bedroom dresser. This conclusion was bolstered by the significant level of alcohol that local authorities had found in Yu's blood. Receiving a severe concussion, he fell to the floor. In a state of confusion from the wound and the loss of blood, Yu wiped his forehead and stumbled into the bathroom, where he attempted to clean himself and stop the bleeding. When he realized the bleeding was not going to stop, he tried to crawl back to his bed but collapsed and died outside of his bathroom instead.

Unfortunately, this was news the Yu family did not want to hear. They wanted to hear about a political assassination and conspiracy, or at least keep that possibility alive until after the election. As we left the morgue to return to our hotel, I received the distinct impression that I was no longer held in very high regard by the family of Teng-fa Yu.

In the days following my return to the United States, I was at dinner with Henry Lee, who told me he was very proud of me and that my conclusion was very courageous.

"How so?" I inquired.

"If you had agreed with the family and said there was a good possibility that Yu's death was a murder, I think that would have sparked riots throughout Taiwan," Dr. Lee said. "Instead, you told them the truth and everything worked out for the best."

TEN

ARSENIC AND OLD BONES

Once or twice every year, I am asked to travel overseas to review or conduct an autopsy. These cases can be very time-consuming and tiring, but they also have provided me with unique educational experiences that I would not have obtained otherwise.

In the late summer of 1993, I was contacted at my office by Shuja Nawaz, an official at the International Monetary Fund. Nawaz's brother was General Asif Nawaz, chief of army staff in Pakistan. Earlier that year, Nawaz told me, his brother had died. Government officials said that the cause was a heart attack, but Nawaz, his family, and apparently many others believed there might have been more involved. "We suspect he may have been murdered," Nawaz told me.

An obviously intelligent and articulate man, Nawaz said he had been referred to me by several lawyers and judges in our country. His request was clear: he wanted me to fly to Pakistan, exhume his brother's body, perform an autopsy, and determine once and for all whether his brother had died of natural causes or had been the victim of a sinister plot.

At this point, he readily admitted, there was little or no evidence to support their suspicions. But his brother had been a strong military leader and had, on several occasions, ex-pressed significant disagreement with many of the politicians who ran the country. In a nation that has changed political leaders thirty times in forty-six years, he reminded me, power-hungry, opportunistic people will do anything to seize control.

"If he did not die naturally, how do you think he died?" I asked. "By gunshot? Could he have been suffocated or drowned? Is there a possibility he was injected with something?"

"We believe he could have been poisoned," Nawaz said. "We don't know how. Maybe he was injected with some kind of poison or maybe it was slipped into something he drank or ate."

In November 1992, the general had fallen seriously ill with many of the same symptoms, I was told. However, he recovered fully within a few days. Still, Nawaz wondered whether that episode had been a failed poisoning attempt. "What can we do to put our suspicions at ease?" he inquired.

I told Nawaz that if they really wanted to pursue this line of inquiry, there were a few steps that definitely should be taken. First, I told him to retrieve a hairbrush that his brother had recently used. "If that first incident was due to some form of poisoning attempt employing heavy metals or certain other toxic compounds, then the chemicals used would have had time to grow into the general's hair," I said. "And if you can find a comb or brush that he used on his hair in the days and weeks following that attack, and if there was a heavy metal poison of some kind, such as arsenic, in his bodily system, it would be detectable in the hairs on the brush."

While Nawaz was searching for a brush or comb belonging to his brother, I called Dr. Fredric Rieders, my friend and colleague who would later testify in the Simpson trial. "If you need a test done on hairs or anything else, just send it to me," he said.

A few days later, Nawaz called me from his home near Washington, D.C., to say that the general's wife had sent him her husband's personal hairbrush. I gave him Dr. Rieders's address and telephone number.

"Send him hair samples from the brush," I told Nawaz. "He will be able to conduct a series of tests on them to determine if there were any unnatural or toxic substances in your brother's body in the days before he died." If the tests come back positive, I explained, we will have preliminary evidence of possible criminal activity and can then talk further about my flying to Pakistan to do the autopsy. Nawaz agreed.

A couple of weeks later, I heard back from both Nawaz and Dr. Rieders. The hair samples from the brush had tested positive for unnaturally high, possibly deadly levels of arsenic. Perhaps the Nawaz family is right, I thought. Perhaps someone had deliberately poisoned the general by periodically placing small amounts of arsenic in his food or beverage. (Several historians and medical scholars believe this was how Napoléon Bonaparte died.) As far as I was concerned, this finding in and of itself was sufficient cause to suspect possible criminal activity. It proved nothing, but it was potential evidence of foul play.

With this new information revealed, federal law enforcement authorities in Pakistan quickly got involved in the investigation. Much to my surprise, they even helped us to take the next step by announcing that they would pay all expenses for me and two other forensic pathologists to fly to their country to examine the body of General Nawaz. I must admit that my initial response to the government's actions was extreme suspicion. If there had been a government plot to eliminate the general, I thought, the Pakistani officials might be attempting to take the lead in the investigation just so they could later derail it themselves.

Some of my reservations were put to rest when I learned that the Pakistani law enforcement officials had also contacted Britain's Scotland Yard and France's Sûreté—two of the most prestigious law enforcement agencies in the world—to help them select forensic pathologists to join me. Scotland Yard chose Dr. John Clark and Sûreté selected Dr. Patrick Lambert, two men with outstanding credentials and professional reputations beyond reproach.

On September 30, I found myself flying across the Atlantic

Ocean en route to Pakistan. Ignoring whatever old movies the
airline was featuring, I spent much of the long flight reading
newspaper and magazine articles about General Nawaz. At
age fifty-six, the military leader was considered "pro-Western"
and had helped foster democracy in Pakistan, a country long
mired in martial law. In 1992, he was promoted to chief of
army staff, a position he held until his death.

But the general was not without his critics. Some articles
blamed him for the tragic Sind Operation, in which the military
moved into the southern province of Sind to quell ethnic
violence between native Sindhis and Mohajir immigrants
from India. The natives had asked for military intervention,
seeking help in deterring a growing problem with murders
and kidnappings. Critics said the operation was politically
motivated and pointed out that most of the three hundred
people killed during the operation were members of the
"leftist" Pakistan People's Party. In the years following the 1990
Sind Operation, leaders of the PPP openly called for General
Nawaz's assassination.

Instantly, I knew this was a realistic and very likely motive,
if indeed we were able to prove that the general had been
murdered. As far as some family members and friends were
concerned, there was no question. The general's wife, Begum
Nuzhat Nawaz, was widely quoted as saying that her husband
had been "assassinated" and that his "murderer must be found
and dealt with."

A country that seems always to be in the midst of political
turmoil, Pakistan was embroiled in another national election
when I arrived in the capital city of Islamabad. Only six days
later the country's voters would decide who their new leaders
would be. The death of General Nawaz and rumors of his
possible murder were a major campaign issue, with both sides
promising to find the truth and punish any wrongdoers.

With its population of 132 million, Pakistan is among the
poorest and most undereducated of independent republics.
The average person makes less than $400 a year, and more
than three of every four people are illiterate. To make matters

worse, Pakistan's population is increasing at a rate of 3.2 percent annually, one of the highest in the world.

Both candidates in the national election were promising voters the sky—that they would implement economic reforms that would offer every hardworking citizen a middle-class lifestyle. Most analysts quoted in the press said that such promises were unachievable, especially since the national government was itself on the verge of bankruptcy, unable to pay interest on the national debt.

During the flight, I also took some time to review General Nawaz's personal medical records, which had been sent to me by his family. He was a strong and robust man who exercised regularly and did not smoke or drink. To be sure, his occupation was stressful, but the general had been the picture of health until November 24, 1992, when he became sick while attending a high-level government meeting. His complaints at that time were a sore throat, dizziness, and tenderness in his legs. The physicians gave him a thorough examination and concluded that he probably had some form of viral illness that had produced an inner-ear infection, thus causing dizziness. They prescribed a small daily dosage of aspirin and warned him not to exercise too extensively for a while. During the next few weeks, he recovered fully and the symptoms quickly disappeared.

Six weeks later, on January 8, 1993, the general was jogging on a treadmill at his home when he started experiencing chest pains, loss of breath, and profuse sweating. His wife helped him to lie down on his bed and began to massage his chest, encouraging him to breathe more slowly. But the sweat never dried up and his speech began to slur severely. When he lost consciousness, Mrs. Nawaz called an emergency crew, who rushed him to a nearby hospital.

When he arrived at the hospital, doctors said that the general appeared to have suffered cardiac arrest. Emergency measures were taken to get his heart beating at a normal rhythm again, but all failed. At 3:55 P.M., seven hours after he had been admitted to the hospital, General Nawaz was declared dead. If the hospital records were accurate, there could be no criticism of the work done by the emergency room doctors. They did everything possible to save his life.

As is the Muslim custom, the Nawaz family buried the general exactly twenty-four hours after he died without an autopsy and without embalming him. His body was wrapped in a white burial shroud and placed in a coffin. As his family looked on, four of his fellow military leaders lowered his casket to its final resting place.

At the airport in Islamabad, I was met by members of the Nawaz family and a handful of government and law enforcement officials. After formal greetings, I was taken to a nearby hotel to get some much-needed rest.

Early the next morning, I and the other forensic pathologists met with Dr. Muhammad Shoaib Suddle, deputy inspector general of police in Pakistan. For two hours, he briefed us on the case. From our conversations, I felt he was quite competent and totally honest; he was objective and open to the possibility that General Nawaz had indeed been the victim of foul play. Furthermore, Dr. Suddle assured us that he planned to take the appropriate steps under his country's laws should we find that he had been murdered.

In the late morning, we were ushered to a military helicopter and flown about one hundred miles to the Nawaz family burial plot near Jhelum, which is about thirty miles from the border of India. Local police, with the assistance of army officials, sealed off the entire area surrounding the burial site, which was a few miles outside of Chakri Rajgan, the general's ancestral village. The area appeared to be farmland, but it was badly in need of irrigation. Huge mountains could be seen off in the distance. Military guards carrying small machine guns and wearing khaki pants, black pullover shirts, and black berets cordoned off the area.

At the grave site, Drs. Clark and Lambert and I were joined by at least a half-dozen other local physicians and medical school professors interested in watching us work. Because of the lack of proper educational facilities, Pakistan is many years behind countries such as the United States, Great Britain, and France in developing sophisticated medical-legal investigative agencies. As novel as it was for the three of us to be in Pakistan for this autopsy, it must have been just as exciting for the local doctors to stand by, watch, and learn.

From the start, we were given lists of questions by both the Pakistani law enforcement authorities and the Nawaz family. Our mission was to answer those inquiries with hard scientific evidence. The questions included the following:

- Did the death of the late general occur due to poisoning or any other unnatural causes?
- If yes, what type of poison was detected?
- When did he ingest the first dose?
- Was the poison administered in a single dose or in multiple doses?
- How was the poison administered? Orally, through skin absorption, through injections, or by inhalation?
- If he was not poisoned, what was the cause of his death?

As the temperature climbed to above one hundred degrees Fahrenheit, we donned our medical attire and prepared to go to work. Dozens of people, including several high-ranking government officials, watched as workers shoveled away the dry, sandy soil that covered General Nawaz's grave. A tent was erected over the grave site to protect workers from the direct sunlight, which added to the intense heat. There were four other graves next to the general's that were designated for other members of his family. Each of these had a granite marker; however, there was no marker for the general's grave.

Approximately three feet down in the ground, the workers uncovered the concrete slabs that made up the roof of the brick-lined vault that housed the wooden coffin. Because it rains so little in this area of Pakistan, the soil all around the tomb was completely dry. That was good news. The damper the soil, the faster the bodies buried therein will decompose. I reached down and scooped up some of the soil from on top and beside the coffin and placed it in a plastic bag for later testing. Some soil may contain arsenic and could thereby contaminate the body, causing erroneous results in subsequent toxicology tests.

The coffin was slowly lifted from the hole in the ground and placed on a makeshift platform nearby. Some of the wooden coffin had eroded and been eaten away by termites. As the workers lifted the top of the coffin, I noticed a thick white fungus lining the inside of the plywood. The general's body was nude, but wrapped in the white shroud, which also was covered by the white fungus.

The shroud was lifted and General Nawaz's partially decomposed body was exposed. His face was blackened and dehydrated. But because the soil was so dry, the body was in much better condition than I had anticipated.

Officials and family members at the scene confirmed that this was the body of General Nawaz. He measured five feet nine inches in height and appeared to be of average build. There was no gray in his hair and his teeth were in very good condition. As I scanned his face, head, torso, and hands, I noticed no obvious scars or other signs of trauma.

The skin was mostly intact, though it had turned brown and dry. His hair and fingernails detached easily from the body, and samples were taken for further laboratory studies, since trace amounts of arsenic and other poisons will usually show up in these tissues within a few days of ingesting the substance.

Using a scalpel, we made an incision from the neck to the pubis so we could examine the internal organs. All of the major organs—the heart, lungs, liver, spleen, pancreas, and kidneys—were clearly identifiable. In order to minimize disfigurement, the family had asked that we make no cuts to the general's head or face unless we deemed it absolutely necessary to examine the brain. Though I considered it to be a rather illogical request—since the body was being exhumed to find out as much as we could to determine the cause of death—we honored the family's wishes.

As we examined the general's chest area, we noted that five of his ribs were fractured on the front of the body. This most likely had occurred when the emergency room doctors tried to resuscitate him. Step by step, we examined every inch of his body internally and externally. There was no evidence of blunt-force trauma or needle injections. I also cut small samples from all of his organs and other tissues to be tested by Dr. Rieders for arsenic and other poisons. Dr. Clark and Dr. Lambert also took similar tissue specimens home with them to be tested.

As we dissected the heart, I noticed that one of the main coronary arteries leading from the aorta had severe narrowing. As we grow older, calcium and fat plaques build up on the inner lining of the coronary arteries, thereby impeding the flow of blood that supplies oxygen to the heart muscle. There are several causes for this plaque buildup. The most important factor is genetics. This was a good possibility. I had been told that the general's family had a history of heart problems. A second risk factor could be a lack of exercise and a sedentary lifestyle. However, family and friends of the general said he worked out almost daily. The third possibility was that General Nawaz simply ate too many rich and fatty foods. However, his religious and cultural background argued strongly against that. I also noticed an excess of fluid in both the chest cavity and the abdomen. When a heart begins to fail, the blood is not pumped out effectively and fluid will back up and collect in organs and body cavities.

Finally, we looked inside the stomach. If the general had been poisoned with a corrosive substance, I hoped the lining of the stomach might provide us with the evidence. However, we could see no inflammation of the stomach lining or anything abnormal within the stomach wall.

After getting additional samples from the general's skin, hair, muscle, and fat, we sewed the body up and stepped back for the workers to return it to the tomb. General Nawaz's body was placed into a new casket and his body was lowered into the concrete vault.

I must admit I was somewhat perplexed. After the initial findings of arsenic by the toxicology laboratory, I had expected to find even more evidence within the body. But it just wasn't there. As we reviewed our preliminary gross findings following the autopsy, we agreed that we had uncovered little of significance that day. However, the ultimate answer would have to await the final toxicology results of the various samples we had taken, as well as the microscopic examination of the body organs and tissues.

About two weeks after I returned to Pittsburgh, Dr. Rieders called me with the results. This time he had found nothing unusual. There were small, insignificant traces of arsenic, but nothing compared to the extremely high amounts previously found in the hair taken from the general's personal hairbrush.

Through telephone conversations and detailed letters about our individual findings, Dr. Clark, Dr. Lambert, and I agreed that there was no evidence of arsenic poisoning or any other toxic substances. We came to the same conclusion: General Nawaz's death was the result of natural causes—specifically, coronary artery insufficiency due to arteriosclerotic cardiovascular disease.

I mailed Shuja Nawaz and law enforcement officials in Pakistan a letter detailing my findings and conclusions, and highlighted the evidence supporting these opinions, as did the other two forensic pathologists.

"The sample findings from the hairbrush were an aberration," I explained. "The high arsenic levels found on those hair samples cannot be explained. However, the results of our own toxicology tests of the samples I personally retrieved from your brother's body clearly show there are no significant amounts of arsenic or any other poisons . . . in General Nawaz's body."

I must say that it would have been extremely dramatic for me to have announced that I had discovered General Nawaz had been the victim of foul play. The same is true for the second case I investigated in Taiwan. If I had not strictly followed my findings and had allowed myself to be used to support the position of those who advocated that these prominent men had been murdered, I would have received a lot more press attention.

There are some people, especially prosecutors, police, and civil-suit defense attorneys, who say that the testimony and findings of expert witnesses are for sale to the highest bidder.

They believe that consultants are willing to take the witness stand and say anything as long as they are being paid to say it. Probably every forensic science expert has been accused of tailoring his or her findings to support the theory that was being advanced by the lawyer who had retained that expert. To these mean-spirited, ill-founded accusations, I have a simple response:

Hogwash.

Certainly, there are a few forensic pathologists and other physicians who are less than credible, who are willing to sell their souls for the almighty dollar, who are willing to be suborned and commit perjury. But if you are one of those professional prostitutes, you will be found out and exposed sooner or later. These "experts" develop a bad reputation quickly, and good lawyers are able to tear them apart on the witness stand on cross-examination. Lawyers who do their homework research the background of every expert witness to make sure his or her testimony in the case at hand is consistent with testimony he or she has given in previous cases involving the same or similar issues. If it is not, that witness will be discredited in depositions or in open court.

In other words, the most valuable commodity in the professional world of forensic science is a reputation for honesty and integrity, as well as competence. Without these, all the fame and money in the world would be meaningless.

ELEVEN

THE HOUSEMAID'S TALE

Lights flashing and sirens blaring, police cars sped to the 147 block of Gangsa Road. Arriving at the flat, the Singaporean authorities found Wong Sing Keong and his wife grasping the limp body of their four-year-old son. Only a few feet away lay the Chinese couple's Filipino maid, an elastic cord wrapped around her neck. Both were dead—she apparently by strangulation, he by drowning in a bucket of water.

In an interview with the police, the Wongs stated that they had come home from a long day at work expecting to be greeted at the front door by their two children. As soon as they stepped inside, however, they knew that something was wrong: the couple could hear the cries of their twenty-two-month-old daughter, whom they soon discovered had been locked inside the bedroom of their maid, Della Maga. Using brute strength, Mr. Wong forced his way in and found his daughter safe but shaken. As he held her in his arms and wiped the tears from her eyes, Mr. Wong heard a scream from elsewhere in the house. In the bathroom, he found his hysterical wife standing over Nicholas, their son. His head was completely inside an overturned bucket of water, his face expressionless, and his body cold and empty of life.

Looking to their right, the Wongs spotted Maga stretched out on the floor on her back. Her head was underneath the sink and both of her knees were slightly flexed. Some type of rope or string was around her throat. Her brown eyes were open, as was her mouth. The look on her face was that of absolute horror. It was as if she knew she was about to die, but fought it with every muscle in her small body.

For much of the evening, detectives questioned the Wongs. Who could have done this? Was anyone mad at Maga? Had she ever been in trouble before? Had they been mad at her for any reason?

The Wongs denied knowing anything about the tragedy and gave police full liberty to search their house for evidence. In Maga's room, they found a diary. Mostly concerned with returning home and seeing her family again, it contained no hint of troubles or problems. But on the page bearing notes from that particular day—May 4, 1991—there was a name and address: "Flor Contemplacion, Blk 633, Veerasamay Rd, #05-122, S'pore." Detectives also found photographs of Maga and Contemplacion together. It appeared as if the two were friends. This lead, Singaporean police would later claim, allowed them to solve the case.

Investigators quickly found Contemplacion at the listed address, which was the home of her employer's parents. She, too, was a Filipino maid working in Singapore to make money to send back to her family in Manila. A search of Contemplacion's room turned up some key evidence: jewelry and other valuables belonging to Maga were hidden under Contemplacion's bed.

At the police station, Contemplacion made a full confession. She admitted to strangling Maga and drowning the boy. She made no excuses for her actions, saying only that she didn't know why she had done it. But the authorities developed their own motive, however unlikely. They claimed that when Contemplacion found out Maga was returning to Manila, she asked her new friend to take back several items to her family. For some unknown reason, Maga had refused. As a result, authorities said, Contemplacion became enraged and strangled Maga. Realizing that four-year-old Nicholas was a potential witness, she killed him too.

On May 5, the day after the bodies were found, Contemplation was officially charged with murder. Prosecutors said they planned to seek the death penalty.

Seven months later, on December 24, Contemplacion appeared for the first time in court. Authorities presented all of their evidence to a magistrate, including her confession. After reviewing the government's case, the magistrate agreed there was enough evidence to put Contemplacion on trial for two counts of murder.

In January 1993, Justice T. S. Sinnathuray presided over Contemplacion's week-long trial. The main evidence against her were the four statements she had made to police in which she admitted her guilt. Equally damning was the testimony of Dr. Wee Keng Poh, the forensic pathologist at Singapore's Institute of Science and Forensic Medicine who had performed the autopsies on Maga and the boy. Dr. Wee told the judge that Maga died after someone placed an elastic cord around her neck and applied force for more than five minutes. Nicholas, he said, died after having his face immersed in water for about five minutes. During the trial, Contemplacion declined to testify on her own behalf.

In the end, it came as no surprise that Contemplacion was found guilty and sentenced to die.

In January 1994, lawyers representing Contemplacion appealed her conviction to Singapore's Court of Appeals. Her newly appointed attorneys claimed that their client was suffering from "diminished responsibility" when she committed the crimes. They even produced an affidavit from Dr. Terence Burke, a psychologist, stating that Contemplacion was suffering from "an abnormality of the mind" on the day she killed the two. (Later, I would find evidence to support this theory.) However, an expert for the government testified that the defendant was not mentally ill, merely suffering from a mild migraine.

In the end, a three-judge panel upheld Contemplacion's conviction, and her execution was set for March 17, 1995. What happened thereafter is truly bizarre.

Seldom does a murder case make headlines worldwide. Maybe the slaying of a world leader or a famous musician.

Or if a renowned athlete is the suspect, then the case might receive some attention. But not everyday homicides and certainly not that of a poor Filipino maid. After all, according to the World Health Organization, someone is murdered every twenty seconds.

But for reasons beyond my comprehension, the Flor Contemplacion case became an international incident. Singapore and the Philippines—two countries with natural economic, historical, and social ties—nearly became enemies overnight because of this case. And in both countries, the death of Della Maga and the sentencing of Flor Contemplacion became the dominant political issue, bigger than unemployment, inflation, or any social controversies.

In 1995, the Filipinos were in the midst of a national election. There was widespread frustration about the economy, and there was even more uneasiness over how Filipinos were being treated in other countries. Those seeking to gain power and oust the existing leadership used the Contemplacion case as a rallying point, blaming President Fidel Ramos and his staff and supporters for not doing a better job of protecting the rights and interests of Filipinos abroad. Why had the government not done more to defend Contemplacion? they asked. Feeling these political pressures, President Ramos fired his longtime and trusted ally, Foreign Affairs Secretary Roberto R. Romulo. For all practical purposes, Ramos shut down communications and relations between the Philippines and Singapore. It was at this point that the feud began gaining worldwide attention.

Outside of the obvious political ramifications, there was yet another reason many people were upset about this case: they believed Singapore may have executed an innocent woman and that the government of Singapore had made this poor woman a scapegoat in the two murders. Interestingly, the people holding this belief were not some ultra-left-wing wackos or wild-eyed conspiracy theorists. They were medical doctors, lawyers, and businessmen and -women who were decrying Singapore's criminal justice system.

A key question early on was "Why?"—Why would Contemplacion have committed this horrible act? To be sure, the alleged motivation that she was mad at Maga for not taking something back to Contemplacion's family in Manila seemed weak. But it is not unbelievable. In the tens of thousands of murder investigations with which I have been associated, I have never failed to be surprised at the reasons people kill other people. I have learned that most homicides occur over matters that 99.99 percent of society would consider silly or ridiculous.

Just six days before the scheduled execution, President Ramos asked Singapore president Ong Teng Cheong to issue a stay, claiming that his government had new evidence that might exonerate Contemplacion. The new evidence was a sworn statement from another Filipino maid who claimed to have overheard Wong Sing Keong, Nicholas's father, admitting that he killed Maga after discovering that she had negligently allowed his son to drown. On March 13, this statement was faxed to President Ong, who turned it over to the police for immediate investigation. The next day, however, investigators informed President Ong that the maid's statement had no merit. With that, the Singaporean leader told President Ramos that he was unable to grant the stay of execution, causing widespread protests in the Philippines and political consternation for Ramos.

At this point, I could not understand why President Ong had not simply agreed to delay the execution for three to six months, until after the Filipino elections were over. The Singaporeans could have publicly said that they were going to take a little more time to investigate the concerns of their Filipino neighbors and friends without having to admit that there were any problems with the case. Such a gesture, I believe, would have done a great deal to calm the emotions of the people of the Philippines and would possibly have laid to rest most of the political friction between the two countries. But that is not how things work in Singapore. It is a country known worldwide for its strict and swift enforcement of its criminal laws.

On March 17, 1995, Flor Contemplacion was hanged. She was forty years old.

As the controversy festered, the Filipino government appointed a panel of its own experts to examine the case.

Political insiders say that Ramos hoped the panel would come to a nebulous conclusion and that the entire affair would be dropped and forgotten. Such was not the case. Instead, when officials exhumed Maga's body on March 28, 1995, pathologists from the Philippines National Bureau of Investigation (NBI) claimed to have noticed several abnormalities not mentioned in the autopsy performed by Dr. Wee. According to their initial report, there was evidence of skull injuries, fractured ribs, and fractured scapulae, or shoulder blades.

The Filipino commission concluded that there was significant evidence pointing toward Contemplacion's innocence and made a simple recommendation: ask Singapore to join them in hiring three independent forensic experts from other countries to examine the physical evidence. Singapore officials immediately agreed to the offer.

It was during the first week of April that I received a telephone call from Dr. Chao Tzee Cheng, an old friend and an internationally respected forensic pathologist who serves as director of the Institute of Science and Forensic Medicine in Singapore.

"We have found ourselves in a complicated situation," Dr. Chao told me. "We need your help."

Dr. Chao said he needed the names of leading forensic experts who would be willing to travel on short notice to Manila to make an independent examination of Maga's remains and other physical evidence. Later that day, I faxed to him a list of several names and telephone numbers of well-respected forensic scientists in the United States, Great Britain, and Japan.

On April 11, I received an overnight letter from Dr. Chao. Fie had made his choice of three experts, and I was on his list. "Dear Cyril," he wrote,

> Thanks for your help. You are requested to resolve the controversy between the autopsy reports of Singapore and Philippines.
> First of all, I will give you the background of the case. The official version of the killing of Della Maga is contained

in the confession to the High Court which has never been retracted or refuted in court.

The alleged version told to the [Filipino] Commission of Inquiry is that the boy had an epileptic fit and drowned in the pail of water. The boy's father came home, saw this, flew into a rage, beat up Della Maga severely and savagely with heavy karate blows or iron pipe rendering her unconscious and finally strangled her in the presence of Flor Contemplacion. He then called police and pointed out to police that Flor Contemplacion was the killer. The boy did not have a history of fits.

At the autopsy when we had a full body, Dr. Wee found only strangulation marks on her neck and signs of asphyxia. There were very little other external injuries, and none of them could be attributed to severe or savage beating by heavy karate blows or iron pipe.

The NBI examined the remains of Della Maga almost four years later when there were only bone remains. In their report they stated that they found: blood clots in the cranial cavity, the right occipital area over the bridge of the nose; severe injuries and clotting in the scapular areas [upper back]; and fractures of four right ribs and one left rib. Later in the oral testimony, it was alleged that multiple fractures of the skull, shoulder and rib cage were present and these were due to severe and savage beating by a man, not a woman.

Therefore it is necessary for you to determine from all the available evidence:

(1) whether Della Maga died of asphyxia due to strangulation.

(2) whether there was evidence of severe and savage beating of Della Maga before her death.

(3) whether the injuries could not have been inflicted by Contemplacion or a woman of her build.

(4) whether fractures and blood clots were antemortem or postmortem.

(5) whether the examination of the remains and

description in the NBI report support the theory that she was beaten up severely and savagely.

Yours sincerely,
Chao Tzee Cheng

Because of various professional commitments, I had not planned on becoming involved in this case. However, it was certainly among the most intriguing cases I had encountered, and I felt honored that Dr. Chao was personally requesting my assistance. I was pleased to learn that the two others who would be joining me in this adventure were both men for whom I have great respect—Dr. Michael Baden and Dr. William Maples.

Michael, who is described in vivid detail in the first chapter of this book, enjoys a reputation as one of the world's preeminent forensic scientists. Likewise, Dr. Maples' reputation as a professional is widely trumpeted. A forensic pathologist and professor at the University of Florida, Dr. Maples played a key role in identifying the skeletal remains of Czar Nicholas and his family in Russia in 1994.

Because officials in Singapore and the Philippines were anxious to get this incident behind them, each country requested that we fly there as soon as possible. Together, we agreed that April 18 would be the best date.

Just a day before our scheduled trip, an interesting development occurred. The Filipino government had decided against being a co-sponsor of our trip. Filipino officials still agreed to welcome us and show us their entire case and the evidence proving that Contemplacion was innocent, but they no longer wanted it to be a joint venture with Singapore. I'm still not sure why the Philippines did this. Undaunted, officials in Singapore said they nevertheless wanted us to come and make an official determination.

Dr. Baden, Dr. Maples, and I rendezvoused at the Singapore Airlines lounge at New York's JFK Airport at 9:45 P.M. on Monday, April 17. From there, it was a seven-hour flight across the Atlantic Ocean to Frankfurt, Germany. After a ninety-minute layover, we reboarded the plane for another eleven hours. With so much time available, I decided to review once more the materials Dr. Chao had mailed to me. The first document I read was the official autopsy report prepared by Dr. Wee. It was simple and to the point:

Name of Deceased: Della M. Maga
Age: 34
Sex: Female
Race: Filipino
Date of Death: May 4, 1991
Time of Death: 2:03 P.M.
Cause of Death: Asphyxia due to strangulation

Dr. Wee's autopsy and examination seemed thorough and complete. Nothing I read caused me any alarm or concern or, for that matter, raised any questions. He had documented every scratch and bruise.

There are, of course, two sides to every story, so I made sure to keep an open mind to any evidence that may have been overlooked or misinterpreted by the Singapore investigators. I reminded myself that the Filipino officials were adamant about Contemplacion's innocence. I was waiting for the other shoe to drop at any moment and anticipating the possibility of some startling revelation to surface that would dramatically change the entire complexion of this case.

Included in the materials I had been sent was Contemplacion's statement to police. In it she mapped out her activities on that day, which appeared to have included the killing of Maga. Reading it, I came to realize why Singaporean officials were so sure of her guilt; it was as damning a confession as confessions can be:

I left my employer's house at 9:30 A.M. to go to my friend's house at Gangsa Road to bring the package I will send to my family. I reached her place at 9:50 A.M. I was met by the small boy Nicholas who upon seeing me called Della. Della let me into the house. She led me into the kitchen because she was doing something. We exchanged stories about our families and her going back.

I even told her that I cannot send the money I intended to send my family because I haven't received the cash advance I had requested from my employer. We then moved into another room which has a very big dining table. I even saw on top of the table things, which according to her she will fix into her shoulder bag, like a camera, watches, makeup set and combs. On the table were also two passports and an air ticket.

We then went back to the kitchen because Della wanted to do something. I then felt like throwing up and very heavy. I was also perspiring with cold sweat. After a few minutes, I finally vomited inside the bathroom. Only saliva came out, no solid foods. I could feel the taste of the pills which I swallowed at my employer's house.

When I came out of the bathroom, I saw her with the bag standing before the kitchen sink. She appeared so small and tiny. I then noticed a rubber string beside the washing machine. I picked it up and I felt I wanted to strangle her like I was so angry and trembling with anger. I felt so strong at that moment.

I wrapped the string around her neck and pulled it as tight as I can. She did not struggle. There was no word from her. I pulled her towards the toilet door.

When I saw the boy inside the bathroom playing with water, I felt the same thing when I saw Della earlier. He looked so small and tiny. So I just pushed him into the pail of water. I held him by the hand and the pail even fell sideways with him.

After that, I walked out and took all the things from the table and placed all the things in a plastic bag. I walked out of the house and closed the door behind me.

A few items in this document immediately leaped out at me. First, there was the matter of Contemplacion having taken some kind of pills. As I later learned, she was referring to medication she took for severe migraine headaches. Still, the fact that a suspect in a highly controversial murder case was under medication for a debilitating neurological disorder was something I thought should have been looked into further. The second puzzle was Contemplacion's statement that the pail in which she had drowned the boy had fallen sideways during his struggle. On its face, this statement seemed to beg the question of how he could have drowned. But then, of course, the bucket could have tipped over after the fact. Also never explained was Contemplacion's observation that there were two passports on Maga's table. If one was Maga's, to whom did the other one belong? Or did they both belong to her employers? This was a question that went unanswered.

Dr. Chao also had sent me a few photographs taken during the autopsy, as well as several newspaper articles written about the controversy. Only then did I realize how serious this affair was. The two countries were close to completely severing diplomatic ties. The politicians, newspapers, and some extreme nationalist groups in the Philippines were stirring up strong emotions in their country.

Upon arriving in Singapore, the three of us were met by Singapore officials, including Dr. Wee and Dr. Chao, as well as a Philippine official who said she would be happy to answer any questions we might have. Overall, the session was quite cordial. After showering, shaving, and changing clothes, we all boarded yet another jet for a three-hour flight to Manila, where we arrived a little after 1 P.M.

As we exited the Manila airport, we were greeted by a huge throng of reporters. Some shouted questions, but most just wanted photographs of us arriving. Because none of us knew anything yet, none of us made any statements. Instead, we were quickly whisked away in three cars, escorted by eight police officers on motorcycles. Traffic was incredibly heavy, and we occasionally had to drive on sidewalks or even the other side of the road to circumvent it.

About forty-five minutes later, we arrived at St. Luke's Hospital, where Filipino officials, physicians, pathologists, and NBI investigators were awaiting our arrival. An elaborate buffet of vegetables and meats had been prepared for us, but because we had eaten on the flight into Manila, the three of us settled for soft drinks. For the first few minutes, we talked informally. The atmosphere was very cordial and relaxed, and no hostilities seemed to be present. Several of the group had even brought copies of my previous book, *Cause of Death,* and Dr. Baden's book, *Confessions of a Medical Examiner,* which they asked us to autograph.

When it came time to get down to business, we seated ourselves around a U-shaped table and freely discussed the evidence. The Filipino officials readily gave us their scenario of what they believed had happened. It was as Dr. Chao and the newspaper articles reported: they believed Contemplacion was framed for the two deaths by the Wongs and that the Singapore government was helping to cover up the entire incident.

Before us on the table were official reports from both sides and more photographs and X rays taken of Della Maga before and during the autopsy, as well as after the exhumation. We also watched a complete videotape of the NBI's exhumation. The remains were basically skeletonized, with only a small amount of soft tissue remaining and in an advanced stage of decomposition. To my surprise, even though the Philippines government had done an exhumation of Maga's body only days earlier, they had reburied most of her remains.

"Why didn't you keep the body so that we could examine it?" I inquired.

The Filipino officials explained that Maga's family had strict religious beliefs and wanted the body immediately reburied. They had, however, kept out a few bones that they believed proved their case.

Brought out and laid before us were Maga's skull, shoulder blades, and five ribs. One by one, we each examined the bones. They had been chemically cleaned and treated by the NBI officials who conducted the exhumation. As I took the skull in my hands, I searched for the fractures that Filipino officials had initially claimed to have found. There were none. Even the NBI pathologists sitting in the room with us admitted as much. But the Filipinos seemed undeterred. They wanted to know our opinion of the bloodstains they had found on

Maga's head in their videotaped examination of the body after the exhumation. They believed that the blood clots were evidence of hemorrhaging from antemortem injury—that is to say, that the trauma occurred while she was still alive.

The Singaporeans took the position that the bloodstains were small and played no role in causing Maga's death. The bloodstains, Dr. Wee opined, could have occurred when Maga's head struck the floor after strangulation, or they could have developed postmortem and simply represented an artefactual suggestion of injury.

As we turned our focus to the shoulder blades, NBI pathologists again quickly backed away from earlier claims that there was evidence of fractures. Indeed, there were no fractures to be seen. But the Filipino officials did contend that they had discovered blood clots on both shoulder blades that could only have been caused by trauma while Maga was alive.

By contrast, Dr. Wee said that if there had been a blood clot from trauma, it would have appeared as a bruise on Maga's skin. However, he said he had seen no bruise during his examination of the body. With that in mind, I thumbed through the autopsy photographs that the Singapore authorities had provided. A close-up of Maga's back and shoulders confirmed Dr. Wee's contentions: there was no bruise.

Finally, we examined the ribs, which were identified by the Filipino doctors as the fifth, sixth, seventh, and eighth ribs on the right side and the eighth rib on the left side. As the NBI experts had claimed, there were indeed small areas of irregular roughening in these ribs, as well as evidence of blood clots which could have been caused by trauma. Responding to this allegation, Dr. Wee argued that he had found no evidence of rib fractures when he performed the autopsy. His position was that if there had been a rib fracture, it would have revealed itself through bruises on Maga's body. Dr. Wee said he had seen no such bruises.

Once again, we went to the photographs. Again, there were no visible bruises to be seen—a fact that the experts from the Philippines did not dispute. At this point, Dr. Baden, Dr. Maples, and I made another quick determination: we believed that the Filipino doctors were confused as to which ribs we were looking at. They were improperly numbered. From the curvature and width of the ribs, we could tell that they were out of order. At this point, however, this discovery was of no great consequence.

In arguing their case, the Filipino pathologists insisted that the skeletal remains showed convincing evidence of bloodstains that were most likely caused by antemortem trauma. These injuries, they contended, were so severe and so savage that they could not have been caused by Flor Contemplacion; only a man, or possibly a woman skilled in the martial arts, could have inflicted such trauma. In addition, they believed that the injuries to Maga's skull, shoulder blades, and ribs indicated that she had been attacked with some kind of iron pipe. Since Contemplacion never mentioned this in her confession, it lent credence to the theory that her confession was either fabricated or coerced, they said.

It soon became evident that simply showing that Singapore officials had done an inadequate autopsy was not enough. The Philippine authorities needed to find a way to physically exculpate Contemplacion. However, they could not argue that the two did not know each other or that Contemplacion had not been in Maga's home. Indeed, there was direct evidence to the contrary. So, the Filipinos used Maga's remains to make the quantum leap that not only had they discovered these additional injuries, but these injuries were of such a severe and extensive nature that they connoted a ferocious and brutal beating of Maga.

As our four-hour meeting came to a close, the two sides were still locked in disagreement as to the cause and extent of the bloodstains and fractures. We three American experts agreed to discuss our thoughts with one another and then issue a complete report. It was our mission to weed out truth from fiction and make an independent determination of the physical evidence.

That night, Singaporean officials had reserved rooms for us at a very nice hotel in Manila. For security reasons, however, they encouraged us to stay at the Singapore embassy. We readily agreed.

The next morning, we awoke to new allegations in the newspapers charging conspiracy and cover-up by the Singapore officials. The new charges were not from the NBI pathologists but from Professor Jerome Bailen, a physical anthropologist with no expertise in forensic sciences. Bailen had been present during our meeting at St. Luke's Hospital but had remained relatively silent. These allegations in the newspaper basically called Dr. Wee and other Singaporean authorities liars.

Professor Bailen said that after re-examining the photographs of Maga taken at the house where she died and comparing them with photographs taken at the autopsy, he determined that the ligature was tighter at the time of the autopsy than it had been at the crime scene. Bailen's obvious implication was that Dr. Wee or some other Singaporean official had deliberately tightened the ligature around Maga's neck to make it more readily apparent that she had died as a result of strangulation.

Professor Bailen's second explosive claim was that Maga's attacker had to have been left-handed. Since Contemplacion was right-handed, the suggestion was that it had to have been someone else. Bailen came to this conclusion based on the fact that photographs showed the cord around Maga's neck to have been wound in a counterclockwise fashion and knotted at the left side of the nape of her neck.

Finally, there was a third allegation made by Bailen that directly questioned our credibility. He told the newspapers that Philippine officials had indicated to us that they had five military helicopters fueled and ready to take us to Maga's burial site if we wished to personally examine the rest of her skeletal remains, but that we, the three independent American forensic scientists, had turned down their offer.

Upon reading this, Dr. Baden, Dr. Maples, and I agreed that no such offer had been made to us at any time. We later discovered that a videotape of the entire meeting also proved that no such offer was tendered. To me, this misrepresentation seriously compromised Bailen's credibility and demonstrated that he was not a reliable scientist searching for the truth.

That day, as we boarded a flight for the return home, I began to re-examine portions of the case. Clearly, the bulk of the evidence against Contemplacion was her own confession. She had supposedly talked to police four times, and each time she told them basically the same story. Indeed, it would have been very easy for Singaporean authorities to fabricate a confession.

However, there are many holes in a coercion or fabrication theory. First and foremost, when testifying in open court, Contemplacion never once indicated that she had been framed or that the police had made up her confession. From the beginning, she had been represented by competent legal counsel who would have instructed her to make such an allegation if it were the truth. Furthermore, Contemplacion was visited more than sixty-eight times in her jail cell by a nun and not once did Contemplacion ever mention having been forced to confess. I also found it interesting that talk of a conspiracy in the Contemplacion case did not surface until just a few weeks before she was executed.

There were, of course, Professor Bailen's comments to contend with. But they were completely without merit. What he did not tell us was how he determined the relative positions of Maga and her assailant at the time of strangulation. Was the attacker in front of or behind her? Was Maga standing, stooping, or sitting? Was Contemplacion incapable of using her left arm and hand for any kind of physical endeavor whatsoever?

And what about the evidence of trauma? The more I re-examined the photographs and the autopsy report, the more I leaned toward a position of "So what?" Even if the allegations of rib fractures and blood clots caused by trauma on the shoulder blades and skull were correct, they were meaningless. First, the staining on the skull was on the outside, and a hemorrhage on the scalp is not going to kill anybody. Secondly, if the ribs were fractured, the worst that would have happened is that Maga would have experienced severe pain. There were no vital organs for them to lacerate because they were not displaced to the slightest degree, merely roughened on the edges. Certainly, they could not have caused or even contributed to her death.

The day after I returned to Pittsburgh, I was eating my customary bagel for breakfast when an article in the *New York Times* caught my attention. It was a column by William Safire entitled "With the Hanging of Flor." Even though I am a longtime admirer of Mr. Safire, I believed this particular column was unfair and imbalanced. Furthermore, I thought he had gotten several of the facts wrong. Feeling that we should respond, Dr. Baden and I called Safire's office and left messages stating that he needed more information.

The next day, I was in my office at St. Francis Central Hospital when my secretary informed me that William Safire was on the line. I picked up the phone and we proceeded to talk for about fifteen minutes. I told him he is one of my heroes, mainly because of his strong support of Israel. We discussed my findings and summary of the Maga case and he seemed to genuinely appreciate the information I had passed on to him. Safire, I later learned, has a general dislike or distrust of the Singaporean government that dates back to that country's alleged mistreatment of journalists and other possible human rights violations.

Less than a week after our return to the United States, Dr. Baden, Dr. Maples, and I drafted a final report containing all of our findings and conclusions and sent it to the appropriate authorities in the governments of Singapore and the Philippines. The seven-page report, which discussed all of the physical evidence we had examined, arrived at the following conclusions:

1. Della M. Maga died as a result of asphyxiation due to ligature strangulation.
2. There were no fractures of Maga's skull.
3. There were no fractures of either scapula [shoulder blade].
4. Apparent damage to the inferior portion of the right scapula represented a postmortem artefact.

5. There were no adherent blood clots or residual blood clots of any kind noted on any of the bones. Furthermore, no blood clots were collected from any of the other remains of Maga's body at the time of the exhumation.
6. There was no evidence in the available skeletal portion of Maga that any injury was present in those bones at the time of death. All damage appeared to be postmortem in nature.

Even after our independent examination of the evidence, the Filipinos were not satisfied. They asked to have three more American forensic pathology experts review their findings. In July 1995, that was done. To no one's surprise, this second panel confirmed each and every finding we had made.

Looking back at this case, I have come to several realizations. First, this was a controversy that could have been completely avoided with a little diplomacy, patience, and sensible thinking. Even if Singaporean officials were absolutely assured of Contemplacion's guilt and wanted to put her to death, they should have recognized the turmoil the case was causing in the Philippines. At the very least, officials in Singapore could have delayed the execution under the pretense of re-examining the claims made by the NBI. A mere three- to six-month stay of execution would have allowed the elections in the Philippines to pass, as well as the intense emotionalism that this case engendered.

However, the bottom line is that the officials in Singapore were right and their counterparts in the Philippines were wrong. Indeed, in August, Singapore's prime minister bestowed upon Dr. Chao the Meritorious Service Award, one of the highest awards offered in that country. I can't imagine that any such awards will be awarded to any of the Filipino doctors. My main question regarding the forensic scientists there is how they could have been so misled. Was their adamant stance created and nurtured by politics, or had they merely misinterpreted the evidence?

Most probably, it was a little of both.

TWELVE

THE KILLER BUGS

A s a forensic pathologist testifying in court, I have seen hundreds of killers. Some of these killers, it turns out, have taken human lives—sometimes those of relatives, lovers, or friends—either accidentally or in a moment of rage. Other killers are quite simply insane or mentally ill, and scarcely know what they've done. And still others can be called evil: they have no conscience or respect for human life whatsoever. From Charles Manson to Jeffrey Dahmer, we have had our share of serial murderers in this country. However, very few, if any of us, have found ourselves living in fear that some stranger might sneak into our homes and end our lives.

But in 1976, such fear existed in every community in our country. A killer was on the loose—uninhibited, uncaring, and unidentified. In fact, this killer created a panic that reached from the average citizen to President Gerald Ford and dominated the thought processes of federal government agencies and officials. The reaction to this killer is unparalleled in American history.

However, there was a basic flaw in this murder mystery. Quite simply, the killer that authorities spent hundreds of millions of dollars to find, catch, and prevent from killing again did not exist. In other words, it was a fantasy murderer.

That's not to say that innocent people were not killed or harmed; indeed, dozens died and as many as 150 more had to be hospitalized. The government just had the wrong suspect. And while authorities focused on this one killer, the real offender was free, receiving no attention, scrutiny, or deterrence. In fact, this attacker is still out there today, preying mainly on the elderly and the ill.

The mystery begins in January 1976. Like all murder dramas, the scene opens with a victim, in this case a U.S. Army private at Fort Dix, New Jersey, reporting at sick call. After a brief examination, the base physician, Colonel Joseph Bartley, diagnosed the soldier's illness as an upper respiratory infection. Nothing serious. Nothing that forty-eight hours of rest wouldn't cure.

Ignoring the doctor's orders, the private decided to participate in a late-night march. About halfway through the procedure, however, he collapsed. He stopped breathing. His heart stopped pounding. The sergeant immediately performed mouth-to-mouth resuscitation, bringing him back to life. The private was rushed to the infirmary, but a few days later he was dead.

Over the next few hours, dozens more soldiers reported at sick call with upper respiratory infections. Some sort of flu was immediately suspected. Alarmed, Dr. Bartley called the New Jersey Public Health Lab, which ordered throat swabs from each of the sick men. The specimens tested at the lab produced a typical flu virus, but also a separate virus that the New Jersey scientists had never seen before and were unable to identify. The specimens were promptly shipped to the Centers for Disease Control (CDC) in Atlanta, which is the federal government's bureau for identifying and managing epidemics.

Within days, the virus was identified; scientists in Atlanta believed they had seen it before. In 1918, two waves of influenza had swept the globe, killing an estimated 20 million people worldwide; 600,000 of those deaths had occurred in the United States. Because of the concurrent effect the influenza had on American hogs at that time, physicians gave it a name: swine flu. This flu, they determined, was a virus that is spread from hogs to humans and between humans. It was mainly an airborne pathogen, meaning that one contracted it from being sneezed upon or from coming into contact with an infected hog's or person's respiratory droplets or spit. As a modern-day comparison, we need look no further than the AIDS epidemic—while the human immunodeficiency virus (HIV) is transmitted person to person, many epidemiologists and researchers believe it originated with monkeys.

Convinced that the new outbreak was a resurgence of the 1918 epidemic, the Food and Drug Administration issued a bulletin: swine flu is lurking in the nation's hogs. Be very careful.

Far from helping matters, however, this FDA announcement only fueled the fire. The entire public health community was in a panic. Certainly, there was cause for concern: tests needed to be run, the problem needed to be studied, a course of action needed to be formed and followed. But everything should have been done with extreme care and caution. Instead, the public health community reacted with fear and alarm. The result would be tragedy.

On February 20, 1976, two weeks after the death at Fort Dix, the CDC searched the country's hospitals for other swine flu victims. That same week, the FDA began discussions on preparing for a national vaccination campaign. It was agreed that plans should be made to head in that direction.

On March 10, the CDC's Advisory Committee on Immunization Practices convened. This group advises the CDC director—at that time, Dr. David Sencer—as to what types of immunization programs should be undertaken by the federal government. The panel's position that day was clear: stockpile a vaccine for swine flu and develop a plan for administering it. But that was all it recommended. The panel did not recommend actually proceeding with a mass vaccination program.

Despite this lack of support from the advisory panel, Dr. Sencer wasted no time in preparing an "action memo" to senior government officials recommending a full-blown immunization program. The memo suggested the strong possibility of a swine flu pandemic and stated that "the Administration can tolerate unnecessary health expenditures better than unnecessary death and illness."

Officials at the U.S. Department of Health, Education and Welfare just as promptly sent a memo to the White House. On March 24, President Ford took to the national television and radio airwaves to announce that every man, woman, and child in the United States would need to receive the vaccination. Certainly, the upcoming election campaign against Jimmy Carter had to have been on the president's mind. This was a natural headline grabber. If a 1977 swine flu pandemic occurred, but Americans were spared due to the speedy efforts of President Ford, he might emerge as a national hero. If not, it could be curtains.

The proposal moved quickly through Washington, D.C., which was now besieged by wild rumors that an epidemic was imminent. The proposal itself was simple: mass-produce the vaccine and ship it to every local health department in the country, which would inject all local citizens with the lifesaving formula. The estimated cost? $135 million. In 1976, that was a lot of money, even for the U.S. government.

From the beginning, the Swine Flu Immunization Program was plagued with problems. One of the manufacturers chosen to produce the vaccine produced 2 million doses of the wrong one. Apparently, the CDC had supplied the company with the wrong virus. However, that was only the beginning. Eventually, even the proper vaccine ran into problems—big problems.

Testing of the vaccine found that the dosage necessary to produce sufficient antibodies to fight the virus created a high probability of negative reactions. The inoculation would cause people to develop temperatures exceeding 100 degrees, as well as headaches and malaise. Even in the government's own tests, as many as 2 percent of all inoculated individuals could expect a severe reaction to the vaccine.

When this news hit the streets, the Swine Flu Immunization Program ran into a big snag. Those companies carrying the liability coverage for the drug manufacturers refused to underwrite the production and sale of the vaccine. The insurers estimated that even if only 2 percent of the people given the vaccine experienced adverse reactions, it would lead to an estimated $5 billion in potential lawsuit liability.

To get around this problem, public health officials proposed legislation whereby the federal government would not only finance the manufacture of the vaccine and administer the inoculation program, but also act as the insurer against all future claims and lawsuits. As might be expected, however, this measure was met with great skepticism in Congress: it would cost too much money and was simply too dangerous.

By July, the entire Swine Flu Immunization Program should have been re-evaluated. Five months had passed since the death of the private and only five others who were admitted to the Fort Dix infirmary were confirmed cases of swine flu. About five hundred soldiers tested did show a rise in the swine flu antibodies, but none reported any illness. At the same time, the CDC's search for swine flu cases throughout the country was turning up empty.

More interestingly, the sergeant who had given the private mouth-to-mouth resuscitation never became ill. These were all facts that were not given proper attention by CDC or other federal public health officials. Instead, they remained committed to the Swine Flu Immunization Program. Nothing would change their minds.

Just as it appeared that the entire program was going to die a bureaucratic death in some obscure subcommittee of Congress, it was given a jolt that breathed new life into the CDC's proposal. Between July 27 and August 6, doctors across Pennsylvania were hit with a medical phenomenon. Patients would initially complain of malaise, muscle aches, and headaches. Within twenty-four hours, symptoms included a rapidly rising fever and chills. Temperatures would run as high as 105 degrees. An early, nonproductive cough that later became productive was also reported. Some victims experienced abdominal pains and gastrointestinal problems.

During this time period, 29 people died and another 147

were hospitalized. They had one thing in common: all had attended or had subsequently been in contact with people who had attended the annual Pennsylvania State Legionnaires Convention in Philadelphia's famous Bellevue-Stratford Hotel.

More than ten thousand veterans had attended the conference. There were immediate fears that all of them were infected with some virus or had been exposed to some unknown toxin. Some people, mainly members of the American Legion, talked of a conspiracy by some foreign, Communist organization to poison these former American soldiers.

This tragedy is exactly what federal public health officials were looking for. They immediately took the public stand that this outbreak could also be swine flu. After all, many of the symptoms were the same. Using the national news media, they promoted an incredible theory: the swine flu virus had jumped the Delaware River and was invading Philadelphia. And now, the conventioneers were spreading it to their hometowns. This line of thinking was designed for two purposes: to scare everyone into calling their local public health officials and members of Congress to inquire about the vaccination, and to push through the inoculation legislation.

While I considered the Swine Flu Immunization Program to be total hogwash, I was dumbfounded. While I had been very critical of the program, this sudden rash of mysterious deaths forced me to reassess my stance. Could I have been wrong?

Within five days of the end of the American Legionnaires convention, I found myself performing autopsies on three people from the Pittsburgh area who had attended the conference. All were older adults. During the course of these examinations, I noticed that all three had significant health problems—enlarged hearts, lung diseases, and so on.

To obtain more information about what we were dealing with, I began making telephone calls to our state health department. I even sent it a telegram seeking information. Never once did I receive a response. What good was a health department, I wondered, if it did not share information on sicknesses and diseases and tell local medical officials how to deal with them? Sadly, I and my staff were on our own, facing some unknown, deadly killer.

In performing the autopsies, we had no idea what we were dealing with. Whatever was causing these illnesses could have been transmitted through blood, bodily fluids, or air. Despite the dangers, however, we pathologists had to do our jobs. We did take extra precautions, of course. We wore masks and double sets of gloves. We went to great lengths to completely cover all open sores and cuts. And we closely examined the laboratory's ventilation system before beginning. Still, we had no idea how or when the disease might strike.

Thinking back on those days, I am reminded now of the more recent case in California in which a woman was brought into an emergency room dying of a metastatic cancer. As hospital emergency room personnel tried to save her, several became violently ill and passed out. The scene turned to panic when hospital officials publicly speculated that the woman's body had emitted some toxic fumes.

The most outrageous aspect of that case was that the physicians at the hospital did not put an end to such hysteria right away. Instead, the rest of the world will always remember the scene in which pathologists dressed in space suits entered the room to do an autopsy on the body. Form day one, I told reporters that bodies don't emit such fumes. It's silly even to suggest such a thing. In the end, medical officials agreed the toxic fumes had come not from the woman, but from another, inanimate source within the hospital.

The first person to link the current rash of sicknesses with the American Legionnaires convention was Dr. Ernest Campbell of Bloomsburg, Pennsylvania. He had grown suspicious after three attendees of the convention came to him with serious pneumonia-like symptoms on the afternoon of Friday, July 30. His first thought was to contact the state health department. However, Dr. Campbell was told that the office was closed for the weekend and that he should wait until Monday to make his report.

During that weekend, a total of eighteen people died. This was completely unacceptable. The state health department should have had officials available twenty-four hours a day, seven days a week, fifty-two weeks a year in the event of emergencies like this. Who knows how many lives were lost due to this inexcusable delay?

However, the folly did not end there. When the state health department learned the news on Monday, August 2, officials immediately contacted the CDC, which came in and took over the probe. The manner in which the investigation was handled was outrageous. Initially, the illnesses were treated as if they were swine flu candidates. This may have been partially political, or perhaps somebody at the CDC actually believed it.

And yet another major flaw in the handling of the situation emerged. Let's say for a minute that the state health department and the CDC were right—that is, that the cause of these deaths was swine flu. Swine flu was being described by the CDC as a highly virulent killer. Yet no attempt was ever made to isolate the Legionnaires from the rest of the population. If the epidemic had indeed been swine flu, as the CDC believed, the consequences of allowing ten thousand potential carriers to come into contact with the rest of the population could have been catastrophic.

With the CDC pushing the swine flu theory in the Pennsylvania cases, President Ford called key members of Congress to the White House to implore them to endorse his vaccination proposal. As reports of people dying continued to surface every day, the Congress passed in record time the National Swine Flu Immunization Program of 1976. It gave the CDC and FDA everything both federal agencies wanted—money and authority.

However, it would also cost the American people a lot of lives.

At first, the investigation into the Bellevue-Stratford Hotel illnesses focused on bacteria and viruses, mainly swine flu. But by August 4, the CDC and the state had eliminated bacteria as a suspected cause of the disease. Two days later, viruses were also eliminated. This left toxins as the likely etiologic culprit.

By this time, the news media had picked up on the story and was trumpeting headlines across the country. It was Laura Foreman, a reporter for the *Philadelphia Inquirer,* who first gave it the label "Legionnaires' Disease." It was a name that was destined to stick.

On August 20, after no new cases of the outbreak had been reported since the program had begun, state health department officials gave the Bellevue-Stratford Hotel a clean bill of health. I could not believe they did this. Twenty-nine people were dead and the only link was that they were all at this hotel. To me, this was reason enough to close the place down. Ironically, the public was much smarter than public health officials and stayed far away from the hotel. It was forced to close down permanently a few weeks later due to lack of business.

By late August, CDC officials were seriously confused. Testing of the hotel, of the water and food, and of the specimens from the dead bodies produced few clues. At this point, most believed toxins were not the cause. After considerable research, scientists identified it as a previously unrecognized microorganism, specifically, a new bacterium. Most of us simply called it "the bug." Scientists at the CDC gave it the name *Legionella pneumophila.* The public stuck with Legionnaires' Disease.

Over the next several months, we would learn that the organism was actually not new at all, that it had, in fact, been around for many years and caused many deaths. In this way, it resembled AIDS; while HIV itself was not discovered and named until the early 1980s, we have been able to look back and identify many previous deaths that can be attributed to it. The same was true of Legionnaires' Disease.

Unfortunately, this story of death and medicine does not end on a happy note with the killer being arrested and eliminated. In fact, the opposite is true.

Legionnaires' Disease is still with us today. It lives in damp air-conditioning units and on showerheads. Who knows how it feeds or how it travels? Who knows why this deadly bacterium pops up in Lansing, Michigan, or Long Beach, California, this year but not in Chattanooga, Tennessee, or Salem, New Jersey?

And when it does reappear, it is still deadly. We have been lucky enough to learn that erythromycin, a lesser-used antibiotic, can effectively fight this bacterium. But if it is not caught and is given free rein in the body, it can and will kill. There is nothing that we as scientists can do about this act of nature.

Even more devastating to me, however, was the swine flu fiasco. I and others were unable to convince public health officials of the dangers of the vaccination program, and the federal government went forward in late November 1976 with its plans. Millions of people were inoculated, despite the fact that the public was never told what swine flu was or how the vaccination worked.

As for me, I simply refused to be inoculated. Vaccines are never completely safe. They are not cure-alls. What happens is that the vaccine actually introduces the offending microorganism into the body, but in an attenuated state, or with significantly diminished virulence. This is done to help the body develop antibodies to the particular virus or bacterium. When the real sickness comes along, the body is thus prepared and can easily produce more antibodies.

Keep in mind, however, that you are still introducing the sickness into the body. Whenever that happens, there are very good chances that the person being injected will actually get the illness. Indeed, this is precisely what happened in this case. On December 6, exactly two weeks after the vaccinations began, three people from Pittsburgh died within six hours of receiving their shots at the same clinic. I immediately called the county health department and we shut down the local program. In reaction, seven other states and several cities promptly halted the inoculations for several days.

I also notified CDC officials instantly, and they sent a group of investigators to Pittsburgh the same day. But just as in Philadelphia, I felt the Pittsburgh deaths were whitewashed over. There were real problems with these vaccinations and no one at the federal level was paying attention.

Finally, a month later, the entire program was halted. There was clear evidence that the Philadelphia deaths had nothing to do with swine flu and that no other confirmed cases had surfaced. What had happened was tragic. At least fifty-two people had died reportedly in connection with the swine flu vaccine. Another six hundred people had been diagnosed with a paralysis called Guillain-Barré Syndrome, the increased incidence of which was linked to the inoculations. The federal government, which had guaranteed to pick up the tab for any liability, ended up paying billions of dollars to victims and their families through medical-malpractice and wrongful-death lawsuits.

In 1977, I was asked to speak in Philadelphia before a congressional committee consisting of both U.S. representatives and senators. In a meeting covered by the national news media, I was given about forty-five minutes to relay my fears and concerns about how public health officials had reacted, or underreacted, to the Legionnaires' emergency. The press attention through this entire event was extraordinary. Because of my lack of hesitancy to speak out and be critical, I was constantly bombarded with requests for interviews from members of the news media. I even remember waking up one morning and seeing my photograph on the front page of the *New York Times*.

There are many lessons to learn from the swine flu fiasco and the Legionnaires' tragedy. We allowed the federal government to implement a nationwide public health policy without raising sufficient questions or providing scientific proof of causation. Where were the news media during this fiasco? Indeed, the swine flu incident may have been the biggest "boy-who-cried wolf" story in recent history. We cannot afford to overreact emotionally to a potential public health hazard. In this case, it ended up costing many more lives than it could have saved.

THIRTEEN

GENTLE GIANT OR COLD-BLOODED KILLER?

One of the most intriguing aspects of my forensic work is the wide range of characters with whom it brings me into contact. Some of them—people guilty of such crimes as child abuse, rape, and premeditated murder, for instance—have been the lowest forms of human life. Others have been so innocent as to seem almost saintly. But the great majority have occupied that gray area in between, and it is their stories that have always intrigued and troubled me the most.

Take the case of Guillermo Aillon. Every holiday, I receive a card or a letter from Gil. He calls every few months, just to see how my family and I are doing. We've spoken for hours on the phone and I even paid him a visit in prison once. From this limited contact, and from having spoken at great length with friends and lawyers who worked with Gil, I've come to see a man of great sensitivity, graciousness, and humility. And yet this man will most likely spend the rest of his life behind bars.

To meet Gil Aillon is to wonder how such a gentle, considerate person could have brutally stabbed his wife and her parents to death. I, for one, am not so certain that he did.

I first met Gil Aillon on August 17, 1972, the very night

he would be arrested and charged with three counts of first-degree murder. I was spending a long weekend with my family at our summer home in Milford, Connecticut, a small, oceanfront community just down the coast from New Haven. Returning home from a restaurant late that evening, I was surprised to see two men sitting on the front stoop of our cottage. As I pulled into the driveway, I recognized one of the men as Howard Jacobs, a well-respected New Haven trial lawyer whom I'd known since childhood. As for the other man, I'd never seen him before.

Getting out of the car, I took a closer look at this stranger. Standing at least six feet five inches and weighing perhaps 250 pounds, he towered over us all. He wore a navy blue suit and had a head of dark, wavy hair that he kept bowed as though he were embarrassed to be intruding in our home at this late hour. Howard introduced him to me as Mr. Gil Aillon, and we shook hands and chatted briefly. From the outset, everything about his demeanor seemed to belie his physical appearance. He spoke only when spoken to, always addressed both me and Howard as "sir," and repeatedly expressed his apologies for visiting so late and unannounced.

Then Howard dropped the bombshell. He and Gil were about to call the police so that Gil could turn himself in. The state had issued an arrest warrant earlier that day in which his client was accused of murdering his wife, Barbara Aillon, and her parents, George and Bernice Montano, who had been found stabbed to death four days earlier in the Montanos' home in nearby North Haven. Howard wanted me to examine a few injuries on Aillon's arms and hands before he was taken into custody.

"When the police and prosecutors see these cuts, no doubt they'll try to use them as evidence against him," Howard said. "I need you to look at these injuries, document them, determine how old they may be, and, if possible, decide what kind of instrument could have caused them."

I agreed to examine Howard's client, but not without a word of warning to both of them. "You must understand that you're potentially making me a witness in this case," I said.

"And I'll have to testify as to exactly what I see. If I examine these wounds and determine that they match the kinds of injuries the police are looking for, I must testify to that effect." Without a moment's hesitation, Howard and Aillon agreed.

Leading Aillon over to a lamp in our living room, I proceeded to take a look at his left index finger. The first injury was located half an inch below the first knuckle joint on the back of the finger, and was roughly half an inch long, a quarter of an inch wide, and maybe an eighth of an inch deep. It had a reddish orange center and showed early signs of scabbing. My initial thought, which I jotted down in a pad for future reference, was that this was the kind of injury a person receives from a burn.

Injury number two was located on Aillon's right forearm, about three and a half inches from the crease in the elbow joint. It measured just over an inch long and maybe an eighth of an inch wide. This injury, too, appeared to be healing, with a pink-red center and an early scab formation. Like the first injury, it reminded me most of a burn.

The third injury I examined was on the back of Aillon's left arm, where the wrist meets the hand. This one measured half an inch long and a little more than an eighth of an inch wide. A scab was also developing on this wound, and it, too, appeared to have been caused by a burn.

As I continued my examination, I noted several superficial epidermal abrasions—better known as scratches—on the palm of Aillon's right hand. There also appeared to be several scratch marks about two and a half inches down from the wrist, just below the base of the thumb. The longest of these was about half an inch long and an eighth of an inch wide. There was early scab formation and no significant depth to these injuries.

Without my even inquiring, Aillon explained that he had received the injuries in different ways over the past two weeks. The burn on the right forearm came while grilling some meat. The injury on the left wrist had been caused by accidentally touching a hot iron while pressing his shirts. The wound on his second finger was caused by touching metal on a heated car engine. And the cuts on his right hand came from the sharp edges of chrome that had started peeling off the gear shift handle of his car. As he talked, I wrote down his explanations.

The examination took a little less than an hour, but during that time, I learned a lot about Aillon. He'd been born in Potosí, Bolivia, on February 1, 1938. His father, a successful lawyer, had paid handsomely for Aillon to get the best education Bolivia had to offer, and Aillon had the equivalent of a bachelor of science degree from the University of San Andrés School of Engineering, which he had attended from 1957 through 1960. Aillon's father had acquired rather large assets throughout his career, but then he had become extremely ill, and the family's life savings were drained trying to save him.

Aillon, who had strong democratic principles in his youth, had been arrested several times for anti-government activities. On many occasions, the Bolivian police would beat him and throw him in jail for days or weeks without food. Finally, in 1960, Aillon fled the country for the United States, where he soon became a naturalized citizen. In 1961 he joined the U.S. Army and served for three years. Afterward, he served an additional four years in the Army Reserves, which awarded him the Good Conduct Medal in 1967.

After leaving the army, Aillon settled in Hartford, Connecticut, where he had friends in the Hispanic community. Using these ties, he found work as a counselor and supervisor of various community service programs. In 1969, he was named housing director of the Urban League of Greater Hartford, where he organized the city's first multifaith, multiethnic, bilingual education and recreation programs. As a result of his commitment to the community, the Connecticut Jaycees in 1972 named Aillon "Outstanding Young Man of the Year," as well as one of three outstanding young men in New England.

During this time, some mutual friends introduced Aillon and Barbara Montano, the beautiful young daughter of a politically well-connected and quite wealthy North Haven family. George Montano, Barbara's father, had started the National Lumber Company of North Haven twenty-five years earlier. Over the years, as his wealth accumulated, he'd bought a couple dozen houses and apartments throughout the New Haven area, which he would then refurbish and rent out.

On April 26, 1971, Gil and Barbara were married, and nine months later Barbara gave birth to a daughter, Catherine Victoria. Together, the family lived in a small apartment in Wallingford, a bedroom community just north of New Haven, and for a while their marriage was the picture of domestic bliss. But in 1972, things started going sour. It was a familiar story: husband loses his job, starts drinking, and before you know it, things begin to take a slide. "Maybe I was not adequately caring for my wife and family," Aillon admitted to me. "But I still loved both of them very much."

Apparently, whatever love Aillon felt was not quite enough to hold the family together; on July 31, 1972, after only sixteen months of marriage, Barbara packed her belongings, took the baby, and moved back in with her parents. Two days later, she contacted a lawyer and started divorce proceedings against Aillon. On August 8, Aillon was officially served with papers informing him of Barbara's intention to obtain a legal separation and to seek full custody of their baby daughter.

Now, Barbara Aillon and her parents were dead. For Aillon, I knew, this meant one thing: prosecutors and police were going to label him an angry, jealous husband who killed his wife and her family to prevent her from divorcing him and taking their child away.

When I finished my examination that night, I saw Aillon and Howard to the door. Howard wanted to know if I'd be willing to review the police and autopsy reports when the district attorney turned them over to him. I agreed to take a look at them, but as I said good-bye, I doubted that it would make much of a difference.

From my house, the two men drove back to Howard's law offices, where they made last-minute preparations. Even though the arrest warrant had been issued earlier in the day, the police had agreed to give Aillon until 2 A.M. to turn himself in. This may sound strange, but when the person being arrested is a well-known and respected member of the community and his lawyer promises to see him into the custody of the police, the authorities are lenient. They will not go banging down the defendant's door to arrest him.

The very same type of situation received quite a bit of publicity in the summer of 1994, when O.J. Simpson was charged with murder and promised to turn himself in to the police. But in that case, when the appointed hour came and the police arrived to take the suspect into custody, they discovered that Simpson had quietly slipped away. As most of us will remember for years to come, TV cameras and a line of police cars caught up with O.J. as he was driven down the freeway, holding a handgun to his own head.

To Aillon's credit, he did not am or hide. When police arrived at Howard's office, they placed Aillon in handcuffs, read him the Miranda warning, and escorted him to the Bridgeport Correctional Facility, where he was held on $25,000 bond.

A few weeks after I'd returned to Pittsburgh, I received a package in the mail from Howard Jacobs that included the reports he had promised. In an accompanying letter, he wrote that the prosecutors were indeed planning on arguing that the wounds to Aillon's hands and arms resulted from a struggle with the victims. "One thing is certain, my friend," Howard wrote. "You will be called as a witness. If you come across anything unusual or out of place when reading through these reports, please let me know."

I spent the next few days reviewing the detailed reports filed by detectives and the crime-scene photos taken by police, trying to figure out what had happened the morning the bodies of Barbara Aillon and George and Bernice Montano were found. The story gathered by the government, I discovered, began and ended with Gil Aillon.

At about 7:30 on the morning of Monday, August 14, 1972, Aillon drove his 1965 Chevy Supersport Impala to the Empire Service Center, an auto repair shop located just down the street from George Montano's lumber company in North Haven. The night before, police officers had given Aillon a warning that one of his taillights was out and that his muffler was broken and causing too much noise.

It had been two weeks since Barbara had taken Catherine and moved in with her parents. As Aillon told the police, he had an appointment with George Montano at 9:30 that morning to discuss what he could do to convince Barbara to give him another chance. When the auto mechanics told Aillon it would be several hours before his car was fixed, Aillon tried to call his father-in-law to confirm their meeting. The line at the Montano residence was busy.

Because the lumber company was only a few hundred yards down the street, Aillon decided to walk there to see if his father-in-law was in. Once there, he learned that Montano had not yet come in. Again, Aillon tried calling his father-in-law's house, but the telephone was still busy. A switchboard operator at the lumber company then tried, but she, too, got a busy signal. After a few more tries, she called the operator, who checked the line and said that it was "definitely busy." During this time, the switchboard operator, who apparently knew Aillon fairly well, described him as being his "normal, cheerful self."

About thirty minutes later, Aillon ran into Donald Montano, George's brother, who also worked at the lumber company. Donald apparently did not know that Barbara had moved out until Aillon told him that morning. When Donald offered Aillon the use of his car to drive to the Montanos' house to see George, Aillon said that would not be a good idea. If Barbara saw him at their house, he explained, she would get very upset and might decide against their getting back together. With that, Donald offered to drive Aillon to his brother's house and run interference for him. Aillon agreed.

When the two were about 150 feet from the Montanos' house on Crestview Drive, Donald stopped the car and Aillon got out. It was about 11 A.M.

"I'll go in and talk with George and see what the story is," Donald reportedly told Aillon. "If the coast is clear, I'll motion for you to come up."

Aillon agreed and waited on the street corner while Donald

drove his car up the Montanos' driveway. He tried the front door first, but it was locked. When no one responded to his knocking, he went around to the garage and entered through a side door that was frequently left unlocked. Within seconds, he had spotted the bloodied bodies of his brother, his sister-in-law, and his niece. Apparently possessing enough presence of mind not to touch anything, he ran next door and called the police. Then he called his wife to break the news. Finally, composing himself, he walked down the driveway toward Aillon.

"Is it OK for me to go in?" Aillon reportedly asked.

"No, not yet," said Montano.

"What's wrong?"

"Nothing's wrong. Just wait here."

At that moment, the two heard sirens and turned to see police cars coming around the corner and pulling into the Montanos' driveway. It was then, according to Montano, that Aillon said something very strange. But whether it was an admission of guilt or a protest against Barbara calling the police on him, Montano was unclear.

"Don't call the police," Aillon reportedly said. "Why the police? We can handle this with lawyers."

"They're dead," Montano told him at this point. "They're all dead."

At that, Aillon started running toward the house. He, too, entered through the side door in the garage, passing through the kitchen and laundry rooms before arriving upon the same spectacle Donald Montano had just seen. As Aillon would later report, he found his daughter crying under a chair on the sun porch, unharmed but her clothes soaked in blood. By that time, the police had entered the house and escorted him outside, his daughter held close to his chest.

According to the report, five of the house's eleven rooms had been ransacked; dresser and nightstand drawers had been emptied on the floor. However, many valuables, including jewelry, antiques, and artwork, remained untouched. Furthermore, there was no sign of forcible entrance; the windows were closed, the shades were drawn, and the doors—

with the exception of the one leading to the garage—were locked. The only light on in the house was a small night-light in the hallway. And the telephone was off the hook. Given this scenario, the police would later say, they had concluded that the murders were not part of a burglary gone bad. Rather, the person or persons who killed the Montanos wanted them to *think* it was a burglary.

To get a clearer picture of the scene, I began looking through the more than fifty black-and-white photographs taken by the North Haven Homicide Squad, matching them up with the autopsy reports filed by the Connecticut state medical examiner, Dr. Elliott Gross.

The first body police came upon was that of Bernice Montano, whom they found lying in the foyer next to the kitchen near the bottom of a set of stairs. She had been stabbed four times in the chest and back. Three of these wounds had penetrated her rib cage, severing the pulmonary vein and piercing one of her lungs. She also had a very bad bruise over her right eye.

The second body was that of Barbara Montano Aillon, who was found lying in a puddle of blood in a hallway only a few feet from her mother. She had been stabbed four times—twice in the upper chest, once beneath the left arm, and once in the right side of her back. Two of the cuts had punctured her lungs, and a third went completely through her heart.

The final victim was forty-nine-year-old George Montano, whose body was found lying face-up in the hallway at the top of the stairs, directly in front of a table on which sat a display of artificial birds of paradise. A ceiling fan above his head was on, as was the air conditioning in his bedroom. Montano was wearing blue pajama bottoms and a wristwatch. The top of his pajamas was a few feet away on the floor. The photographs showed dried blood on his face and chest.

George Montano had been stabbed at least twenty-one times, and many of the wounds appeared to be defensive in nature. Nine of them were to his chest, mostly between the midline and nipples. The knife had sliced through his heart five times and lacerated his lungs twice. A tenth injury was found on his left temple, and there were several cuts to the palm of his left hand. One of his fingers had been sliced off and was apparently found a couple of feet away from his body. From the description, it was obvious that he had put up a strong fight and that his attacker might have been injured as well.

As I sat back to assimilate this information, two things were certain: the scene inside that house had been a horrific one, and the injuries to all the victims were so severe that they must have died very quickly, probably within minutes. From the reports I'd read, it was also clear to me why the police were working on the premise that Aillon was the killer. For one thing, the fact that he and Barbara were on the cusp of potentially devastating divorce proceedings did make him a suspect. And the injuries to his hands and arms, at least to the untrained eye, did not paint a favorable picture either. Still, as far as I'm concerned, the detectives committed an all too common error by focusing exclusively on Aillon and not looking into the possibility of other suspects.

Much of the police suspicion about Aillon, according to reports, surrounded his activities during the previous twelve hours and his conduct at the crime scene. According to Donald Montano, for example, as he drove Aillon back to his apartment that night, Aillon started muttering, "I should have stopped. I should have stopped."

"When I asked him what he meant," Montano told police, "Gil said he had driven near the house the previous night and thought about stopping in but decided it was too late."

Meanwhile, the police had made another interesting discovery. Word of the tragedy had quickly made its way to the Empire Service Center, where mechanics had finished working on Aillon's car. Curious, one of the mechanics glanced into the back seat and spotted a twelve- or thirteen-inch serrated knife with a wooden handle wrapped in bloodstained aluminum foil, both its ends sticking out. Within minutes, police were at the garage to confiscate the car.

When questioned about the knife by police, Aillon said he had visited his sister the night before and taken her a roast for dinner. The knife, he said, had accompanied the roast. Not surprisingly, the police did not believe Aillon and were convinced they had found the murder weapon.

Simultaneously, detectives discovered that Aillon had been seen in the neighborhood of the Montanos' house about midnight. In fact, police records revealed that because of Aillon's missing taillight and noisy muffler, North Haven patrolman Edward Murphy had pulled Aillon over in that area sometime between 12:30 and 1 A.M. When Aillon agreed to have his car fixed the next morning, the officer let him go with a warning. However, five minutes later, a report of a burglary giving a description of a car matching that of Aillon's came across the police radio. Immediately, Officer Murphy and two other patrolmen, Officer Kerwyn Daniels and Sergeant Haynes Gibson, located Aillon pulling into a nearby coffee shop and pulled him over again.

As the officers began to question Aillon, one of them shined a flashlight into the back seat and spotted the butt end of a knife. When the officers asked Aillon to let them see the knife, Aillon was initially reluctant. In the end, though, he did show them the knife, accounting for the bloodstains by telling the officers that he had used it to cut rare roast beef at his sister's house that night. Lacking sufficient evidence to question him further, the officers let Aillon go.

As far as I was concerned, this looked bad for Aillon, very bad. First, there was the extremely damaging evidence of a bloody knife. And secondly, the police could place Aillon near the scene of the crime around the time the murders were said to have been committed; indeed, Dr. Gross had made an unofficial determination that the victims died sometime between 10 P.M. Sunday and 2 A.M. Monday. But as I continued to review the reports, I saw that the case was perhaps not so open-and-shut.

On Tuesday, the day after the bodies were found, detectives obtained a search warrant from a New Haven judge to comb Aillon's apartment for evidence. There, they seized a six-inch serrated knife, but it was too small to match with the wounds on the victims, and no other evidence was found.

Back at the crime scene, detectives confiscated the drains and filters from sinks in the kitchen and bathrooms, as well as the filter from a washing machine and dryer. They were hoping that the killer had washed his hands or had even attempted to wash blood spatter off his clothes. However, neither skin nor blood was found, and a check of the garbage disposal proved similarly fruitless.

Police also took samples of more than a hundred blood spatters throughout the Montano house, hoping that at least one of them would prove to be from the attacker. The samples were sent to the Federal Bureau of Investigation crime laboratory near Washington, D.C., for testing and examination. This was proper procedure and a smart move, but the police erred when they used the same razor blade to scrape twenty-five different blood samples without washing or sterilizing the blade between scrapings. As a result, all twenty-five samples were contaminated and could not be used in a court of law. Who knows what they might have shown?

In the end, the only significant evidence discovered at the crime scene was a drop of blood on the fingertip of a rubber glove found near Bernice Montano's body. All the other bloodstains were found to be either type O or type A—the former compatible with George Montano and his daughter, the latter with Bernice Montano. But the blood sample found on the rubber glove was type B. The obvious next step for police was to determine what blood type Aillon had. Aillon volunteered the information himself: type B.

With this, I knew, police believed they had hit the evidentiary jackpot. However, keep in mind that this was before the days of DNA fingerprinting; no one could say with certainty whose blood it was. And in fact, a quick call to the Centers for Disease Control in Atlanta would have informed the police that more than 10 percent of the American population has type B blood. Based on this particular piece of evidence, then, Aillon or any one of 20 million other people could have committed the murders. In that sense, the drop of blood was a somewhat less than convincing piece of evidence.

The investigation went on to hit a few more snags. For

example, tests conducted by the Connecticut State Police Forensic Science Lab showed that the stains on the knife found in Aillon's car were indeed from animal blood, just as Aillon had stated they were. And in a separate report, a fingerprint expert noted that of all the prints recovered from the Montanos' home, none matched Aillon's. Even more interesting was the expert's discovery of several sets of prints that did not match any of the victims either. Taking his experiment a step further, he obtained fingerprints from more than fifty members of the Montano family and others who may have been in the house in the days prior to the slaying. None matched the mystery fingerprints.

Despite the presence of so much contradictory evidence, prosecutors and police presented their case to a New Haven grand jury on November 29, 1972.

At the risk of getting sidetracked, I want to take a moment to say that the grand jury is perhaps the most misunderstood aspect of our criminal justice system. Most people believe that this group, usually consisting of sixteen to twenty-four local residents chosen through the voter registration system, listens to all the evidence in a case before deciding whether to issue an indictment. That simply is not true. Usually, the only evidence grand juries hear comes from the police or from witnesses carefully selected by prosecutors. In fact, defense counsel is not even allowed to take part in grand jury proceedings, which are completely confidential. In other words, the jurors hear only one side of a case. To be sure, defendants are permitted to testify. But in reality few do, since most defense attorneys feel that this would place their clients at the mercy of prosecutors.

At any rate, the prosecution in this case must have done a credible job of presenting the evidence, for later that same day the grand jury returned what is known as a "true bill," indicting thirty-four-year-old Gil Aillon for triple homicide.

The trial itself, held before an all-white jury of six men and six women, finally got under way in July of 1973. Connecticut prosecutor Arnold Markle started the trial by saying that the defendant had murdered his wife and in-laws in a moment of anger and greed. He admitted up front that there were no eyewitnesses to these crimes, but emphatically stated that all of the available evidence pointed to Aillon.

"The defendant had the motive, the opportunity, and the means to kill these people," Markle told the jury. "Circumstantial evidence is as good as direct evidence."

In response, Howard Jacobs told jurors in his opening statement that the state's case was "full of holes," and that the evidence collected by the police would "fall through the cracks of one of those holes when closely examined."

"Here sits a man," Jacobs said, pointing to his client, "who has been wrongfully accused of a terrible crime. He is a man of flaws and with problems. But he loved his wife and daughter very much and would never do anything to harm them."

To his credit, Markle went on to do a workmanlike job of presenting the prosecution's case. He started by placing Aillon near the scene of the crime around the time police believed the murders had occurred. One by one, the three patrolmen who had pulled Aillon over because of the bad taillight and muffler recalled seeing a knife with blood on it in the back of Aillon's car that night. Next, Markle informed the jury that a bloodied knife was found in the back of Aillon's car the next morning. However, the prosecutor noted, the bloodstains from that knife came from a roast beef. Carefully picking up the knife that was seized, Markle showed it to the officers.

"Is this the knife you saw in the back of Aillon's car the night of the murder?"

"No," responded each officer.

The knife they had seen, the patrolman said, was a little bit longer and had more serrated edges. This meant that there was yet another knife out there—the killer's knife. Markle admitted that the police had never found the murder weapon, and speculated that Aillon had gotten rid of the real knife and substituted this knife covered with beef blood to confuse police.

Markle's next witness was the Montanos' next-door neighbor, nineteen-year-old James Davidson. He told jurors that he had been up watching TV at about 12:30 A.M. when a car with its headlights on pulled into the Montanos' driveway.

But Davidson went on to surprise the prosecutor by saying that the car he had seen appeared to be a Plymouth Fury, not the 1965 Chevy that Aillon drove.

Moving on, Markle presented to the jury photographs of Aillon's hands and arms that had been taken by police the day he was arrested. The injuries, Markle told the court, were evidence that Aillon had recently been in a struggle and that a knife was probably involved. With that testimony now officially before the jury, Howard informed me, he would have to call me in as a witness. But it was not my turn just yet.

The prosecution's next witness was a powerful one. Arthur A. Abehouse, a well-respected and experienced attorney, had represented Montano's lumber company for years. More relevant to this trial, he was the man Barbara Aillon had consulted about getting a divorce. Now on the stand, Abehouse related to the jury what had transpired when Mrs. Aillon first contacted him on July 27—seventeen days before she was murdered.

MARKLE: Did she say why she wanted a divorce?

ABEHOUSE: Yes. She told me all of the problems of her married life. She said she was having a lot of problems. She said Gil had lost his job in Hartford and was trying to sell real estate and insurance in Wallingford and now wanted to go to embalming school.

MARKLE: What were the particular problems she and Mr. Aillon were experiencing?

ABEHOUSE: She said her husband was never at home at night and that when she tried to discuss their problems with him to save their marriage, he would clam up and walk out of the house.

MARKLE: Did she say she was afraid of her husband?

ABEHOUSE: She said she was scared. She said he had threatened her life—threatened, but didn't strike her. She said he had a fixation on the baby. He wouldn't let anyone near her. She said he would take the baby to South America and that if he couldn't have the baby, nobody would. She said that if Aillon knew she was seeing a lawyer, she didn't know what he would do.

MARKLE: What was your response?

ABEHOUSE: I told her to be calm and think about what she was doing. On July 31, she called me saying she had moved out of the apartment she and Aillon shared and that she wanted me to proceed with suing for divorce.

Abehouse went on to tell the jury that Aillon was officially served with divorce papers on August 8, accusing him of "intolerable cruelty" and requesting that Barbara be granted full custody of their daughter. The next day, Abehouse said, he received a telephone call at his law office from a "very upset" Gil Aillon.

MARKLE: What did he want?

ABEHOUSE: He said he had lost his job and was trying to get a job as an embalmer. He said he had lost [custody of] a son in a previous marriage and that if he lost his daughter, he didn't know what he would do.

MARKLE: What was your response?

ABEHOUSE: I advised Aillon to get some counseling in an attempt to save his marriage and Aillon indicated he would do that.

From the jury's standpoint, Abehouse was an effective witness. He had no motive to perjure himself, and I do believe he was telling the entire truth. However, keep in mind that he was only repeating what Barbara Aillon had told him over the phone, and that she was extremely distraught when she spoke with him.

Normally, witnesses are not allowed to testify in court as to what someone else said or told them. Under the law, such evidence is called "hearsay" and is considered inadmissible. However, there are exceptions to the hearsay rule. One is that anything supposedly said by the defendant is considered fair game. Another is that anything said by a homicide victim that may establish his or her state of mind before being killed is admissible. In other words, the testimony of Mr. Abehouse was meant only to demonstrate the thoughts and fears Mrs. Aillon was experiencing in the days leading up to her murder. The words themselves are not to be accepted as truth, the judge instructed the jury.

In my opinion, such an approach is analogous to the situation in a trial when a lawyer objects to something a witness has said before a jury and the judge sustains the objection. Frequently, the judge will tell the jurors that they are to "disregard" the witness's statement. Technically, this may make sense, but as I see it, if a reasonable person hears something interesting, he or she isn't going to be able to forget about it just because a judge says it should be forgotten. Once something has been said, it cannot just be taken back. Of course, there's no way to foresee objectionable statements. But when it comes to hearsay, I believe judges should consider the obviously prejudicial effect such evidence can have in an emotional murder trial, and that they should be stricter about letting a jury hear it.

Following Abehouse's testimony, several family members took the stand to tell their stories. Damaging testimony came from Montano relatives who said that George Montano had promised to give Aillon $1,600 so that he could attend embalming school. But when Barbara decided to get a divorce, they said, her father changed his mind, thus making Aillon very angry.

The testimony that I thought hurt Aillon the most, however, was that of Dr. Charles Jones, a pediatrician who frequently saw Catherine Aillon. On the witness stand, Dr. Jones said Aillon called him at 7 A.M. on August 14, a few hours before the Montano bodies were found.

MARKLE: What did he say?
JONES: He asked if I thought he could hurt anyone. I said no.
MARKLE: Did he call again later?
JONES: Yes, the next day. He asked if I knew how big George Montano was. I said yes. He asked me if I thought a man his size could alone overpower George Montano.

No matter what side you were on, you had to respect the method, if not the manner, in which Markle presented the state's case. He called witness after witness, more than a dozen in all, to give testimony that portrayed Guillermo Aillon as an evil, violent man who had executed the murders of his wife and her parents to near perfection, almost without leaving behind any physical evidence of his involvement in the crimes. But while the prosecutor admitted that his case was based on circumstantial evidence—"mountains of it," as he put it—he was able to completely gloss over the physical, medical, and scientific evidence which either did not point at Aillon or, in some cases, actually pointed away from him.

For example, police found four hairs at the Montanos' house that an FBI hair analyst determined had the same or similar microscopic characteristics to Aillon's. These hairs had been found in a blanket and on a sheet in George Montano's bedroom, as well as in the washer and dryer. Furthermore, the analyst testified that a strand of hair found on trousers in Aillon's car matched the characteristics of George Montano's hair. At the same time, a search of these pants for textile fibers from the clothes of other people in the Montano household turned up nothing.

To me, this evidence was particularly disturbing—not because it pointed to Gil Aillon, but because the judge would even allow it to be presented to the jury in the first place. Remember, this was before DNA fingerprinting had been perfected and could be used as evidence in court. In 1972, the only way to identify body hair was to look at it through a microscope and compare it to other body hairs to determine whether it had similar characteristics. The procedure was archaic, and certainly less than scientifically foolproof—a point the FBI analyst readily admitted on the stand.

But even if you put the scientific challenges to the testing aside, and accept for a moment that it could be proven without a shadow of a doubt that these were Aillon's hairs, so what? What did that prove? Several witnesses had already testified that Gil and Barbara lived with the Montanos during the first few months of their marriage, and two more witnesses said that Aillon and George Montano had met twice the week before the slaying. With these facts in mind, take into account that hair sticks to almost everything and can be transferred numerous times. There were any number of reasonable and physically plausible ways in which Aillon's hair could have made it into the Montano house or that Montano's hair could have ended up on Aillon's pants. From the jury's standpoint, however, this was just another smoking gun.

With this in mind, I referred Howard to Wellon Collum, a Pittsburgh criminalist who specialized in hair analysis. He closely examined each of the hairs and said that they in no way matched. Interestingly, the FBI's analyst also testified that he'd found several hairs at the Montano house that did not match those of Aillon or any member of the Montano family. This evidence, however, was not pursued by the police.

The final witnesses for the prosecution focused on the time of death and the size of the knife. Dr. Gross, the forensic pathologist who headed the Connecticut Medical Examiner's Office, testified that the death "most likely" occurred between 10 P.M. and 2 A.M.—a time frame in which the police could place Aillon near the scene of the crime with a bloodied knife in his back seat. And FBI agent Edmund W. Kelso, Jr., a specialist in tool mark identification, testified that law enforcement officers had taken from the Montanos' home three sections of wallboard containing knife marks. These marks, he said, showed serrations that were larger than those of the knife recovered in the back of Aillon's car the next morning.

When Arnold Markle rested the prosecution's case, Howard Jacobs called to tell me that he felt encouraged. "They left the door open," he said. "The question is how much we will be able to get through it."

One of the first witnesses called for the defense, I took the stand on Thursday, August 2, 1973. The courtroom was filled. As usual, members of the victims' family and police officers sat on one side, friends and family of the defendant on the other. A handful of reporters was scattered throughout the room.

Following the tedious but necessary recitation of my

credentials, training, and experience, as well as a condensed dissertation on what pathology and forensic pathology are, Howard took me back to that evening nearly a year earlier when I'd found him sitting with his client on the stoop of my cottage.

> JACOBS: Have you ever seen my client before?
> WECHT: I saw Mr. Aillon for the first and only time prior to today at my home in Milford on the evening of Thursday, August 17, 1972, at approximately 10 P.M., when you came with him.
> JACOBS: About how long did you spend with us?
> WECHT: I'd say roughly an hour.
> JACOBS: Did I request you to do something?
> WECHT: You asked me to look specifically at injuries on Mr. Aillon's hands and forearms, and you had me look at his upper torso.

For the next twenty minutes, I meticulously described each injury I'd seen on Gil Aillon. As expected, most of Howard's questions and prosecutor Markle's cross-examination related to the cuts on Aillon's hand.

> JACOBS: Doctor, I'm going to show you State's Exhibit RRRR, which has been testified to as being the knob from the shifting lever on Mr. Aillon's car. Have you examined this?
> WECHT: It was shown to me this morning before court started.
> JACOBS: Doctor, do you have an opinion with reasonable medical probability as to whether or not the contact between Mr. Aillon's right palm and this gear shift lever could have caused these superficial skin marks that you have described?
> WECHT: My opinion is that they could have been caused by contact with this rough, irregular surface.

.   .   .   .

MARKLE: But, Doctor, those marks could have been caused by anything, couldn't they?

WECHT: No, not anything.

MARKLE: Are those marks as consistent with holding a knife and hitting a bone as with the car gear shift theory?

WECHT: My answer is no, they are not as consistent with holding a knife. Assuming that someone is holding a knife by the handle, and the handle is smooth, as it was described by the police officers, then it would not have caused the scratch marks or abrasions displayed by Mr. Aillon.

MARKLE: Could you tell whether the abrasions on the palms were fresh?

WECHT: In my opinion, they had not just occurred. Based on the scabs that were already present or developing, and the coloring of those injuries, I would have aged them up to a couple of weeks old.

With that out of the way, Jacobs moved on to more significant matters.

JACOBS: You have examined the sizes, angles, and tears that each knife wound made on each victim, and you have examined the knife seized in Mr. Aillon's car and a knife similar to that seen by police the night of the murders in Mr. Aillon's possession. Can you tell me if any or all of these wounds were caused by any one of these knives?

WECHT: If the knife the police saw in Mr. Aillon's car had the deep and pronounced serrations the police say it did, then in my opinion, based upon a reasonable degree of medical probability, it could not have produced all the wounds to the three victims.

JACOBS: Why is that, Doctor?

WECHT: Two reasons. The first is the pattern. If a serrated knife were used, there would be some irregularity in the cuts on the skin—something other than a smooth straight line of the cutting edges. There would be some rough edges in some of the wounds. That is not the case here.

The second reason is the length of the incised wounds or cuts.

I wrapped up my testimony by explaining that the lengths of the incisions, as well as the depths of some of the wounds as determined by internal examination, did not correlate with the physical dimensions of either knife. Finally, after two days on the witness stand going over each autopsy and medical report, I was excused. That afternoon, as I left for Athens, Greece, where I would be participating in a medicolegal seminar, I felt that I had done all I could for Mr. Aillon.

Over the next few days, Howard Jacobs called upon several witnesses to offset the state's barrage of circumstantial evidence against his client. Two of George Montano's neighbors, testifying separately, said they were up late the night of the murders and did not hear a car with a loud muffler drive onto their street. "If there had been a car with a defective muffler," one neighbor said, "I would have heard it."

Gil Aillon's sister, Dr. Luz Aillon, testified that her brother had come over to her house that evening with a roast beef and a carving knife. She also testified that she did not clean the knife, but wrapped it in aluminum foil for him to take home.

Joseph Delaney, a Wallingford lawyer whom Aillon consulted when he was served with divorce papers, testified that Aillon's only concern was "reconciling with his wife and visitation rights with his daughter."

And Dr. Marlin Dearden, a high priest, or elder, in the Mormon church, told the jury that Aillon had visited him the week before the killings seeking advice on how to patch things up with his wife.

The last witness Howard Jacobs called for the defense was the defendant himself. The moment Aillon sat down in the witness chair, Howard got to the point.

JACOBS: Were you the husband of Barbara?
AILLON: Yes.
JACOBS: Did you kill her?

AILLON: No, I did not. I loved her very much.
JACOBS: Were you the son-in-law of George Montano?
AILLON: Yes, I am.
JACOBS: Did you kill him?
AILLON: No, I did not.
JACOBS: Were you the son-in-law of Bernice Montano?
AILLON: Yes.
JACOBS: Did you kill her?
AILLON: I did not.

Aillon went on to tell the jury about the origin of the cuts on his hands and about the arguments he'd had with Barbara in the days prior to the murders. He told them about eating dinner at his sister's house on the night of the murders and about being pulled over by police. And he stated once more that the knife in the back seat of his car had been used only to cut roast beef.

When Howard finished examining Aillon, Markle took over. For two days, the prosecutor grilled Aillon, trying to pressure him into making contradictory statements. But despite the intensity, Aillon never wavered from his original statement. Finally, the only remaining question was whether the jury believed him or considered him a cold-blooded murderer.

The jury's first set of deliberations lasted more than thirty-seven hours. Finally, hopelessly deadlocked, they sent a note to the judge saying they didn't think they would be able to reach a verdict. The judge told them they had better reach a verdict and sent them back in to deliberate. Eighteen hours later, at 4:30 A.M. on Saturday, September 1, the jury found Aillon guilty on three counts of murder. The judge immediately sentenced him to seventy-five years in prison—essentially a death sentence.

The fate of Gil Aillon would not prove to be quite so simple, however. A short time later, word leaked out that the guilty verdict had come only after the judge secretly and illegally talked with a member of the jury panel during deliberations. The Connecticut Supreme Court promptly reversed the conviction and ordered Aillon to be released from jail until a new trial could be held.

In 1979 Connecticut prosecutors again put Aillon on trial, and once again, I was called as a witness. For ten weeks, both sides presented evidence. But in the end, it was all for naught. After deliberating for more than fifty-six hours, the jurors sent foreman William Keel, a thirty-nine-year-old bus driver from New Haven, to tell the judge they were hopelessly deadlocked. Seven jurors were for conviction, while five felt Aillon was innocent and remained steadfast in their votes for acquittal. The court ordered Aillon released again, and for the next several years, he raised his daughter and worked full-time trying to pay his lawyers' fees.

In 1984, Aillon faced a judge and jury for the third time. This trial was an absolute farce. For starters, many of the defense's witnesses were unavailable to testify and a few had died. The judge assigned to handle the case was known for his pro-prosecution leanings, and the prosecutor, who had come to view this case as his life's work, handled much of the evidence in a less than straightforward fashion. More importantly, before the trial even began, the state forced Howard Jacobs, who'd defended Aillon every step of the way, to quit the case. No conflict of interest was discovered. Nothing unsavory was revealed. Quite simply, the state made it impossible for him to work on the case by refusing to pay him adequately for his services.

In cases where criminal defendants are poor or indigent, the state is required by the Constitution's Sixth Amendment to provide a lawyer to the defendant. During the first two trials and the subsequent appeals, Aillon was fortunate to have been appointed a very good local attorney. However, Howard was paid so little to defend his client that it barely covered his expenses. If one takes into account the fact that Howard could have been representing a paying client during the thirteen years he defended Aillon, it can be argued that he actually lost tens of thousands of dollars.

At any rate, because of the financial strain the Aillon case put on Jacobs's law practice and the state's refusal to pay him any additional money, he had no choice but to withdraw. Personally, I think the prosecutors knew they did not have enough evidence to gain a conviction against Aillon as long as he had such an experienced attorney at his side. And because they could not simply fire him or remove him from the case, they took this back-door approach instead.

The upshot of all this was that, only three months before the third trial was scheduled to begin, the judge ended up appointing two lawyers from the public defender's office to represent Aillon. Without impugning the important work that such lawyers do, it can be said that most public defenders are younger, less experienced, more overworked, and have fewer resources at their disposal than private lawyers. And while I have no doubt about the legal abilities of these two particular lawyers, it was clear to me that they were not nearly as experienced as Jacobs, nor were they prepared to defend him properly at trial. As a result, they were extremely ineffective, something they publicly admitted to. Important evidence, totally refuted at the first two trials, went unchallenged. Key witnesses were either unprepared or were not called at all. In the end, it took less than five hours for this jury to find Aillon guilty.

The U.S. Constitution requires that the burden of proving a person guilty of a crime lies completely and solely on the government. It is up to prosecutors and police to prove "beyond a reasonable doubt" that the person accused of a crime did it. The defendant, on the other hand, is not legally required to prove anything.

That having been said, we do not live in a perfect world, and the criminal case against Gil Aillon is a perfect example of its imperfection. I have seen case after case in which jurors, after finding someone guilty of a crime, comment publicly that while the state's case was poor and the evidence completely unconvincing, the defendant did nothing to prove his innocence. Therefore, they decided, he must be guilty. Successful criminal defense attorneys have learned that in the real world they must do more than simply argue that the government has not proven its case beyond a reasonable doubt; they must give jurors a reason to find the defendant not guilty.

In a murder case, there are five basic arguments that can be advanced to achieve this goal: the defendant didn't do it because he wasn't there; the defendant did it, but it was in self-defense; the killing was an accident; the victim was a bad person who deserved to be killed; and lastly, the "Perry Mason defense."

In the Perry Mason television series, as in many other popular crime shows, the lawyer goes through the dramatics of actually solving the crime for the police and getting the real murderer to confess on the witness stand. Contrary to what TV may have us believe, however, the number of times this has happened in the history of our criminal justice system can probably be counted on two hands. It is almost completely unheard of, yet jurors today, probably because of TV and the movies, expect defense lawyers to do just that.

In research for this book, we contacted six of the jurors who voted to find Aillon guilty. All of them had vivid memories of the case. Two of the jurors said they regretted voting to find him guilty, and only one of the six said he remained convinced of Aillon's guilt. The other three jurors said they had serious doubts about Aillon's guilt, and did not think the evidence proved he was the responsible party.

Why, then, did they agree to convict him?

"Who else could it have been?" one juror asked.

"If his lawyers had just been able to show us why someone else would have done it or showed us some evidence of another suspect, I think that would have been very convincing," commented another.

The bottom line is that in murder cases, particularly brutal ones involving innocent victims, jurors want to be able to blame someone for the deaths. And if there is no one else to take the blame, the defendant is going to have to.

Something that good defense attorneys can and will do, however, is to show that there are reasons why people other than the defendant might want to kill the victim. Perhaps the victim was a gambler and had a debt he couldn't pay. Maybe the victim had been involved in suspicious business dealings or was having an extramarital affair. The lawyers representing Gil Aillon had the opportunity to take this tack but simply failed to do so. If they'd succeeded, Aillon might be a free man today.

In the years since the final Aillon trial, I have learned that many people in New Haven suspected there were multiple attackers, and that none was Gil Aillon. Even back in 1972, I am told, there was talk that this was a "mob hit."

In the summer of 1992, I made a trip to Somers, Connecticut, the home of the state's main prison, to visit with Gil and to see how he was doing. For about half an hour, we were allowed to sit in the prison cafeteria and talk. Aillon looked good and said he'd been working in the prison's law library. And Aillon said that he, too, had heard from fellow prison inmates that the murders were at the hands of the Mafia.

"In 1976," Aillon told me, "this prisoner who knew everybody told me he was sorry I was in jail because he knew I didn't do it and he knew who did. I asked him who did it. At first, he wouldn't tell me, but I persisted. Finally, the man said the order to kill my father-in-law came from New York and that a policeman was involved. The man said he would deny everything if I ever asked him about it again."

The next day, I visited with Aillon's appellate lawyer, John Williams of New Haven. He, too, had heard about the possible involvement of the Mafia, many powerful members of which have made Connecticut their home since the 1940s.

"There has always been this underlying suspicion that these murders had something to do with organized crime," Williams said. "The Montano family was involved in vending machines, and the mob's attraction to the vending machine business is well known. But while there have always been these whispers and gossip around town about this, no hard evidence has ever surfaced."

As I think about this case, my questions about it seem to boil down to these: Is Gil Aillon guilty of these murders? and Did he receive a fair trial?

Only Gil Aillon knows the answer to the first question;

I personally have no insight into whether he participated in these terrible crimes, although I pray that he did not. As for the second question, some may argue that if Aillon did kill these people, then why does it matter whether his trial was fair? Was justice not served?

In pondering this, I am reminded of something the great Georgia trial lawyer Bobby Lee Cook once said: "If you can railroad a bad man to prison, you can railroad a good man to prison." Indeed, the Sixth Amendment of our Constitution, which guarantees a fair trial and that a person is innocent until proven guilty, must apply to those who are truly guilty if it is going to protect those of us who are innocent but who may one day be accused of a crime.

Unfortunately, the three people found dead in 1972 were not the only victims of this crime. Catherine Victoria Aillon was only seven months old when she was found in a puddle of blood a few feet from her mother's cold body. Even today, she cries over the mother she never had. Now in her twenties, Ms. Aillon has read and reread every line of transcript in her father's three trials. She has examined every piece of evidence. She has questioned her father about it at length, and she has come to one definite conclusion:

"My father didn't do it," she says. "They've got the wrong person."

FOURTEEN

POSTMORTEM ENCOUNTER
OF A THIRD KIND

On July 4, 1947, a violent electrical storm battered Corona, New Mexico. It is a day that locals, as well as people the world over, talk about even now. Their conversations, however, do not revolve around thunder and lightning.

The next day, legend has it, William "Mac" Brazel toured his ranch to survey the damage. What he found was not just blown-over trees. Instead, he came across unusual debris littering more than a half mile of his property. One piece, which looked like an I-beam, bore a strange print on one side that looked like hieroglyphics. Other fragments appeared to be threads of silk or fishing line. But the most unusual item, witnesses say, was a foil-like substance that was both stronger and lighter than aluminum foil. It could not be cut, burned, or shredded. According to one eyewitness, when you wadded this foil up into a ball, it became so small that "you had to look to see if it was still there. But when you dropped it, it spread out all over the floor."

Never having seen such materials before, Brazel collected a small sample and took it to Chaves County sheriff George Wilcox. Although similarly unable to identify the debris, Wilcox suspected that it had come from some kind of experimental aircraft being developed at nearby Roswell Army Air Field, home of the elite 509th Bomber Group and of World War II's legendary *Enola Gay*. Wilcox immediately called the base for verification.

The moment Major Jesse Marcel, the base's senior security intelligence officer, spotted the materials, he knew they were not of military origin. Within a half hour, top brass from Roswell had descended upon Brazel's ranch. The site was sealed, the civilians were cleared off, and high-ranking military and government officials began to fly in. For hours, they searched for and gathered the debris, which they then transported via B-29 to Fort Worth, Texas, for further examination.

On July 8, Colonel William Blanchard, the U.S. Army's top officer at Roswell, issued a statement to the press that his bomber group had recovered a "flying disc." The next day, newspapers across the country, including the reputable *New York Times*, featured headlines to this effect.

The same day, however, the story began to change. Twenty-four hours after the arrival of the "flying disc," Major Marcel was flown to Fort Worth Army Air Field to meet with his superiors. There, General William Ramey, commander of the 8th Airborne Division, told him that he and the other military personnel at Roswell had been wrong—the debris had not come from some flying saucer after all; it was nothing more than the scattered remains of a weather balloon and radar reflector that tracked wind velocity and direction.

Whatever the case, neither Major Marcel nor Colonel Blanchard would ever speak publicly of the incident again. There is tremendous speculation among those who have studied the so-called Roswell incident that the two men were sworn to secrecy regarding this matter.

In the decades since, the question of what happened that night in the New Mexican desert has attracted the serious attention of thousands of individuals from across the United States and beyond, and has become the subject of countless books, movies, and articles. What the case lacks in the way of available physical evidence, it more than makes up for in eyewitness accounts and the speculation fueled by nearly a half century of official silence. Indeed, UFO buffs consider Roswell the crown jewel in their search for evidence of extraterrestrial life.

Forty-eight years and a few weeks after that mysterious night, I found myself in the thick of the controversy, a place I'd never imagined I'd find myself. I must admit that I've never spent much time thinking about the possibilities of UFOs. My life's work has been focused on bodies of this world and how they died or became ill, not on little green men with big heads and superior intellects. As they say, however, you live and you learn.

My involvement in the world of UFOs began on Tuesday, August 1, 1995. Tom Seligson, a producer from Fox TV, had asked me to meet him at 1 P.M. at the historic Willard Hotel in Washington, D.C., where he and his crew had rented a suite. There, they showed me one of the most remarkable series of images I have ever seen.

The video, which lasted about eighteen minutes, showed two people, their faces obscured by protective hoods and their bodies covered by what looked like anti-contamination suits, performing an autopsy on what appeared to be either a deformed human being or a creature from someplace other than Earth. A third person stood behind a glass partition, observing the proceedings. Shot in black and white, the images captured on the video appeared to be old. The lighting was poor and the shots frequently went out of focus.

The video, I was told, was a copy of a film shot in 1947 during the postmortem examination of an alleged space alien recovered from the wreckage at Roswell. According to Mr. Seligson, military officials had flown in a freelance cameraman with top military clearance to film the autopsy, which supposedly took place in either Fort Worth or at Wright Army Air Field in Dayton, Ohio. Afterward, the story goes, the military had neglected to collect several cans of exposed film from the cameraman.

For nearly five decades, the mystery photographer secretly held onto the film. Then, in 1994, he met Ray Santilli, the owner of a small video and film distribution company in London who was in the United States scouring for vintage footage of singer Elvis Presley. Very little is known about the relationship or deal cut between the two men, but it is believed that Santilli paid the cameraman a sizable amount of money for the film and promised to keep his identity confidential. For that matter, I knew nothing about the circumstances under which Fox had acquired the film. Nor did I ask.

I viewed the video several times, pausing and rewinding whenever I wished to get a better view. The television producers simply wanted me to offer my opinion, based on my experience examining the bodies of human beings, as to whether this film depicted an actual autopsy of a flesh-and-blood being. Beyond that, they wanted to know whether the being that was examined was human or something else entirely.

The video, which had no accompanying audio, opened with a shot of what appeared to be a completely nude body, or a very close facsimile thereof, lying on its back on an autopsy table, mouth and eyes opened wide. Completely hairless and featuring a disproportionately large head and eyes, it looked very much like the stereotypical being from outer space that the mass media have impressed upon our collective mind's eye over the years. This one, however, had a feature I'd never seen before: six fingers on each hand and six toes on each foot, a condition known in medical literature as polydactyly.

Upon closer viewing, the body appeared to be that of a young adult or teenage female with significant abdominal distension, perhaps in the late stages of pregnancy. However, there was no development of the breasts and no pubic hair was visible. Although no measurements were shown, I would estimate, based on the relative size of the autopsists and the table, that the body was about five feet in length. There was no evidence of decomposition.

In close-ups of the head, I could not see any teeth in the being's mouth, which had an inward puckering effect. There were no eyelids or eyebrows, and the ears were small and somewhat narrow and angular. At a later point in the external examination, the autopsists used tweezers to remove a soft, dark-colored film from the surface of each orbital socket, which they then placed in a jar. I had no idea what this material could be, but once it had been removed, the eyes appeared starkly white, with no pupils visible.

The only noticeable external injury appeared on the inside of the right thigh, extending from a point below the groin to the knee level. The wound had a blackened or charred effect, suggesting that it had been caused by something that was on fire. It appeared to be deep, with widespread bleeding. Strangely, however, the surrounding areas of skin on the right leg showed no evidence of injury. Nor was I able to spot any other lacerations, abrasions, or apparent fractures on the body, although there did appear to be some dark discoloration on the left side of the trunk that could have represented a large area of contusion. Based on my experience examining victims of motor vehicle accidents, this kind of isolated injury did not suggest the type of trauma one might receive in the crash of an aircraft.

The body was opened with an extended Y-shaped incision—an infrequently seen procedure in which the autopsist begins behind the lower portion of each ear, brings the incisions together at the neck, then proceeds downward to open the chest and abdominal cavities. As the incisions were made, a dark fluid consistent in appearance with blood started running down the side of the neck and torso, as it would from a recently deceased body, as opposed to one that had been mummified or preserved in some kind of solution.

What impressed me more, however, was the fact that these cuts were made in such a way as to suggest that the people in the space suit-like outfits were actually pathologists, if not exactly master surgeons. Quite simply, I find it highly unlikely that actors would have thought to make an incision that is used only by forensic pathologists in a limited number of cases—unless, of course, they were being directed by forensic pathologists. Who knows what some of my colleagues do in their spare time?

Due to the poor camera work, I was unable to tell whether the organs demonstrated in the chest cavity were the heart and lungs. Later, a small, cyst-like structure appeared to be carefully cut from the area of the heart and placed in an open jar. Once again, however, the poor quality of the film made it impossible to see these organs and the surrounding rib cage clearly.

The puzzle became even greater when the abdominal cavity was opened. From what I could tell, there was no evidence of loops of intestines, either large or small. There was a large organ that could have been the liver, except that it was located much more to the midline and toward the left than would be normally expected. It also appeared to be firmer and less well-defined than a normal human liver.

No other specific abdominal organs or tissues could be identified. A moment later, however, the film showed the physicians removing and dissecting a large tissue mass from the abdominal cavity. At one point I saw what looked like the back of a fetal head. As the autopsy continued, there emerged a rather large, sac-like structure, consistent with a large placenta, which was removed and placed in a container. It had fairly well-defined borders and was easily removed from the abdominal cavity.

If this had been some type of tumor or unnatural growth, it would have required much more dissection and would have had less well-defined borders. It could have been a fetus. But there was essentially no bleeding as the doctors dissected the tissue. This was strange for a recently deceased being, and was inconsistent with the blood I saw when incisions were made on the sides of the neck and chest.

The physicians then moved to the head, which showed no sign of trauma. Incisions were made from behind one ear to the other, again suggesting some knowledge of basic autopsy techniques. As the front of the scalp was peeled back, a darkly discolored surface was revealed, giving a more thickened, roughened, and granular appearance than would be expected on the undersurface of a human scalp. The discoloration was also far too intense and total to be consistent with a hemorrhage, especially when I considered the fact that there was no evidence of external trauma on the face or scalp. The back of the head, however, was never shown being opened.

Next, a handsaw was used to remove the calvarium, and a mass was lifted from the cranial vault. Again, the film was so dark and poorly focused that I could not adequately identify the tissue. However, its shape and consistency did not appear to be those of a human brain. It was much too firm and easily removed than one would expect from a fresh brain. Furthermore, no blood was seen dripping from the object as it was lifted from the cranial vault and placed in a large tray.

As I viewed the video, I made sure to pay close attention to the background as well, searching for some inconsistency or anomaly that might reveal it to be a hoax. There was an old-fashioned microphone hanging from the ceiling, and a round wall clock that indicated the passage of time. Moreover, everything about the operating room appeared to be consistent with the era in which the film was purportedly shot—from a large, black telephone mounted on the wall to the autopsy instruments and the sunken rectangular metal tray in which they lay.

However, there were several aspects of the video that brought out the skeptic in me. First, there was the fact that every time the camera moved in for a close-up of an injury or internal organ, the shot quickly went out of focus. Secondly, only the front of the body was shown. It was never turned laterally to display the back; in fact, the surgeons did not move the body at all and manipulated it only to a limited extent. Even more troubling was the haste with which the procedure was apparently performed. If the subject of the autopsy was truly a previously unseen life-form, I would expect the government to spend weeks, months, maybe even years dissecting and studying it. There was certainly something fishy about the whole thing. And yet its technical execution was impressive enough to make one want to consider the full possibilities.

When I had finished my viewing, the lights went on and the Fox producers turned to me. What was this thing we were watching? Was it from outer space? Was it a complete hoax? What, they wanted to know, was my expert opinion?

"The most that can be said from viewing the film," I said, "is that the body is humanoid, which is to say it is something like a human being but not definitely a human being."

Then I gave them several possibilities to consider:

1. This was an extremely clever hoax that demonstrated remarkable technical skill and expertise on the part of those who put it together.
2. This represented a dysmorphic human being who suffered from various congenital abnormalities, either genetic or chromosomal.
3. This was a human being who had been subjected to the ravages of some disease process or processes, and possibly external and/or internal radiation effects. In fact, the possibility that this was the subject of a radiation experiment gone awry would answer many questions, including the absence of hair and the deformed head, and the need for the autopsists to wear anti-contamination suits.
4. This body represented something other than a human being.

In a written report submitted a couple of days later, I suggested that the film be shown to appropriate U.S. government officials and that a specific request be made to have the film studied by forensic pathologists at the Armed Forces Institute of Pathology (AFIP). Also, I said, since the Armed Forces Institute of Technology at Wright-Pattern Air Force Base—where the film was allegedly shot—was the predecessor to the AFIP, the AFIP should be asked whether it has any records of this autopsy.

At the end of the month, Fox presented its program *Alien Autopsy: Fact or Fiction?* Hosted by Jonathan Frakes, a co-star on the popular science fiction television series *Star Trek: The Next Generation,* it had all the elements of popular appeal. Not surprisingly, the hour-long program was the highest-rated documentary and the second-highest-rated show of any kind that Fox had ever featured. The show was so popular, in fact, that Fox has since rebroadcast the program several times, achieving equally high ratings, and is now selling a videotape of the show containing unedited footage of the alleged autopsy itself.

The success of the television show, of course, does not grant legitimacy to the theory that the subject was indeed a space alien. But I thought the producers did an excellent job of confirming as much as they possibly could. Interviewed on the show were local residents who claimed to have seen pieces of the wreckage, a former public relations officer at Roswell, photography and special effects experts, even another forensic pathologist. Although the deck was a bit stacked in favor of the extraterrestrial believers, I thought that the professional stature and diversity of the sources, as well as the clarity and objectivity with which they spoke, lent the show a credibility that served it well.

Among the more titillating comments was one from Stan Winston, the man who created the dinosaurs in *Jurassic Park* and the monster in *Aliens*, among many other Hollywood beings. After viewing the film in the company of several professional colleagues, he did not believe that the autopsy was a hoax. "Knowing how difficult it is to simulate skin and blood," Winston said, "I started looking at this and thinking, 'If this isn't real, I'd be real proud of creating an image like that today.' If this is a hoax, it is one of the greatest pieces of artwork I have ever seen."

Another example of the show's appeal came in a comment by Paulo Cherchi, a senior curator at Eastman Kodak: "If it's a true document, it is a document of exceptional importance. If it's a fake, it should be hailed as one of the most extraordinary fakes ever put together by a filmmaker."

Predictably, this film has been the subject of countless discussions on the Internet and elsewhere. The latest thought was that the whole incident was indeed a hoax, albeit one concocted by the U.S. government with the intention of later revealing that the whole thing was phony and thereby discrediting UFO believers. The result would be a chilling effect upon demands for further disclosures regarding the Roswell incident. This explanation seems to be outrageously paranoid. But then, of course, our government has done stranger things. And in the world of UFOs, who really knows where the truth may lie?

Thankfully, forensic pathologists do not typically find themselves confronted with such cosmic mysteries. There are more than enough problems right here on Planet Earth and enough puzzles involving human flesh and blood to keep us busy and intellectually stimulated. In fact, as we prepare to enter a new millennium, forensic medicine finds itself armed with such exciting new tools as DNA testing, computer simulation, and positron emission tomography—tools that are certain to vastly expand the horizons of our profession.

As technologically advanced as forensic medicine has become, however, it is still a field grounded in concepts and principles that have been around since some of the earliest human civilizations. Nevertheless, as many of the cases presented in this book have illustrated, these fundamental concepts are all too frequently ignored. The consequences, as we have seen, are often devastating.

Now, as we stand on the brink of a whole new era in legal medicine, it is more important than ever that forensic scientists remember the fundamental tools of their professions. Diligent adherence to sound forensic scientific procedures enhanced by new concepts and technological developments will lead to an even larger role for the forensic scientist in the civil and criminal justice systems and will enable us to make an even greater contribution to the causes of justice and social welfare.

INDEX

ABOUT THE AUTHOR

Cyril H. Wecht received his M.D. degree from the University of Pittsburgh and his J.D. Degree from the University of Maryland. He is certified by the American Board of Pathology, the American Board of Disaster Medicine, and the American Board of Legal Medicine.

Dr. Wecht is actively involved as a medical-legal and forensic science consultant, author, and lecturer, and was the elected Coroner of Allegheny County for twenty years. He has performed approximately 20,000 autopsies, and reviewed or been consulted on roughly 40,000 additional post-mortem examinations, including cases in several foreign countries.

Dr. Wecht holds several professorial faculty positions at the University of Pittsburgh, Duquesne and Carlow Universities. He is the author or co-author of more than 620 professional publications, and editor or co editor of forty-six books.

Dr. Wecht has appeared as a frequent guest on numerous national TV and radio shows, discussing famous cases, many of which are discussed in his books, *Cause of Death*, *Grave Secrets*, *Who Killed JonBenet Ramsey?*, *Mortal Evidence*, *Tales from the Morgue*, *From Crime Scene to Courtroom*, *A Question of Murder*, and *Final Exams*.